THE STORY OF GREECE

She changed her into a spider

THE STORY OF GREECE

Told to Boys and Girls by

MARY MACGREGOR

With illustrations by Walter Crane

YESTERDAY'S CLASSICS

CHAPEL HILL, NORTH CAROLINA

Cover and arrangement © 2006 Yesterday's Classics.

This edition, first published in 2006 by Yesterday's Classics, is an unabridged republication of the work originally published by Thomas Nelson and Sons Ltd. in 1914. The color illustrations by Walter Crane in that volume are rendered in black and white in this edition. For a listing of books published by Yesterday's Classics, visit www.yesterdaysclassics.com. Yesterday's Classics is the publishing arm of the Baldwin Project which presents the complete text of dozens of classic books for children at www.mainlesson.com under the editorship of Lisa M. Ripperton and T. A. Roth.

ISBN-10: 1-59915-033-6

ISBN-13: 978-1-59915-033-8

Yesterday's Classics
PO Box 3418
Chapel Hill, NC 27515

TO

JOYCE MOFFAT SCOTT

DEAR LITTLE JOYCE,—One of the reasons why this book is to be your very own is that the story it tells begins in Wonderland, and that is a land in which you and all other little people wander at will.

Grown up children, men and women as we call them, do not know the secrets of this strange land, yet there are a few who can always find their way across its border, as they used to do when they were small like you. Some few others there are who remember its secrets well.

Shall I tell you some of the things you hear and see and do in Wonderland?

Why, when the wind blows soft, faint whispers reach your ear, but you alone know what the whispers tell. When the brooks gurgle you hear joyous laughter, and in the springs of water you see the sparkle of elfin eyes.

As the bluebells shake in the breeze, your tiny feet march to the music of fairy hands, as the raindrops fall you gather pearls with your little hands.

The secrets of this strange Wonderland make you so glad that you laugh and dance and sing.

> "Great, wide, beautiful, wonderful world,
>   With the wonderful water round you curled,
>   And the wonderful grass upon your breast,
>   World you are wonderfully drest."

The ancient Wonderland of Hellas, of which this story tells, was unlike your Wonderland in this, that men and women dwelt in it as well as boys and girls, and they, too, saw and heard its secrets. And this was because, in a way not known to-day, each had kept the heart of a little child.

So it was that these men and women heard voices in the wind and laughter in the streams, so it was that they saw eyes in water springs and pearls in raindrops.

More even than these things the Hellenes saw. For across lone hillsides, through busy fields, in sacral groves and flower-sweet meadows, radiant figures sped. And the simple folk catching glimpses of these flitting forms said one to the other, "The gods have come to live among us. Their presence it is that makes the earth so fair, so wonderful." As the years passed and the Hellenes grew older, sterner times came. Cities sprang up on hillsides and by riverbanks, and the gods were seldom seen. Men went to war, battles were lost and won.

But never, in victory or in defeat, did the people lose their early love of beauty, or that strange, dreamy sense of wonder, which from the beginning was ever plucking at their hearts.

They longed to fulfil their dreams of beauty, they wished to re-shape the world.

But, because the world was so great, so wide, they began with one of their cities, the one of which a poet sang,

"O rich and renowned and with violets crowned,
 O Athens the envied of nations."

Here they built temples which became the wonder of the world, and in them they placed statues of the old gods of Hellas, beautiful statues wrought by master hands out of ivory and gold.

Poets and philosophers lived in Athens, too, and so literature and art spread the glory of Greece far and wide, moulding the thoughts and quickening the deeds of many peoples.

Before the glory of Greece faded, Europe had learned from her to follow truth, to love beauty.

This story tells but a small part of the wonder of this land, yet I hope that it will make you love her and wish to learn more about her.—Your friend,

MARY MACGREGOR.

CONTENTS

		Page
I.	WONDERLAND	1
II.	THE GREAT GOD PAN	4
III.	THE SIX POMEGRANATE SEEDS	9
IV.	THE BIRTH OF ATHENE	16
V.	THE TWO WEAVERS	19
VI.	THE PURPLE FLOWERS	23
VII.	DANAE AND HER LITTLE SON	27
VIII.	THE QUEST OF PERSEUS	34
IX.	ANDROMEDA AND THE SEA-MONSTER	39
X.	ACRISIUS IS KILLED BY PERSEUS	43
XI.	ACHILLES AND BRISEIS THE FAIRCHEEKED	47
XII.	MENELAUS AND PARIS DO BATTLE	56
XIII.	HECTOR AND ANDROMACHE	61
XIV.	THE HORSES OF ACHILLES	65
XV.	THE DEATH OF HECTOR	70
XVI.	POLYPHEMUS THE GIANT	78
XVII.	ODYSSEUS ESCAPES FROM THE CAVE	84
XVIII.	ODYSSEUS RETURNS TO ITHACA	88
XIX.	ARGUS THE HOUND DIES	92
XX.	THE BOW OF ODYSSEUS	97
XXI.	THE LAND OF HELLAS	105
XXII.	LYCURGUS AND HIS LITTLE NEPHEW	110

CONTENTS

XXIII.	Lycurgus Returns to Sparta	114
XXIV.	The Training of the Spartans	119
XXV.	The Helots	124
XXVI.	Aristomenes and the Fox	129
XXVII.	The Olympian Games	136
XXVIII.	The Last King of Athens	141
XXIX.	Cylon Fails to Make Himself Tyrant	145
XXX.	Solon Frees the Slaves	148
XXXI.	The Athenians Take Salamis	155
XXXII.	Pisistratus Becomes Tyrant	159
XXXIII.	Harmodius and Aristogiton	165
XXXIV.	The Law of Ostracism	169
XXXV.	The Bridge of Boats	172
XXXVI.	Darius Rewards Histiaeus	176
XXXVII.	Histiaeus Shaves the Head of his Slave	179
XXXVIII.	Sardis is Destroyed	183
XXXIX.	The Sandal Sewn by Histiaeus	187
XL.	Darius Demands Earth and Water	190
XLI.	The Battle of Marathon	194
XLII.	Miltiades sails to the Island of Paros	199
XLIII.	Aristides is Ostracised	203
XLIV.	The Dream of Xerxes	209
XLV.	Xerxes Orders the Hellespont to be Scourged	213

CONTENTS

XLVI.	"The Bravest Men of All Hellas"	219
XLVII.	The Battle of Thermopylae	224
XLVIII.	The Battle of Artemisium	231
XLIX.	Themistocles Urges Eurybiades to Stay at Salamis	234
L.	Themistocles Tricks the Admirals	240
LI.	The Battle of Salamis	243
LII.	The Battle of Plataea	249
LIII.	The Delian League	256
LIV.	Themistocles Deceives the Spartans	262
LV.	Themistocles is Ostracised	266
LVI.	The Eloquence of Pericles	272
LVII.	Pericles and Elpinice	279
LVIII.	The City of Athens	282
LIX.	Great Men of Athens	288
LX.	The Thebans Attack the Plataeans	291
LXI.	Attica is Invaded by the Spartans	295
LXII.	The Last Words of Pericles	298
LXIII.	The Siege of Plataea	303
LXIV.	The Sentence of Death	308
LXV.	Brasidas Loses his Shield	313
LXVI.	The Spartans Surrender	318
LXVII.	Brasidas the Spartan	324
LXVIII.	Amphipolis Surrenders to Brasidas	328
LXIX.	Alcibiades the Favourite of Athens	334

CONTENTS

LXX.	Socrates the Philosopher	340
LXXI.	Alcibiades Praises Socrates	345
LXXII.	The Images of Hermes are Destroyed	351
LXXIII.	Alcibiades escapes to Sparta	355
LXXIV.	The Siege of Syracuse	358
LXXV.	The Athenian Army is Destroyed	362
LXXVI.	Alcibiades Returns to Athens	367
LXXVII.	Antiochus Disobeys Alcibiades	373
LXXVIII.	The Walls of Athens are Destroyed	377
LXXIX.	The March of the Ten Thousand	381
LXXX.	Pelopidas and Epaminondas	388
LXXXI.	The Seven Conspirators	394
LXXXII.	The Battle of Leuctra	399
LXXXIII.	The Death of Epaminondas	405
LXXXIV.	The Two Brothers	411
LXXXV.	Timoleon Send Dionysius to Corinth	416
LXXXVI.	Icetes Tries to Slay Timoleon	421
LXXXVII.	The Battle of Crimisus	426
LXXXVIII.	Demosthenes wishes to become an Orator	431
LXXXIX.	Demosthenes the Greatest Orator of Athens	434
XC.	The Sacred War	439
XCI.	Alexander and Bucephalus	443
XCII.	Alexander and Diogenes	449

CONTENTS

XCIII.	THE BATTLE OF GRANICUS	454
XCIV.	THE GORDIAN KNOT	458
XCV.	DARIUS GALLOPS FROM THE BATTLEFIELD	462
XCVI.	TYRE IS STORMED BY ALEXANDER	467
XCVII.	THE BATTLE OF GAUGAMELA	471
XCVIII.	ALEXANDER BURNS PERSEPOLIS	476
XCIX.	ALEXANDER SLAYS HIS FOSTER-BROTHER	480
C.	PORUS AND HIS ELEPHANT	486
CI.	ALEXANDER IS WOUNDED	491
CII.	THE DEATH OF ALEXANDER	495
CIII.	DEMOSTHENES IN THE TEMPLE OF POSEIDON	501

CHAPTER I

WONDERLAND

THE story of Greece began long, long ago in a strange wonderland of beauty. Woods and winds, fields and rivers, each had a pathway which led upward and onward into the beautiful land. Sometimes indeed no path was needed, for the rivers, woods, and lone hill-sides were themselves the wonderland of which I am going to tell.

In the woods and winds, in the trees and rivers, dwelt the gods and goddesses whom the people of long ago worshipped. It was their presence in the world that made it so great, so wide, so wonderful.

To the Hellenes, for that is the name by which the Greeks called themselves, there were eyes, living eyes in flowers, trees and water. "So crowded full is the air with them," wrote one poet who lived in the far-off days, "that there is no room to put in the spike of an ear of corn without touching one."

When the wind blew soft, the Hellenes listened to the whispering of a voice. When it blew rough, and snatched one of the children from their midst, they did not greatly grieve. The child had but gone to be the playmate of the gods.

The springs sparkled clean, for in them dwelt the Naiads or freshwater nymphs, with gifts as great as the river gods, who were ofttimes seen and heard amid the churning, tossing waters.

In the trees dwelt the Dryads, nymphs these of the forest, and whom the Hellenes saw but seldom. Shy nymphs were the Dryads, born each one at the birth of a tree, in which she dwelt, fading away when the tree was felled, or when it withered and died.

Their revels were held in some wooded mountain, far from the haunts of men. Were a human footfall heard, the frolics ceased on the instant, while each Dryad sped swift for shelter to the tree of her birth.

So the gods wandered though the land, filling the earth with their presence. Yet there was one lofty mountain in central Greece, named Mount Olympus, which the Hellenes believed was the peculiar home of the gods. It was to this great mount that the actual roads on which the Hellenes walked each day seemed ever to lead.

On the sides of the mountain, green trees and dark pines clustered close. The summit reached high up, beyond the clouds, so used the ancient people to tell. Here, where no human foot had ever climbed, up beyond the twinkling stars, was the abode of the gods.

WONDERLAND

What the Hellenes never saw with their eyes, they saw quite clear with their imagination. Within the clouds, where the gods dwelt, they gazed in this strange way, upon marble halls, glistening with gold and silver, upon thrones too, great white thrones, finer far than those on which an earthly king might sit. The walls gleamed with rainbow tints, and beauty as of dawns and sunsets was painted over vast arches of Olympus.

CHAPTER II

THE GREAT GOD PAN

THE supreme god of the Hellenes was Zeus. He dwelt in the sky, yet on earth, too, he had a sanctuary amid the oak-woods of Dodona.

When the oak-leaves stirred, his voice was heard, mysterious as the voice of the mightiest of all the gods.

In days long after these, Phidias, a great Greek sculptor, made an image of Zeus. The form and the face of the god he moulded into wondrous beauty, so that men gazing saw sunshine on the brow, and in the eyes gladness and warmth as of summer skies.

Even so, if you watch, you may catch on the faces of those whose home is on the hill-side, or by the sea, a glimpse of the beauty and the wonder amid which they dwell.

It was only in very early times that the chief sanctuary of Zeus was at Dodona. Before they had dwelt long in Hellas, the Hellenes built a great temple in the plain of Olympia to their supreme god and named it the Olympian temple.

Here a gold and ivory statue of the god was placed, and to the quiet courts of the temple came the people, singing hymns and marching in joyous procession.

Zeus had stolen his great power from his father Kronus, with the help of his brothers and sisters. To reward them for their aid the god gave to them provinces over which they ruled in his name. Hera, Zeus chose as queen to reign with him. To Poseidon was given the sea, and a palace beneath the waves of the ocean, adorned with seaweed and with shells.

Pluto was made the guardian of Hades, that dark and gloomy kingdom of the dead, beneath the earth, while Demeter was goddess of the earth, and her gifts were flowers, fruits, and bounteous harvests.

Athene was the goddess of war and wisdom, yet often she was to be seen weaving or embroidering, while by her table sat her favourite bird, an owl.

Hermes was known as the fleet-footed, for on his feet he wore winged sandals to speed him swiftly on the errands of the gods.

Apollo, the Sun-god, was the youngest of all the Olympian deities. He dwelt at Parnassus on the eastern coast of Greece, and his sanctuary was at Delphi.

The fairest of the goddesses was Aphrodite, Queen of Love. Her little son was named Eros, and he never grew up. Always he was a little rosy, dimpled child, carrying in his hands a bow and arrows.

Many more gods and goddesses were there in the wonder days of long ago, but of only one more may I stay to tell you now.

The great god Pan, protector of the shepherds and their flocks, was half man, half goat. Everyone loved this strange god, who yet ofttimes startled mortals by his wild and wilful ways. When to-day a sudden, needless fear overtakes a crowd, and we say a panic has fallen upon it, we are using a word which we learned from the name of this old pagan god.

Down by the streams the great god Pan was sometimes seen to wander—

> "What was he doing, the great god Pan,
> Down in the reeds by the river?
> Spreading ruin and scattering ban,
> Splashing and paddling with hoofs of a goat,
> And the breaking the golden lilies afloat,
> With the dragon-fly on the river.
>
> "He tore out a reed, the great god Pan,
> From the deep cool bank of the river,"

and then sitting down he "hacked and hewed, as a great god can," at the slender reed. He made it hollow, and notched out holes, and lo! there was a flute ready for his use.

Sweet, piercing was the music of Pan's pipe

Sweet, piercing sweet was the music of Pan's pipe as the god placed his mouth upon the holes.

> "Blinding sweet, O great god Pan!
> The sun on the hill forgot to die,
> And the lilies revived, and the dragon-fly
> Came back to dream on the river."

On the hill-sides and in the fields of Hellas, the shepherds heard the music of their god and were merry, knowing that he was on his way to frolic to dance among them.

Pan lived for many, many a long year; but there is a story which tells how on the first glad Christmas eve, when Jesus was born in Bethlehem, a traveller, as he passed Tarentum, the chief Greek city in Italy, heard a voice crying, "The great god Pan is dead."

And when this same Jesus had grown to be a Man, and "hung for love's sake on a Cross," one of our own women poets sings that all the old gods of Greece

> "fell down moaning,
> Each from off his golden seat;
> All the false gods with a cry,
> Rendered up their deity,
> Pan, Pan was dead."

And the reason that the old gods fell was that the strange Man upon the Cross was mightier than they. But in the days of ancient Greece the gods were alive and strong; of that the Hellenes were very sure.

CHAPTER III

THE SIX POMEGRANATE SEEDS

DEMETER, the goddess of the earth, was often to be seen in the fields in springtime. As the Greek peasants sowed their seed they caught glimpses of her long yellow hair while she moved now here, now there, among them. It almost seemed to these simple folk as though already the bare fields were golden with the glory of harvest, so bright shone the yellow hair of the goddess. Then they smiled hopefully one to the other, knowing well that Demeter would give them a bounteous reaping-time.

In the autumn she was in the fields again, the peasants even dreamed that they saw her stoop to bind the sheaves. Certainly she had been known to visit their barns when the harvest was safely gathered. And stranger still, it was whispered among the womenfolk that the great Earth-Mother had entered their homes, had stood close beside them as they baked bread to feed their hungry households.

It was in the beautiful island of Sicily, which lies in the Mediterranean Sea, that the goddess had her home. Here she dwelt with her daughter Persephone, whom she loved more dearly than words can tell.

Persephone was young and fair, so fair that she seemed as one of the spring flowers that leaped into life when her mother touched the earth with her gracious hands.

Early as the dawn the maiden was in the fields with Demeter, to gather violets while the dew still lay upon them, to dance and sing with her playmates. At other times she would move gravely by the side of her mother to help her in her quiet labours.

All this time, Pluto, King of Hades, was living in his gloomy kingdom underground, longing for some fair maiden to share his throne. But there was not one who was willing to leave the glad light of the sun, no, not though Pluto offered her the most brilliant gems in his kingdom.

One day the dark king came up out of the shadows, riding in his chariot of gold, drawn by immortal horses. Swifter was their pace than that of any mortal steeds.

Persephone was in a meadow with her playfellows when the king drew near. The maiden stood knee-deep amid the meadow-grass, and, stooping, plucked the fragrant sweet flowers all around her—hyacinth, lilies, roses, and pale violets.

Pluto saw the group of happy maidens, beautiful each one as a day in spring, but it was Persephone who charmed him more than any other.

"She shall be my queen and share my throne," muttered the gloomy king to himself. Then, for he knew that to woo the maiden would be in vain, Pluto seized Persephone in his arms, and bore her weeping to his chariot.

Swift as an arrow the immortal steeds sped from the meadow, where Persephone's playmates were left terror-stricken and dismayed.

On and on flew the chariot. Pluto was in haste to reach Hades ere Demeter should miss her daughter.

A river lay across his path, but of this the king recked naught, for his steeds would bear him across without so much as lessening their speed.

But as the chariot drew near, the waters began to rise as though driven by a tempest. Soon they were lashed to such fury that Pluto saw that it was vain to hope to cross to the other side. So he seized his sceptre, and in a passion he struck three times upon the ground. At once a great chasm opened in the earth, and down into the darkness plunged the horses. A moment more and Pluto was in his own kingdom, Persephone by his side.

When the king seized the maiden in the meadow, and bore her to his chariot, she had cried aloud to Zeus, her father, to save her. But Zeus had made no sign, nor had any heard save Hecate, a mysterious goddess, whose face was half hidden by a veil.

None other heard, yet her piteous cry echoed through the hills and woods, until at length the faint echo reached the ear of Demeter.

A great pain plucked at the heart of the mother as she heard, and throwing the blue hood from off her shoulders, and loosening her long yellow hair, Demeter set forth, swift as a bird, to seek for Persephone until she found her.

To her own home first she hastened, for there, she thought, she might find some trace of the child she loved so well. But the rooms were desolate as "an empty bird's nest or an empty fold."

The mother's eyes searched eagerly in every corner, but nothing met her gaze save the embroidery Persephone had been working, "a gift against the return of her mother, with labour all to be in vain." It lay as she had flung it down in careless mood, and over it crept a spider, spinning his delicate web across the maiden's unfinished work.

For nine days Demeter wandered up and down the earth, carrying blazing torches in her hands. Her sorrow was so great that she would neither eat nor drink, no, not even ambrosia, or a cup of sweet nectar, which are the meat and drink of the gods. Nor would she wash her face. On the tenth day Hecate came towards her, but she had only heard the voice of the maiden, and could not tell Demeter who had carried her away.

Onward sped the unhappy mother, sick at heart for hope unfulfilled, onward until she reached the sun. Here she learned that it was Pluto who had stolen her daughter, and carried her away to his gloomy kingdom.

Then in her despair Demeter left all her duties undone, and a terrible famine came upon the earth. "The dry seed remained hidden in the soil; in vain the oxen drew the ploughshare through the furrows."

As the days passed the misery of the people grew greater and greater, until faint and starving they came to Demeter, and besought her once again to bless the earth.

But sorrow had made the heart of the goddess hard, and she listened unmoved to the entreaties of the hungry folk, saying only that until her daughter was found she could not care for their griefs.

Long, weary days Demeter journeyed over land and sea to seek for Persephone, but at length she came back to Sicily.

One day as she walked along the bank of a river, the water gurgled gladly, and a little wave carried a girdle almost to her feet.

Demeter stooped to pick it up, and lo! it was the girdle that Persephone had worn on the day that she had been carried away. The maiden had flung it into the river as the chariot had plunged into the abyss, hoping that it might reach her mother. The girdle could not help Demeter to recover her

Demeter rejoiced for her daughter was by her side

daughter, yet how glad she was to have it, how safe she treasured it!

At length, broken-hearted indeed, Demeter went to Zeus to beg him to give her back her daughter. "If she returns the people shall again have food and plenteous harvests," she cried. And the god, touched with the grief of the mother and the sore distress of the people, promised that Persephone should come back to earth, if she had eaten no food while she had lived in the gloomy kingdom of Hades.

No words can tell the joy with which Demeter hastened to Hades. Here she found her daughter with no smile upon her sweet face, but only tears of desire for her mother and the dear light of the sun. But alas! that very day Persephone had eaten six pomegranate seeds. For every seed that she had eaten she was doomed to spend a month each year with Pluto. But for the other six months, year after year, mother and daughter would dwell together, and as they clung to one another they were joyous and content.

So for six glad months each year Demeter rejoiced, for her daughter was by her side, and ever it was spring and summer while Persephone dwelt on earth. But when the time came for her to return to Hades, Demeter grew ever cold and sad, and the earth too became weary and grey. It was autumn and winter in the world until Persephone returned once more.

CHAPTER IV

THE BIRTH OF ATHENE

ONE day Zeus was ill. To us it is strange to think of the gods as suffering the same pains as mortals suffer, but to the Hellenes it seemed quite natural.

Zeus was ill. His head ached so severely that he bade all the gods assemble in Olympus to find a cure for his pain. But not one of them, not even Apollo, who was god of medicine as well as Sungod, could ease the suffering deity.

After a time Zeus grew impatient with the cruel pain, and resolved at all costs to end it. So he sent for his strong son Hephaestus, and bade him take an axe and cleave open his head.

Hephaestus did not hesitate to obey, and no sooner had the blow descended than from his father's head sprang forth Athene, the goddess of war and wisdom. She was clad in armour of pure gold, and held in her hand a spear, poised as though for battle. From her lips rang a triumphant war-song.

THE BIRTH OF ATHENE

The assembled gods gazed in wonder, not unmixed with fear at the warrior goddess, who had so suddenly appeared in their midst. But she herself stood unmoved before them, while a great earthquake shook the land and proclaimed to the dwellers in Hellas the birth of a new god.

Athene was a womanly goddess as well as a warlike one. She presided over all kinds of needlework, and herself loved to weave beautiful tapestries.

Soon after the birth of the goddess a man named Cecrops came to a province in Greece, which was afterwards known as Attica. Here he began to build a city, which grew so beautiful beneath his hands that the gods in Olympus marvelled. When it was finished, each of the gods wished to choose a name for the city Cecrops had built.

As only one name could be used, the gods met in a great council to determine what was to be done. Soon, one by one, each gave up his wish to name the city, save only Athene and Poseidon.

Then Zeus decreed that Athene and Poseidon should create an object which would be of use to mortals. To name the city and to care for it should be the prize of the one who produced the more useful gift.

Poseidon at once seized his three-pronged fork or trident, which was the sign that he was ruler of the sea. As he struck the ground with it lo! a noble horse sprang forth, the first horse that the gods had seen.

As Poseidon told the gods in how many ways the beautiful animal could be of use to mortals, they thought that Athene would not be able to produce anything that could help men more.

When she quietly bade the council to look at an olive-tree, the gods laughed her to scorn. But they soon ceased to laugh. For Athene told them how the wood, the fruit, the leaves, all were of use, and not only so, but that the olive-tree was the symbol of peace, while the horse was the symbol of war. And war did ever more harm than good to mortals.

So the gods decided that it was Athene who had won the right to name the city, and she gave to it her own name of Athene, and the citizens ever after worshipped her as their own peculiar goddess.

Of this city, which we know as Athens, you will hear much in this story.

CHAPTER V

THE TWO WEAVERS

ATHENE could not only wield the sword, she could also ply the needle.

In these olden days there lived in Greece a Lydian maid who could weave with wondrous skill. So beautiful were the tapestries she wrought that her fame spread far and wide, and lords and ladies came from distant towns to see the maiden's skilful hands at work.

Arachne, for that was the maiden's name, lived in a cottage with her parents. They were poor folk, and had often found it hard to earn their daily bread. But now that their daughter was famous for her embroidery their troubles were at an end. For not only lords and ladies, but merchants, too, were glad to pay well to secure the young maid's exquisite designs.

And so all would have been well with Arachne and her parents had not the foolish girl become vain of her work. Soon her companions began to weary of her, for of nothing could she talk save of her own deft fingers, of her own beautiful embroideries.

Those who loved Arachne grew sad as they listened to her proud words, and warned her that "pride ever goes before a fall."

But Arachne only tossed her pretty head as she listened to the wisdom of older folk. Nor did she cease to boast, even saying that she could do more wonderful work than the goddess Athene.

Not once, but many times did Arachne say that she wished she might test her skill against that of the goddess. And should a prize be offered, proudly she declared that it was she who would win it.

From Olympus Athene heard the vain words of the maid. So displeased was she with her boldness that she determined to go to see Arachne, and if she did not repent to punish her.

She changed herself into an old white-haired dame, and came to earth. Leaning upon a staff she knocked at the door of the cottage where Arachne lived, and was bidden to enter.

Arachne was sitting in the midst of those who had come to see and to praise her work. Soon she began to talk, as she was quick to do, of her skill, and of how she believed that her work surpassed in beauty any that Athene could produce.

The old woman pushed her way through the group that surrounded the maid, and laying her hand upon the shoulder of Arachne she spoke kindly to her.

"Be more modest, my child," she said, "lest the anger of the gods descend upon you, lest Athene take you at your word, and bid you to the contest you desire."

Impatiently Arachne shook off the stranger's hand, and answered, "Who are you who dare speak to me? I would Athene might hear my words now, and come to test her skill against mine. She would soon see that she had a rival in Arachne."

Athene frowned at the insolence of the maiden. Then the little company were startled to see the old woman suddenly change into the glorious form of the goddess Athene. As they gazed they were afraid and fell at her feet.

But Arachne did not worship the goddess. Foolish Arachne looked boldly in her face, and asked if she had come to accept her challenge.

Athene's only answer was to sit down before an empty loom. Soon each, in silence, had begun to weave a wondrous tapestry.

Swift and more swift moved the fingers of the weavers, while the group of strangers, gathered now near to the door, watched the webs as they grew and grew apace.

Into her tapestry Athene was weaving the story of her contest with Poseidon for the city of Cecrops. The olive-tree, the horse, the gods in the council, all seemed to live as they appeared on the web of the goddess.

The tapestry woven by Arachne was also beauteous as her work was wont to be. In it you saw the sea, with waves breaking over a great bull, to whose horns clung a girl named Europa. And Europa's curls blew free in the wind.

At length Athene rose from the loom, her work complete. Arachne, too, laid down her spindle, and as she turned to look upon the tapestry of the goddess her courage suddenly failed.

A glance had been enough to show her that her skill was as nothing before the wonder and the beauty of Athene's work.

Too late the maiden repented that she had defied the goddess. In her despair she seized a rope and tied it round her neck to hang herself.

But the goddess saw what Arachne meant to do, and at once she changed her into a spider, bidding her from henceforth never cease to spin.

And so when you see a spider weaving its beautiful embroidery on a dewy morning in the garden, or when you find a delicate web in your lumber-room, you will remember how Athene punished poor foolish Arachne in the days of old.

CHAPTER VI

THE PURPLE FLOWERS

APOLLO, the youngest and most beautiful of all the gods, dearly loved a boy named Hyacinthus.

Ofttimes he would leave the other gods sipping nectar in Mount Olympus, ofttimes he would forsake the many beautiful temples in which he was worshipped on earth, that he might be free to wander through the woods with his little friend.

For Hyacinthus was only a merry little lad, who loved to roam over hill and dale, and when the fancy seized him to hunt in the woods.

Apollo was never happier than when he was with the boy. Sometimes he would go hunting with him, and then Hyacinthus was merrier than ever, for the world seemed more full of brightness when the Sun-god was by his side. Sometimes the friends would walk together over hill and dale, followed by the dogs Hyacinthus loved so well.

One day they had wandered far, and the little lad was tired, so he flung himself down in a grassy meadow to rest, Apollo by his side. But the Sun-god was soon eager for a game. He sprang to his feet, crying, "Hyacinthus, let us play at quoits before the shadows fall."

Quoits were flat, heavy discs, and the game was won by the player who could fling the quoits the farthest through the air.

Hyacinthus was ever willing to do as Apollo wished, and the game was soon begun. After a throw of more than usual skill and strength the friends laughed gleefully.

O but it was good to be alive in such a happy world, thought Hyacinthus. And Apollo, as he looked at the merry face of the little lad, rejoiced that he was not sitting in the cold marble halls of Olympus, but was here on the glad green earth.

By and by while they still played, Zephyrus, the god of the south wind, came fleeting by. He saw the Sun-god and his little playmate full of laughter and of joy.

Then an ugly passion, named jealousy, awoke in the heart of the god, for he too loved the little hunter Hyacinthus, and would fain have been in Apollo's place.

Zephyrus tarried a while to watch the friends. Once as Apollo flung his disc high into the air, the Wind-god sent a gust from the south which blew the quoit aside. He meant only to annoy Apollo, but Hyacinthus was standing by, so that the quoit struck him violently on the forehead.

THE PURPLE FLOWERS

The wind god sent a gust from the south

The boy fell to the ground, and soon he was faint from loss of blood.

In vain Apollo tried to staunch the wound; nothing he could do was of any use. Little by little the boy's strength ebbed away, and the Sun-god knew that the lad would never hunt or play again on earth. Hyacinthus was dead.

The grief of the god was terrible. His tears fell fast as he mourned for the playmate he had loved so well.

At length he dried his tears and took his lyre, and as he played he sang a last song to his friend. And all the woodland creatures were silent that they might listen to the love-song of the god.

When the song was ended, Apollo laid aside his lyre, and, stooping, touched with his hand the blood-drops of the boy. And lo! they were changed into a cluster of beautiful purple flowers, which have ever since been named hyacinths, after the little lad Hyacinthus.

Year by year as the spring sun shines, the wonderful purple of the hyacinth is seen. Then you, who know the story, think of the days of long ago, when the Sun-god lost his little friend and a cluster of purple flowers bloomed upon the spot where he lay.

CHAPTER VII

DANAE AND HER LITTLE SON

THE stories I have told you are about the gods of ancient Greece; the story I am going to tell you now is about a Greek hero.

When you think of a hero, you think of a man who does brave, unselfish deeds. But to the Hellenes or Greeks a hero was one who was half god, half man—whose one parent was a god while the other was a mortal. So the god Zeus was the father of Perseus, the hero of whom I am going to tell, while his mother was a beautiful princess named Danae.

From morning to night, from night till morning, Acrisius, the father of Danae, was never happy. Yet he was a king.

A king and unhappy? Yes, this king was unhappy because he was afraid that some day, as an oracle had foretold, he would be slain by his grandson.

The ancient Greeks often sent to sacred groves or temples to ask their gods about the future, and the answer, which was given by a priestess, was called an oracle.

Now Acrisius, King of Argos, had no grandson, so it was strange that the oracle should make him afraid. He hoped that he never would have a grandson.

His one child, beautiful, gentle Danae he had loved well until he had heard the oracle. Now he determined to send her away from the palace, to hide her, where no prince would ever find her and try to win her for his bride.

So the king shut the princess into a tower, which was encased in brass and surrounded it with guards, so that no one, and least of all a prince, could by any chance catch a glimpse of his beautiful daughter.

Very sad was Danae, very lonely too, when she was left in the brazen tower, and Zeus looking down from Olympus pitied her, and before long sent a little son to cheer her loneliness.

One day the guards saw the babe on his mother's knee. Here was the grandson about whom the king had hoped that he would never be born.

In great alarm they hastened to the palace to tell the king the strange tidings. Acrisius was so frightened when he heard their story that he flew into a passion, and vowed that both Danae and Perseus, as her little son was named, should perish. So he ordered the guards to carry the mother and her babe to the seashore, and to send them adrift on the waters in an empty boat.

For two days and two nights the boat was tossed hither and thither by the winds and the waves, while Danae, in sore dismay but with a brave heart, clasped her golden-haired boy tight in her arms.

The child slept soundly in the frail bark, while his mother cried to the gods to bring her and her treasure into a safe haven.

On the third day the answer to her prayers came, for before her Danae saw an island with a shore of yellow sand. And on the shore stood a fisherman with his net, looking out to sea. He soon caught sight of the boat, and as it drew near he cast his net over it, and gently pulled it to the shore.

It seemed to Danae almost too good to be true, to stand once again on dry land. She thought it was but a dream, from which she would awake to find herself once more tossing on the great wide sea.

But there stood Dictys, the fisherman, looking at her in wonder. Then Danae knew that she was indeed awake. She hastened to thank him for his help, and to ask him where she could find shelter for herself and her child.

Then the fisherman, who was the brother of Polydectes, king of the island on which Danae had landed, said that if she would go with him to his home he would treat her as a daughter. And Danae went gladly to live with Dictys.

For two days and two nights the boat was tossed
hither and thither

DANAE AND HER LITTLE SON

So Perseus grew up in the island of Seriphus, playing on the sands when he was small, and when he had grown tall and strong going voyages to other islands with Dictys, or fishing with him nearer home. Zeus loved the lad and watched over him.

Fifteen years passed, and then the wife of Polydectes died, and the king wished to marry Danae, for he loved her and knew that she was a princess.

But Danae did not wish to wed Polydectes, and she refused to become his queen, for indeed she loved no one save her son Perseus.

Then the king was angry, and vowed that if Danae would not come to the palace as his queen, he would compel her to come as his slave.

And it was even so, as a slave, that Perseus found her, when he returned from a voyage with Dictys.

The anger of the lad was fierce. How dare any one treat his beautiful mother so cruelly! He would have slain the king had not Dictys restrained him.

Subduing his anger as well as he could, Perseus went boldly to the palace, and taking no heed of Polydectes, he brought his mother away and left her in the temple of Athene. There she would be safe, for no one, not even the king, would enter the sanctuary of the goddess.

"Perseus must leave the island," said Polydectes when he was told of the lad's bold deed. He thought that if her son were banished Danae would be willing to become his queen.

But Polydectes was too crafty to issue a royal command bidding Perseus leave Seriphus. That, he knew, would make Danae hate him more than ever, so he thought of a better way to get rid of the lad. He arranged to give a great feast in the palace, and proclaimed that each guest should bring a gift to present to the king.

Among other youths, Perseus, too, was invited, but he was poor and had no gift to bring. And this was what the unkind king wished.

So when Perseus entered the palace empty-handed, Polydectes was quick to draw attention to the boy, laughing at him and taunting him that he had not done as the other guests and brought with him a gift. The courtiers followed the example of their king, and Perseus found himself attacked on every side.

The lad soon lost his temper and, looking with defiance at Polydectes, he cried, "I will bring you the head of Medusa as a gift, O King, when next I enter the palace!"

"Brave words are these, Perseus," answered the king. "See that you turn them into deeds, or we shall think you but boast as does a coward."

Then as Perseus turned and left the banqueting-hall the king laughed well pleased, for he had goaded the lad until he had fallen into the trap prepared for him. If Perseus went in search of the head of Medusa, he was not likely to be seen again in Seriphus, thought the king.

And Perseus, as he walked away toward the sea, was saying to himself, "Yes, I shall go in search of Medusa, nor shall I return unless I bring her head with me, a gift for the king."

CHAPTER VIII

THE QUEST OF PERSEUS

MEDUSA and her two sisters were named the Gorgons. The sisters had always been plain and ever terrible to see, but Medusa had once been fair to look upon.

When she was young and beautiful her home was in a northern land, where the sun never shone, so she begged Athene to send her to the south where sunshine made the long days glad. But the goddess refused her request.

In her anger Medusa cried, "It is because I am so beautiful that you will not let me go. For if Medusa were to be seen who then would wish to look at Athene."

Such proud and foolish words might not be suffered by the gods, and the maiden was sharply punished for her rash speech. Her beautiful curly hair was changed into serpents, living serpents that hissed and coiled around her head. Nor was this all, but whoever so much as glanced at her face was at once turned into stone.

Terrible indeed was Medusa, the Gorgon, whose head Perseus had vowed to bring as a gift to Polydectes. She had great wings like eagles and sharp claws instead of hands.

Now as Perseus wandered down to the shore after he had defied the king, his heart began to sink. How was he even to begin his task? He did not know where Medusa lived, nor did any one on the island.

In his perplexity he did as his mother had taught him to do; he prayed to Athene, and lo! even as he prayed the goddess was there by his side. With her was Hermes, the fleet-footed, wearing his winged sandals.

"The gods will aid you, Perseus," said Athene, "if you will do as they bid you. But think not to find their service easy. For they who serve the gods must endure hardship, and live laborious lives. Will this content you?"

Perseus had no fears now that he knew the gods would help him, and with a brave and steadfast heart, he answered, "I am content."

Then Pluto sent to the lad his magic helmet, which made whoever wore it invisible. Hermes gave to him the winged sandals he wore, so that he might be able to fly over land and sea, while Athene entrusted to him her shield, the dread Ægis, burnished bright as the sun. The shield was made from the hide of a goat, but the Hellenes thought of it as the great storm-cloud in which Zeus hid himself when he was angry. For it was the shield of her father Zeus that Athene used.

Upon Medusa herself Perseus would not be able to cast a glance lest he be turned to stone, but looking at the shield he would see her image as in a mirror.

The lad was now armed for his quest, but not yet did he know whither it would lead.

But Athene could direct him. She said that the abode of the Gorgons was known to none save three sisters called the Grææ. These sisters had been born with grey hair, and had only one eye and one tooth between them, which they used in turn. Their home was in the north, in a land of perpetual darkness, and it was there that Perseus must go to learn the dwelling-place of the Gorgons. So at length the lad was ready to set out on his great adventure.

On and on, sped by his winged sandals he flew, past many a fair town, until he left Greece far behind. On and on until he reached the dark and dreary land where the Grææ dwelt. He could see them now, the three grey sisters, as they sat in the gloom just outside their cave.

As Perseus drew near, unseen by them, because of his magic helmet, the sisters were passing their one eye from hand to hand, so that at that moment all three were blind.

Perseus saw his chance, and stretching out his hand seized the eye. They, each thinking the other had it, began to quarrel. But Perseus cried, "I hold the eye in my hand. Tell me where I may find Medusa and you shall have it back."

The sisters were startled by a voice when they had neither seen nor heard any one approach; they were more startled by what the voice said.

Very unwilling were they to tell their secret, yet what could they do if the stranger refused to give back their one eye? Already he was growing impatient, and threatening to throw it into the sea. So lest he should really fling it away they were forced to tell him where he would find the Gorgon. Then Perseus, placing the eye in one of the eager, outstretched hands, sped swiftly on his journey.

As he reached the land of which the Grææ had told him, he heard the restless beating of the Gorgon's wings, and he knew that his quest was well-nigh over.

Onward still he flew, and then raising his burnished shield he looked into it, and lo! he saw the images of the Gorgons. They lay, all three, fast asleep on the shore.

Unsheathing his sword, Perseus held it high, and then, keeping his gaze fixed upon the shield, he flew down and swiftly cut off Medusa's head and thrust it into a magic bag which he carried slung over his shoulder.

Now as Perseus seized the terrible head, the serpents coiled around the Gorgon's brow roused themselves, and began to hiss so fiercely that the two sisters awoke and knew that evil had befallen Medusa.

They could not see Perseus, for he wore his magic helmet, but they heard him, and in an instant they were following fast, eager to avenge the death of their sister.

For a moment the brave heart of the hero failed. Was he doomed to perish now that his task was accomplished?

He cried aloud to Athene, for he heard the Gorgons following ever closer on his path. Then more swiftly sped the winged sandals, and soon Perseus breathed freely once again, for he had left the dread sisters far behind.

CHAPTER IX

ANDROMEDA AND THE SEA-MONSTER

As Perseus journeyed over land and sea on his great quest, he often thought of the dear mother he had left in Seriphus. Now that his task was done he longed to fly over the blue waters of the Mediterranean to see her, to know that she was safe from the cruel King Polydectes. But the gods had work for Perseus to do before he might return to his island home.

Again and again he struggled against wind and rain, trying ever to fly in the direction of Seriphus, but again and again he was beaten back.

Faint and weary he grew, tired too of striving, so that he thought he would die in the desert through which he was passing.

Then all at once it flashed across his mind that Hermes had told him that as long as he wore the winged sandals he could not lose his way. New courage stole into his heart as he remembered the words of the god, and soon he found that he was being carried with the wind toward some high mountains. Among them he caught sight of a Titan or giant named Atlas, who had once tried to dethrone Zeus, and who for his daring had been doomed to stand,

> "Supporting on his shoulders the vast pillar
> Of Heaven and Earth, a weight of cumbrous grasp."

The face of Atlas was pale with the mighty burden he bore, and which he longed to lay down. As he caught sight of Perseus he thought that perhaps the stranger would be able to help him, for he knew what Perseus carried in his magic bag. So as he drew near Atlas cried to him, "Hasten, Perseus, and let me look upon the Gorgon's face, that I may no longer feel this great weight upon my shoulders."

Then in pity Perseus drew from his magic bag the head of Medusa, and held it up before the eyes of Atlas. In a moment the giant was changed into stone, or rather into a great rugged mountain, which ever since that day has been known as the Atlas Mountain.

The winged sandals then bore Perseus on until he reached a dark and desolate land. So desolate it was that it seemed to him that the gods had forsaken it, or that it had been blighted by the sins of mortals. In this island lived Queen Cassiopeia with her daughter Andromeda.

ANDROMEDA AND THE SEA-MONSTER

Cassiopeia was beautiful, but instead of thanking the gods for their gift of beauty, she used to boast of it, saying that she was fairer than the nymphs of the sea.

So angry were the nymphs when they heard this, that they sent a terrible monster to the island, which laid it waste, and made it dark and desolate as Perseus had seen.

The island folk sent to one of their temples to ask what they could do to free their island from the presence of the sea-serpent.

"This monster has been sent to punish Cassiopeia for her vain boast," was the answer. "Bid her sacrifice her daughter Andromeda to the sea-serpent, then will the nymphs remove the curse from your homes."

Andromeda was fair and good, and the people loved her well, so that they were greatly grieved at the oracle. Yet if they did not give up their princess their homes would be ruined, their children would perish before their eyes.

So while the queen shut herself up in her palace to weep, the people took the beautiful maiden down to the shore and chained her fast to a great rock. Then slowly, sorrowfully, they went away, leaving her a prey to the terrible monster.

As Perseus drew nearer to the sea he saw the maiden. The next moment he was gazing in horror at the sea-serpent, as with open, hungry jaws it approached its victim.

Quick as lightning, Perseus drew his sword and swooped down toward the monster, at the same moment holding before him the head of Medusa.

As the eyes of the serpent fell upon that awful sight, it slipped backward, and before Perseus could use his sword, it was changed into a rock, a great black rock. And if you go to the shore of the Levant you may see it still, surrounded by the blue waters of the Mediterranean.

CHAPTER X

ACRISIUS IS KILLED BY PERSEUS

As soon as Perseus saw that the monster was harmless, he took off his magic helmet, and hastening to Andromeda he broke the chain that held her to the rock. Then bidding her fear no more he led her back to the palace, where the queen sat weeping for her lost daughter.

When the door of her room was opened Cassiopeia never stirred. Andromeda's arms were around her, Andromeda's kisses were on her cheek before she could believe that her daughter was in very truth alive. Then, indeed, the mother's joy was boundless.

So fair, so good was the maiden that Perseus loved her, and thanked the gods who had led him to that desolate land. Before many weeks had passed the princess was wedded to the stranger who had saved her from the terrible sea-monster.

Twelve months later they left Cassiopeia, and sailed away to Seriphus, for Perseus longed to see his mother, and to bring to her his beautiful bride.

Seven long years had passed since Perseus set out on his quest, and Danae's heart was glad when she saw her son once more.

As soon as their greetings were over, Perseus left Andromeda with his mother, and went to the palace, carrying with him the head of Medusa in the magic bag.

The king was feasting with his nobles when Perseus entered the banqueting-hall. Long, long ago he had ceased to think of Perseus, for he believed that he had perished on his wild adventure. Now he saw him, grown to be a man, entering the hall, and he grew pale with sudden fear.

Paying no heed to any, Perseus strode through the throng of merry courtiers until he stood before the throne on which sat Polydectes.

"Behold the gift I promised you seven years ago, O King!" cried Perseus, and as he spoke he drew forth the head of Medusa and held it up for the king to see.

Polydectes and his startled nobles stared in horror at the awful face of the Gorgon, and as they gazed the king and all his followers were changed into figures of stone.

Then Perseus turned and left the palace, and telling the island folk that Polydectes was dead, he bade them now place Dictys, the fisherman, upon the throne.

He then hastened to the temple of Athene, and with a glad heart gave back to the goddess the gifts which had served him so well—the helmet, the sandals, the shield.

As his own offering to Athene he gave the head of the Gorgon. She, well pleased, accepted it, and had it placed in the centre of her shield, so from that day the Ægis became more terrible than before, for the Gorgon's head still turned to stone whoever looked upon it.

Danae had often talked to Perseus when he was a boy of Acrisius, her father, and of Argos, the city from which he had been banished when he was a babe. Perseus now resolved to sail to Argos with Danae and Andromeda. During these years Acrisius had been driven from his throne by an ambitious prince. He was in a miserable dungeon, thinking, it may be, of his unkindness to his daughter Danae, when she once again reached Argos.

Perseus soon drove away the usurper, and for his mother's dear sake he took Acrisius out of his dungeon and gave him back his kingdom. For Danae had wept and begged Perseus to rescue his grandfather from prison.

It seemed as though the oracle that long ago had made Acrisius act so cruelly would now never be fulfilled. But sooner or later the words of the gods come true.

One day Perseus was present at the games that were held each year at Argos. As he flung a quoit into the air a sudden gust of wind hurled it aside, so that it fell upon the foot of Acrisius, who was sitting near.

The king was an old man now, and the blow was more than he could bear. Before long he died from the wound, and thus the oracle of the gods was fulfilled.

Perseus was kind as he was brave, and it grieved him that he had caused the death of his grandfather, although it had been no fault of his own.

Argos no longer seemed a happy place to the young king, so he left it, and going to a city called Mycenæ, he made it his capital. Here, after a long and prosperous reign, Perseus died. The gods whom he had served loyally, placed him in the skies, among the stars. And there he still shines, together with Andromeda and Cassiopeia.

CHAPTER XI

ACHILLES AND BRISEIS THE FAIRCHEEKED

THE story of Perseus belongs to the Heroic Age of Greek history, to the time when heroes were half mortal, half divine. Many other wonderful tales belong to the Heroic Age, but among them all none are so famous as those that are told in the *Iliad* and the *Odyssey*. The *Iliad* tells of the war that raged around the walls of the city of Troy; the *Odyssey* of the adventures of the goodly Odysseus.

In the north-west corner of Asia, looking toward Greece, the ruins of an ancient city have been discovered. It was on this spot that Troy or Ilium was believed to have stood.

Strange legends gathered round the warriors of the Trojan War, so strange that some people say that there never were such heroes as those of whom the *Iliad* tells. However that may be, we know that in long after years, when the Greeks fought with the people of Asia, they remembered these old stories, and believed that they were carrying on the wars which their fathers had begun.

The *Iliad* and the *Odyssey* were written by a poet named Homer, so many wise folk tell. While others, it may be just as wise, say that these poems were not written by one man, but were gathered from the legends of the people, now by one poet, now by another, until they grew into the collection of stories which we know as the *Iliad* and the *Odyssey*.

At first these old stories were not written in a book; they were sung or told in verse by the poets to the people of Hellas. And because what is "simple and serious lives longer than what is merely clever," these grave old stories of two thousand years ago are still alive, and people are still eager to read them.

Some day you will read the *Iliad* and the *Odyssey*. In this story I can only tell you about a few of the mighty warriors who fought at Troy, about a few of their strange adventures.

If you look at a map of Greece you will easily find, in the south, the country called Peloponnesus. In Peloponnesus you will see Sparta, the capital city, over which Menelaus was king, when the story of the *Iliad* begins.

Menelaus was married to a beautiful queen named Helen. She was the fairest woman in the wide world.

One day there came to the court of the king a prince named Paris. He was the second son of

Priam, King of Troy. Menelaus welcomed his royal guest and treated him with kindness, but Paris repaid the hospitality of the king most cruelly. For when affairs of State called Menelaus away from Sparta for a short time, Paris did not wait until he returned. He hastened back to Troy, taking with him the beautiful Queen of Sparta, who was ever after known as Helen of Troy.

When Menelaus came home to find that Helen had gone away to Troy, he swore a great oath that he would besiege the city, punish Paris, and bring back his beautiful queen to Sparta; and this was the beginning of the Trojan War.

Menelaus had not a large enough army to go alone against his enemy. So he sent to his brother Agamemnon, who was the chief of all the mighty warriors of Hellas, and to many other lords, to beg them to help him besiege Troy, and if it might be, to slay Paris.

The chiefs were eager to help Menelaus to avenge his wrongs, and soon a great army was ready to sail across the Hellespont to Asia, to march on Troy.

But before the army embarked, the warriors sent, as was their custom, to an oracle, to ask if their expedition would be successful.

"Without the help of goodly Achilles, Troy will never be taken," was the answer.

Achilles was the son of Thetis, the silver-footed goddess, whose home was in the depths of the sea. Well did she love her strong son Achilles. When he was a babe she wished to guard him from the dangers that would surely threaten him when he grew to be a man, so she took him in her arms and carried him to the banks of the river Styx. Whoever bathed in these magic waters became invulnerable, that is, he became proof against every weapon. Silver-footed Thetis, holding her precious babe firmly by one heel, plunged him into the tide, so that his little body became at once invulnerable, save only the heel by which his mother grasped him. It was untouched by the magic water.

Achilles set sail with the other chiefs for Troy, so it seemed as though the city would be taken by his help, as the oracle foretold. With him Achilles took his well-loved friend Patroclus.

For nine long years was the city of Troy besieged, and all for the sake of Helen the beautiful Queen of Sparta. Often as the years passed, she would stand upon the walls of Troy to look at the brave warriors of Hellas, to wonder when they would take the city. But when nine years had passed, no breach had yet been made in the walls.

When the Hellenes needed food or clothing, they attacked and plundered the neighbouring cities, which were not so well defended as Troy.

The plunder of one of these cities, named Chryse, was the cause of the fatal quarrel between Agamemnon and Achilles.

In Chryse there was a temple sacred to Apollo, guarded by a priest named Chryses. His

ACHILLES AND BRISEIS THE FAIRCHEEKED

Often she would stand upon the walls of Troy

daughter Chryseis, and another beautiful maiden named Briseis the Faircheeked, were taken prisoners when the town was sacked by the Hellenes. Agamemnon claimed the daughter of the priest as his share of the spoil, while Briseis he awarded to Achilles.

When Chryses the priest found that his daughter had been carried away by the Greeks, he hastened to the tent of Agamemnon, taking with him a ransom great "beyond telling." In his hands he bore a golden staff on which he had placed the holy garland, that the Greeks, seeing it, might treat him with reverence.

"Now may the gods that dwell in the mansions of Olympus grant you to lay waste the city of Priam and to fare happily homeward," said the priest to the assembled chiefs, "only set ye my dear child free and accept the ransom in reverence to Apollo."

All save Agamemnon wished to accept the ransom and set Chryseis free, but he was wroth with the priest and roughly bade him begone.

"Let me not find thee, old man," he cried, "amid the ships, whether tarrying now or returning again hereafter, lest the sacred staff of the god avail thee naught. And thy daughter will I not set free. But depart, provoke me not, that thou mayest the rather go in peace."

Then Chryses was angry with Agamemnon, while for his daughter's sake he wept.

ACHILLES AND BRISEIS THE FAIRCHEEKED

Down by the "shore of the loud-sounding sea" he walked, praying to Apollo, "Hear me, god of the silver bow. If ever I built a temple gracious in thine eyes, or if ever I burnt to thee fat flesh .... of bulls or goats, fulfil thou this my desire; let the Greeks pay by thine arrows for my tears."

Apollo heard the cry of the priest, and swift was his answer. For he hastened to the tents of the Greeks, bearing upon his shoulders his silver bow, and he sped arrows of death into the camp.

Dogs, mules, men, all fell before the arrows of the angry god. The bodies of the dead were burned on great piles of wood, and the smoke rose black toward the sky.

For nine days the clanging of the silver bow was heard. Then Achilles called the hosts of the Greeks together, and before them all he spoke thus to Agamemnon: "Let us go home, Son of Atreus," he said, "rather than perish, as we surely shall do if we remain here. Else let us ask a priest why Apollo treats us thus harshly."

But it was easy to tell why Apollo was angry, and Calchas, a seer, answered Achilles in plain-spoken words. "The wrath of the god is upon us," he said, "for the sake of the priest whom Agamemnon spurned, refusing to accept the ransom of his daughter. Let Chryseis be sent back to her father, and for sacrifice also a hundred beasts, that the anger of the god may be pacified."

Deep was the wrath of Agamemnon as he listened to the words of Calchas.

"Thou seer of evil," he cried, his eyes aflame with anger, "never yet hast thou told me the thing that is pleasant. Yet that the hosts of our army perish not, I will send the maiden back. But in her place will I take Briseis the Faircheeked, whom Achilles has in his tent."

When Achilles heard these words he drew his sword to slay Agamemnon. But before he could strike a blow he felt the locks of his golden hair caught in a strong grasp, and in a moment his rage was checked, for he knew the touch was that of the goddess Athene. None saw her save Achilles, none heard as she said to him, "I came from heaven to stay thine anger. . . . Go to now, cease from strife, and let not thine hand draw the sword."

Then Achilles sheathed his sword, saying, "Goddess, needs must a man observe thy saying even though he be very wroth at heart, for so is the better way."

Yet although Achilles struck no blow, bitter were the words he spoke to the king, for a coward did he deem him and full of greed. "If thou takest from me Briseis," he cried, "verily, by my staff, that shall not blossom again seeing it has been cleft from a tree, never will I again draw sword for thee. Surely I and my warriors will go home, for no quarrel have we with the Trojans. And when Hector slaughters thy hosts, in vain shalt thou call for Achilles."

Well did Agamemnon know that he ought to soothe the anger of Achilles and prevail on him to stay, for his presence alone could make the Trojans fear. Yet in his pride the king answered, "Thou mayest go and thy warriors with thee. Chieftains have I who will serve me as well as thou, and who will pay me more respect than ever thou hast done. As for the maiden Briseis, her I will have, that the Greeks may know that I am indeed the true sovereign of this host."

The Assembly then broke up, and Chryseis was sent home under the charge of Odysseus, one of the bravest of the Greek warriors.

When the priest received his daughter again, he at once entreated Apollo to stay his fatal darts, that the Greeks might no longer perish in their camp. And Apollo heard and laid aside his silver bow and his arrows of death.

Then Agamemnon called heralds, and bade them go to the tent of Achilles and bring him Briseis of the fair cheeks. "Should Achilles refuse to give her up," said the angry king, "let him know that I myself will come to fetch the maiden."

But when the heralds told Achilles the words of the king, he bade Patroclus bring the damsel from her tent and give her to the messengers of Agamemnon. And the maiden, who would fain have stayed with Achilles, was taken to the king.

CHAPTER XII

MENELAUS AND PARIS DO BATTLE

WHEN the heralds of Agamemnon had led Briseis away, Achilles stripped off his armour, for not again would he fight in the Trojan War. Down to the seashore he went alone to weep for the loss of Briseis the Faircheeked.

As he wept he called aloud to his mother Thetis. From the depths of the sea she heard his cry, and swift on a wave she reached the shore. Soon she was by the side of her son, and taking his hand, as when he was a boy, she asked, "My child, why weepest thou?"

Then Achilles told how Agamemnon had taken from him Briseis, whom he loved.

"Go to the palace of Zeus," he entreated her, "and beseech Zeus to give me honour before the hosts of the Greeks. Let him grant victory to the Trojans until the king sends to Achilles to beg for his help in the battle."

MENELAUS AND PARIS DO BATTLE

So Thetis, for the sake of her dear son, hastened to Olympus, and bending at the knee of Zeus she besought the god to avenge the wrong done to Achilles.

At first Zeus, the Cloud-gatherer, was silent, as though he heard her not. "Give me now thy promise," urged Thetis, "and confirm it with a nod or else deny me."

Then the god nodded, and thereat Olympus shook to its foundations. So Thetis knew that she had found favour in the eyes of Zeus, and leaving the palace of the gods she plunged deep into the sea.

Zeus hastened to fulfil his promise, and sent to Agamemnon a "baneful dream."

As the king dreamed, he thought he heard Zeus bid him go forth to battle against the Trojans, for he would surely take the city. But in this Zeus deceived the king.

When Agamemnon awoke in the morning he was glad, for now he hoped to win great honour among his warriors. Quickly he armed himself for battle, throwing a great cloak over his tunic, and slinging his sword, studded with silver, over his shoulder. In his right hand he bore the scepter of his sires, the sign of his lordship over all the great hosts of Hellas.

Then when he was armed, the king assembled his great army, and after telling his dream, he bade it march in silence toward the city.

But when the Trojans saw the Hellenes drawing near, they came out to meet them "with clamour and with shouting like unto birds, even as when there goeth up before heaven a clamour of cranes which flee from the coming of winter and sudden rain."

As the Trojans approached, Menelaus saw Paris who had stolen his fair wife, and he leaped from his chariot that he might slay the prince. But Paris, when he saw the wrath of Menelaus, was afraid and hid himself among his comrades.

Then Hector, his brother, who was the leader of the Trojans, mocked at him for his cowardice, until Paris grew ashamed.

"Now will I challenge Menelaus to single combat," he cried. And Hector rejoiced at his words and bade the warriors stay their arrows.

"Hearken, ye Trojans and ye Greeks," he cried, "Paris bids you lay down your arms while he and his enemy Menelaus alone do battle for Helen and for her wealth. And he who shall be victor shall keep the woman and her treasures, while we will make with one another oaths of friendship and of peace." So there, without the walls of the city, oaths were taken both by the Greeks and the Trojans. But the heart of Priam, King of Troy, was heavy lest harm should befall Paris, and he hastened within the gates of the city that he might not watch the combat. "I can in no wise bear to behold with mine eyes my dear son fighting with Menelaus," he said. "But Zeus knoweth, and all the immortal gods, for whether of the twain the doom of death is appointed."

Then Menelaus and Paris drew their swords, and Menelaus cried to Zeus to grant him his aid, so that hereafter men "may shudder to wrong his host that hath shown him kindness."

But it seemed that Zeus heard not, for when Menelaus flung his ponderous spear, although it passed close to Paris, rending his tunic, yet it did not wound him, and when he dealt a mighty blow with his sword upon the helmet of his enemy, lo, his sword broke into pieces in his hand.

Then in his wrath, Menelaus reproached the god: "Father Zeus," he cried, "surely none of the gods is crueler than thou. My sword breaketh in my hand, and my spear sped from my grasp in vain, and I have not smitten my enemy."

Yet even if Zeus denied his help, Menelaus determined to slay his foe. So he sprang forward and seized Paris by the strap of his helmet. But the goddess Aphrodite flew to the aid of the prince, and the strap broke in the hand of Menelaus. Before the king could again reach his enemy, a mist sent by the goddess concealed the combatants one from the other. Then, unseen by all, Aphrodite caught up Paris, "very easily as a goddess may," and hid him in the city within his own house.

In vain did Menelaus search for his foe, yet well did he know that no Trojan had given him shelter. For Paris was "hated of all even as black death," because it was through his base deed that Troy had been besieged for nine long years.

CHAPTER XIII

HECTOR AND ANDROMACHE

THE gods were angry with Aphrodite because she had hidden Paris from the king, and they determined that, in spite of their oath, the two armies should again begin to fight.

So Athene was sent to the Trojan hosts, disguised as one of themselves. In and out among the soldiers she paced, until at length she spoke to one of them, bidding him draw his bow and wound Menelaus.

The soldier obeyed, and the arrow, guided by Athene, reached the king, yet was the wound but slight.

When the Greeks saw that the Trojans had disregarded their oath, they were full of wrath, and seizing their arms they followed their chiefs to battle. "You had thought them dumb, so silent were they," as they followed. But as the Trojans looked upon the enemy there arose among them a confused murmur as when "sheep bleat without ceasing to hear their lambs cry."

Fierce and yet more fierce raged the battle. Valiant deeds were done on both sides, but when Hector saw that the Greeks were being helped by the gods, he left the battlefield and hastened to the city.

At the gates, wives and mothers pressed around him, eager to hear what had befallen their husbands, their sons. But Hector tarried only to bid them go pray to the gods.

On to the palace he hastened to find Hecuba, his mother. She, seeing him come, ran to greet him and beg of him to wait until she brought honey-sweet wine, that he might pour out an offering to Zeus, and himself drink and be refreshed.

But Hector said, "Bring me no honey-sweet wine, my lady-mother, lest thou cripple me of my courage and I be forgetful of my might. But go thou to the temple with all thy women, to offer gifts to Athene and to beseech her aid."

Then leaving his mother, Hector went to the house of Paris, and bitterly did he rebuke him, because he was not in the forefront of the battle.

"Stay but till I arm and I will go with thee," answered Paris. But Hector heeded him not, for he was in haste to find his dear wife Andromache and their beautiful boy, Skamandriss. By the people the child was called Astyanax, the City King, for it was his father who guarded Troy.

HECTOR AND ANDROMACHE

Andromache was not in their house, but on the wall of the city, watching the battle, fearing lest harm should befall her lord. With her was her little son, in the arms of his nurse.

Hector dared not linger to search for his wife, but as he hastened back to the gates she saw him and ran to bid him farewell ere he returned to battle.

Close to his side she pressed, and her tears fell as she cried:

> "Too brave! thy valour yet will cause thy death.
> Thou hast no pity on thy tender child,
> Nor me, unhappy one, who soon must be
> Thy widow. All the Greeks will rush on thee
> To take thy life. A happier lot were mine
> If I must lose thee to go down to earth,
> For I shall have no hope when thou art gone—
> Nothing but sorrow. Father have I none,
> And no dear mother. . . .
>   Hector, thou
> Art father and dear mother now to me,
> And brother and my youthful spouse besides,
> In pity keep within the fortress here,
> Nor make thy child an orphan nor thy wife
> A widow."

But Hector, though he dearly loved his wife, could not shrink from battle. As Andromache ceased to plead with him, he held out his arms to his little son, but the child drew back in fear of the great plumes that waved on his father's shining helmet.

Then Hector took off his helmet and laid it upon the ground, while he caught his child in his arms and kissed him, praying Zeus and all the gods to defend him.

Andromache gazed pitifully at her husband as, at length, he gave the child to its nurse, and he seeing her great grief, took her hand and said:

> "Sorrow not thus, beloved one, for me.
> No living man can send me to the shades
> Before my time; no man of woman born,
> Coward or brave, can shun his destiny.
> But go thou home and tend thy labours there,
> The web, the distaff, and command thy maids
> To speed the work. The cares of war pertain
> To all men born in Troy, and most to me."

Then springing into his chariot, Hector drove swiftly back to the field of battle.

CHAPTER XIV

THE HORSES OF ACHILLES

HECTOR and Paris reached the battlefield at the same moment. The Trojans were encouraged to fight yet more fiercely when they saw the two princes, and soon so many of the Greeks were slain that Agamemnon grew afraid.

"Zeus hath sent me a deceiving dream," he said to his counselors. "If the gods send not their help we must perish, unless indeed Achilles will forget his anger and come to our aid. Verily, Zeus loveth Achilles, seeing that he putteth the Greeks to flight that he may do him honour. But even as I wronged him in my folly, so will I make amends and give recompence beyond all telling."

Then, casting aside his pride, the king sent messengers to the tent of Achilles, to say that he would send back Briseis and give to him splendid gifts if he would but come to the help of the Greeks, for they were flying before the enemy.

But the heart of Achilles was too bitter to be touched by the fair promises of the king, for had he not taken from him Briseis, the lady of his love? So he bade the messengers go back to Agamemnon and say that he would not fight, but he would launch his ships on the morrow and sail away to his own land.

When the king heard that Achilles spurned his gifts, and refused to come to his aid, he was afraid. But his counsellors said, "Let us not heed Achilles, whether he sail or whether he linger by the loud-sounding sea. When the gods call to him, or when his own heart bids, he will fight. Let us go once more against the Trojans, and do thou show thyself, O king, in the forefront of the battle."

Then Agamemnon rallied his men and led them against the foe, yet again he was driven back. Chief after chief was wounded, and at length the Hellenes fled to their ships to defend them from the Trojans. But Patroclus determined to plead with Achilles to save his countrymen from defeat. When he entered the tent of his friend he was weeping for pity of the dead and wounded.

"Wherefore weepest thou, Patroclus, like a fond little maid that runs by her mother's side?" asked Achilles as he looked up at the entrance of his friend and saw his tears.

"Never may such wrath take hold of me as that thou nursest, thrice brave, to the hurting of others," answered his comrade. "The Greeks are lying wounded and dead. If thou wilt not come to their help, let me lead thy men so that the enemy may be beaten back...."

> "And give
> The armour from thy shoulders. I will wear
> Thy mail, and then the Trojans, at the sight,
> May think I am Achilles, and may pause
> From fighting."

Even as Patroclus pleaded with his friend, a great light flared up against the sky. The Trojans had set fire to the Greek ships.

Then, at length, Achilles was roused. He would not go himself to the help of Agamemnon, but he bade Patroclus put on his armour, while he called together his brave warriors and commanded them to follow his friend to battle.

Quickly Patroclus donned the well-known armour of Achilles, then calling to Automedon, the chariot driver, he bade him harness Xanthus and Balius, the immortal horses of his friend, for their speed was swift as the wind.

As Patroclus vanished from sight in the chariot drawn by Xanthus and Balius, Achilles prayed to Zeus. "O Zeus," he cried, "I send my comrade to this battle. Strengthen his heart within him, and when he has driven from the ships the war and din of battle, scathless then let him return to me and my people with him."

Down upon the Trojans swept the warriors led by Patroclus. They, seeing the armour of Achilles were afraid, and fled from the ships. But ere long they discovered that it was not Achilles but Patroclus who wore the well-known armour, and they returned to fight with new courage. And ever, where the battle raged most fiercely, did Patroclus bid Automedon drive his chariot.

Then the gods bade Hector find Patroclus and slay him. Little trouble had the prince in finding the warrior who wore the armour of Achilles. Bravely the two heroes fought, but Patroclus was not able to stand against the great strength of Hector. Moreover, the gods betrayed him, striking him from behind on the head and shoulders, so that the helmet of Achilles fell in the dust. Apollo also snatched his shield from his arm and broke his spear in two.

When Hector saw that his enemy was disarmed, he took his spear and struck him so fiercely that Patroclus fell

> "With clashing mail, and all the Greeks beheld
> His fall with grief."

The friend of Achilles was wounded to death.

In his triumph Hector was merciless. He mocked at his fallen foe saying, "Patroclus, surely thou saidst that thou wouldst sack my town, and from Trojan women take away the day of freedom, and bring them in ships to thine own dear country. Fool, ... I ward from them the day of destiny, but thee shall vultures here destroy."

Faint though he was, Patroclus answered, "It was not thou, Hector, who didst slay me, but Apollo, who snatched from me my shield and brake my sword in twain." Then his strength failed and he breathed his last.

No pity yet showed Hector, for he stripped off the armour of Achilles from the body of Patroclus that he might wear it himself. But Zeus, as he looked upon the haughty victor, was displeased.

"Ah, hapless man," said the god to himself, "no thought is in thy heart of death that yet draweth nigh unto thee; thou doest on thee the divine armour of a peerless man before whom the rest have terror. His comrade, gentle and brave, thou hast slain, and unmeetly hast stripped the armour from his head and shoulders."

The immortal horses of Achilles wept when they knew that Patroclus was slain. Automedon lashed them, he spoke kindly to them, yet would they not move. As a pillar on a tomb, so they stood yoked to the chariot. From their eyes big teardrops fell, their beautiful heads hung down with grief so that their long manes were trailed in the dust. Thus sorely did the immortal steeds grieve for the death of Patroclus.

CHAPTER XV

THE DEATH OF HECTOR

FIERCE and long raged the battle around the body of Patroclus. And while the armies fought, a messenger hastened to the tent of Achilles to tell him that his comrade was slain and that the Trojans fought for his body as it lay naked on the ground, stripped of its armour. "Thy armour," said the messenger, "Hector has taken for himself."

When Achilles heard the bitter tidings he took dust and poured it with both hands upon his head. "As he thought thereon, he shed big tears, now lying on his side, now on his back, now on his face, and then anon he would rise upon his feet, and roam wildly beside the beach of the salt sea." As he cried aloud in his grief his mother, Thetis, heard in her home beneath the sea. Swiftly she sped to her son that she might learn why he wept.

Achilles told her all that had befallen Patroclus, and how he himself cared no longer to live, save only that he might slay Hector who had killed his friend.

THE DEATH OF HECTOR

Thetis bade her son wait but till the morrow before he went to battle and she would bring him armour made by the great Fire-god.

Then she left him and prayed the god Hephaestus, keeper of the forge, to give her armour for her dear son.

Hephaestus was pleased to work for so goodly a warrior as Achilles. Quickly he set his twenty bellows to work, and when the fire blazed in the forge, he threw into it bronze and silver and gold. Then taking a great hammer in his hand he fashioned a marvellous shield, more marvellous than words can tell. Before morning a complete suit of armour was ready for Achilles.

Meanwhile Hector had all but captured the body of Patroclus. But the gods spoke to Achilles, bidding him now succour the body of his friend. Without armour Achilles could not enter the fray, yet he hastened to the trenches that the Trojans might see him.

Around his head gleamed a golden light, placed there by Athene. When the Trojans saw the flame and heard the mighty cry of Achilles, they drew back afraid.

Three times the warrior shouted, and three times the Trojans drew back in fear. While they hesitated the Greeks rushed forward and carried away the body of Patroclus, nor did they lay it down until they laid it in the tent of Achilles.

On the morrow Thetis came back to her son, bringing with her the armour made by Hephaestus. She found him weeping over the body of his friend.

"My child," she said, "him who lieth here we must let be, for all our pain. Arm thyself now and go thy way into the fray."

Then Achilles put on the armour of the god in haste, for he feared lest another than he should slay Hector.

With Achilles once again at their head, the Greek warriors attacked the Trojans with redoubled fury. But it was Hector alone whom Achilles longed to meet, and soon he saw his enemy near one of the gates of Troy. Now he would avenge the death of Patroclus. But when Hector saw the great hate in the eyes of his enemy, lo, he turned and fled.

"As a hawk, fastest of all the birds of the air, pursues a dove upon the mountains," so did Achilles pursue the prince until he was forced to stand to take breath. Then Hector, encouraged by the gods, drew near to him and spoke, "Thrice, great Achilles, hast thou pursued me round the walls of Troy, and I dared not stand up against thee; but now I fear thee no more. Only do thou promise, if Zeus give thee the victory, to do no dishonour to my body, as I also will promise to do none to thine should I slay thee."

But Achilles, remembering Patroclus, cried out in anger that never would he make a covenant with him who had slain his friend.

THE DEATH OF HECTOR

Then with fierce blows each fell upon the other, until at length Achilles drove his spear through the armour that Hector wore, and the Trojan prince fell, stricken to the ground.

Achilles, his anger still burning fiercely, stripped the dead man of his armour, while many Greek warriors standing near thrust at him with their spears, saying to one another, "Go to, for easier to handle is Hector now, than when he burnt the ships with blazing fire."

Then Achilles tied the dead man to his chariot with thongs of ox-hide and drove nine times round the city walls, dragging the fair head of Hector in the dust.

From the tower Priam and Hecuba saw the body of their son dragged in the dust, and bitter was their pain.

But Andromache knew not yet what had befallen her lord, for she sat in an inner chamber wearing a purple cloth. Soon she bade her maids prepare a bath for Hector, for she thought that he would return ere long from the battle. She knew not yet that Hector would never return, but as the noise of the wailing of the people reached the room in which she sat, her heart misgave her. In haste she ran to the wall of the city, only to see the chariot of Achilles as it dragged Hector down to the loud-sounding sea.

Then fainting with grief, Andromache fell to the ground, and the diadem which Aphrodite had given to her on her wedding morn dropped from her head, to be worn by her no more.

Down by the seashore Achilles burned the body of Patroclus with great honour, and when the funeral rites were ended, he dragged the dead body of Hector round the tomb, weeping for the loss of his dear comrade.

But Zeus was angry with Achilles for treating the Trojan prince so cruelly, and he sent Thetis to bid her son give back Hector's body to Priam, who would come to offer for it a ransom. "If Zeus decrees it, whoever brings a ransom shall return with the dead," answered Achilles.

Then Zeus sent a messenger to the house of Priam, where the mother and the wife of Hector wept, saying, "Be of good cheer in thy heart, O Priam. . . . I am the messenger of Zeus to thee, who though he be afar off, hath great care and pity for thee. The Olympian biddeth thee ransom noble Hector's body, and carry gifts to Achilles that may gladden his heart."

So Priam set out alone, save for the driver of the wagon which was to bring Hector again to Troy, for so had the messenger commanded. But Hecuba feared to let the old man go alone to the tent of the enemy. When he reached the camp of the Greeks, Priam hastened to the tent of Achilles, and entering it before his enemy was aware, the old king fell at the feet of his enemy and begged for the body of his dear son.

THE DEATH OF HECTOR

Achilles could not look upon the grief of the old man unmoved, but when Priam offered him gifts he frowned and haughtily he answered, "Of myself am I minded to give Hector back to thee, for so has Zeus commanded."

Then a truce for nine days was made between the Greeks and the Trojans, so that King Priam and his people might mourn for Hector and bury him undisturbed by fear of the enemy.

Priam tarried with Achilles until night fell. Then while he and his warriors slept, the king arose and bade the driver yoke the horses and mules. When this was done they laid the body of Hector upon the wagon, and in the silence of the night set out on their homeward journey.

At the gates of Troy stood Andromache and Hecuba watching until Priam returned. And when the wagon reached the city the Trojans carried Hector into his own house. Then Andromache took the head of her dear husband in her arms and said, "Husband, thou art gone young from life and leavest me a widow in thy halls. And the child is yet but a little one . . . nor methinks shall he grow up to manhood, for ere then shall this city be utterly destroyed. For thou art verily perished who didst watch over it and guard it, and keptest safe its noble wives and infant little ones."

The following morning Priam bade his people go gather wood for the burial, and after nine days the body of Hector was laid on the pile and burned. Then his white bones, wrapped in purple cloth, were placed in a golden chest. Above the chest a great mound was raised, and thus, Hector, the brave prince of Troy, was buried.

Soon after the burial of Hector Achilles was killed by a poisoned arrow which Paris aimed at his heel, the one spot of his body that Thetis had failed to bathe in the magic waters of the river Styx. Paris himself perished soon after the death of Achilles.

Troy still remained untaken. Then goodly Odysseus told the Greeks that although they could not take the city by storm, they might take her by a stratagem or trick.

So the Greeks, as he bade them, built a huge wooden horse, which was hollow within. Here they hid a number of their bravest warriors, and then the main body of the army marched away, as though they were tired of trying to take the city. The wooden horse they left as an offering to Poseidon. Only a slave named Sinon was left behind to persuade the Trojans to drag the horse into the city. But the Trojans needed little persuasion. They came out of the city, gazed at the strange horse, half feared a trick, and then, like children amused with a new toy, they pulled it within the walls of Troy.

So glad were the Trojans that the enemy had gone away, that they made a great feast. While they ate and drank, careless of danger, Sinon helped the Greek warriors out of the hollow wooden horse. They waited until it was late and all was quiet, then they slipped down to the gates and flung them open, while their comrades, who had not marched far away, rushed in to plunder and burn the city. Thus after many long years Troy was taken by the counsel of Odysseus.

One of the first to sail away from the city was Menelaus, with his beautiful queen safe at his side. After many adventures he reached Sparta and lived with Helen "in peace, comfort, and wealth, and his palace shone in its splendour like the sun or the moon."

CHAPTER XVI

POLYPHEMUS THE GIANT

THE Greek warriors burned and sacked the city of Troy, and then they set sail for the sunny isles of Greece. But storms overtook some, the gods sent misfortune to others, so that but few reached their own land in safety.

Odysseus, King of Ithaca, an island on the western coast of Greece, suffered greater hardships than any other. For ten years he was either tossed by the gods on stormy seas, or kept a captive in strange countries. Of some of his adventures I shall tell you now.

When Odysseus and his comrades sailed away from Troy, they were driven by a fair wind to the shore of Ismarus. Here dwelt a rich and prosperous people called the Cicones.

The Greeks wished to take much spoil back with them to their homes, so they resolved to slay the Cicones and plunder their city.

POLYPHEMUS THE GIANT

Some of the citizens escaped the sword of the adventurers and hastened to their kinsmen who dwelt farther from the shore. When they had told their terrible tidings, their comrades armed themselves and sped to the shore to punish the strangers.

Odysseus had tried in vain to make his followers go back to their ships. They had refused to be hurried, and were now sitting on the seashore eating and drinking, heedless of danger.

Before they were aware the kinsmen of the Cicones had fallen upon them, and when the sun went down they had slain six men out of each of the strangers' ships. The rest barely escaped with their lives.

Scarcely had the Greeks reached their vessels and sailed away from Ismarus, when Zeus sent a north wind against them. For nine days their ships were driven hither and thither. Their sails were torn to shreds, when on the tenth day the sailors caught sight of land. It was the land of the lotus-eaters, where the people fed only on the fruit of the lotus, a fruit that brought sleep and forgetfulness to the eater.

Odysseus sent three sailors on shore to find out what manner of people the lotus-eaters were. No sooner had they landed than the inhabitants brought them fruit, which they ate with delight. But the honey-sweet flowers made them forget Odysseus, their comrades, and their ships. They had no wish save to stay for ever with the lotus-eaters to share their magic food.

At length, Odysseus grew tired of waiting for the three sailors to return, and he himself with a few armed men went on shore to look for them. He thought that perhaps they had been taken prisoners and had been bound with chains, but he found them lying on the yellow sand, dreamy and content.

> "And sweet it was to dream of Fatherland,
> Of child, and wife, and slave; but evermore
> Most weary seem'd the sea, weary the oar,
> Weary the wandering fields of barren foam."

When the three sailors saw Odysseus they cried:

> " 'We will return no more.'
> And all at once they sang, 'Our island home
> Is far beyond the wave; we will no longer roam.' "

Odysseus and his comrades were offered fruit by the kindly lotus-eaters, but Odysseus waved it aside and bade his men drag away the three sailors who had already eaten. The sailors wept sore, for fain would they have dwelt for ever in the land of dreams. But when they were once more on their vessels and had put out to sea, the breezes brought back health to their bodies, vigour to their minds. Soon they were able to rejoice that they had left the enchanted lotus-land far behind.

POLYPHEMUS THE GIANT

Westward sailed the fleet of Odysseus, until it reached the island of Sicily, where the Cyclopes dwelt. The Cyclopes were giants who had each but one eye, fixed in the middle of his brow.

Odysseus, taking with him only his own crew, landed on the island, for he wished to see the Cyclopes. He had walked but a little way when he came to a great cave, in which stood baskets filled with cheeses and milkpans filled with milk. In this cave dwelt Polyphemus, one of the sons of Poseidon, and the fiercest of all the fierce Cyclopes.

Into this cave went Odysseus and his comrades. Polyphemus was not within; he was out on the hills with his flocks.

"Let us take the cheeses and drive away the lambs and the kids that are here, before the giant returns," said the sailors. But Odysseus would not do as they wished, for, said he, "I greatly wish to see the giant shepherd who dwells in the cave."

"Verily," said Odysseus, as he told the tale in after days, "verily, his coming was not to be a joy to my company."

Evening drew on apace, and Polyphemus, driving his flocks before him, reached the cave. When he had driven his flocks in before him, the giant took a huge rock and placed it in the doorway.

Odysseus and his comrades had hidden themselves in the dimmest corners of the cave when Polyphemus entered. The giant lighted a great fire of pine wood and began to milk the ewes. Soon the flames lighted up every corner of the cave, and Polyphemus saw his unexpected guests.

In a voice that struck terror even into the brave hearts of the Greeks, so gruff, so loud it was, the giant demanded, "Strangers, who are ye? Whence sail ye over the watery ways? On some trading enterprise or at adventure do ye rove, even as sea-robbers over the brine?"

Boldly then answered Odysseus, "*No Man*' is my name. My ship, Poseidon, the shaker of the earth, broke it to pieces, for he cast it upon the rocks at the border of your country, and brought it nigh the headland, and a wind bore it thither from the sea. But I, with these my men, escaped from utter doom. Give us, we beseech thee, food and shelter."

As you know, Odysseus had not been shipwrecked, his vessel, safely anchored, awaited his return, nor was his true name *No Man*. He dared not tell the giant the truth, lest he should go in search of his ship and take it for firewood, while he and his companions were kept prisoners in the cave.

The giant said not a word when Odysseus ended his tale, but he stretched out his great hand, seized two of the strangers, and devoured them before the eyes of their horrified companions. Then, well satisfied with his meal, he fell fast asleep.

In the morning the giant finished his breakfast by eating two more of his guests, then, moving away the stone at the entrance of the cave as easily as if it had been a feather, he drove his flocks to pasture.

He did not forget to replace the stone in the doorway before he turned away.

CHAPTER XVII

ODYSSEUS ESCAPES FROM THE CAVE

ODYSSEUS was determined that he and his comrades should escape from the cave of the dread Cyclops. Hour after hour he pondered how he might persuade the giant to let them go, but at length he thought, "I will not persuade him, I will force him to let us go."

At that moment, his eye fell upon a great staff or club in a corner of the cave. He bade his companions make a sharp point to it. When this was done he hardened it in the fire and then hid it from sight.

The day passed slowly, but at length evening came and Polyphemus returned to the cave. His guests shrank into the farthest corner as the giant began his supper, but ere he finished, he again stretched out his hand, seized two of his prisoners, and devoured them. Then Odysseus offered him a draught of wine which he had brought with him from Ismarus.

ODYSSEUS ESCAPES FROM THE CAVE

Deep drank the giant, and ere he fell into a sound sleep he turned to Odysseus saying, "*No Man,* thee will I eat last in return for thy gift of wine."

Odysseus waited until he saw that Polyphemus was fast asleep, then he bade his comrades put the point of the great staff in the fire. When it was red hot he told them to thrust it deep into the eye of the giant. So great was the pain that the Cyclops heaped up from his sleep and hurled away the staff, uttering loud cries of agony.

The giants who dwelt on the mountains round about heard the voice of Polyphemus, and together they hastened to the doorway of the cave.

"What hath so distressed thee, Polyphemus," they cried, "that thou criest thus aloud through the immortal night and makest us sleepless? Surely no mortal driveth off thy flocks against thy will; surely none slayeth thyself by force or craft?"

"*No Man* is slaying me by guile, nor at all by force," answered Polyphemus, proud even in his pain.

"If no man is harming thee, it may be that Zeus has sent sickness upon thee," answered the giants. "Pray thou then to thy father Poseidon for aid. As for us, we will go back to our slumbers."

Odysseus laughed to himself as he heard their retreating feet, for now he was sure that he would be able to save himself and his comrades.

When morning dawned, Polyphemus, still groaning with pain, groped his way to the door. Having found it he pushed the stone a little way to the side to allow his flocks to pass out of the cave. To make sure that his prisoners did not escape with the animals, he sat down by the entrance and touched the back of each ram as it passed. But Odysseus had tied his followers with osier twigs beneath the rams, and so, in spite of the care of the giant, all his prisoners escaped. Odysseus himself was the last to leave the cave, holding fast to the fleece of the largest ram.

No sooner had Odysseus rejoined his companions than he loosened the twigs with which he had bound them. Then together they ran to the shore, driving before them many of the giant's best sheep. These they took on board their ship, and then rowed out some way from land.

Polyphemus soon found that he had been outwitted, and he began to stumble down toward the sea.

When Odysseus saw him, he bade his men rest on their oars, while he spoke to the giant in a loud voice.

"Cyclops," he cried, "so thou wert not to eat the company of a weakling by main might in thy hollow cave. Thine evil deeds were very sure to find thee out, thou cruel man, who hadst no shame to eat thy guests within thy gates, wherefore Zeus hath requited thee and the other gods."

ODYSSEUS ESCAPES FROM THE CAVE

In his rage Polyphemus took a great rock off the top of a mountain and hurled it in the direction from which the voice came. The rock fell near to the bow of the ship, so that the waters rose and pushed the vessel toward the shore.

But Odysseus seized a pole and swiftly thrust the ship back from the land. Then he bade the sailors pull for the open sea with might and main.

When the ship was once more some distance from the shore, Odysseus taunted the giant yet again with his evil deeds.

"Cyclops," he cried, "if any one of mortal men shall ask thee of the unsightly blinding of thine eye, say that it was Odysseus who blinded it, the Waster of Cities, son of Laertes, whose dwelling is in Ithaca."

Then the giant, in impotent anger, stretched out his hands to the heavens and cried, "Hear me, Poseidon, girdler of the earth, god of the dark hair, if indeed I be thy son.... Grant that he may never come to his home, even Odysseus, waster of cities, son of Laertes, whose dwelling is in Ithaca; yet if he is ordained to see his friends and come into his well-builded house and his own country, late may he come, and in evil case, with the loss of all his company, in the ship of strangers, and find sorrows in his house."

And so it came to pass, even as the Cyclops prayed, for only after many wanderings did Odysseus reach his home, to find it in the hands of those who prayed that the king might never return to Ithaca.

CHAPTER XVIII

ODYSSEUS RETURNS TO ITHACA

THE small island of Ithaca, of which Odysseus was king, lay on the western shore of Greece. His subjects deemed that their king was dead, for ten years had passed since Troy had been destroyed, and yet he had not come home.

But Penelope, the wife of Odysseus, would not believe that her lord was dead; she clung to the hope that he would yet return. Princes came to the palace to beg the queen to wed, but in vain did each urge his suit, for hope whispered in the heart of Penelope, "My lord is still alive."

Laertes, the father of Odysseus, was too old, her little son Telemachus was too young, to help the queen, when the princes rudely insisted on living in the palace and in wasting the goods of Odysseus. Again and again they entreated her to wed one among them. But the queen grew angry and rebuked them for their insolence in living in the palace. From day to day, from week to week, from month to month, even from year to year, Penelope mocked at the impatience of her suitors.

For she set up in the hall of the palace a large loom and began to weave a beautiful robe. "Ye princely youths, my wooers," she said, "now that Odysseus is dead, as ye declare, do ye abide patiently, how eager soever on this marriage of mine, till I finish the robe."

The princes agreed to wait until the robe was finished, but little did they dream how long the queen would take to her task.

Day after day, day after day, they watched as Penelope sat at her web weaving, ever weaving. But night after night, night after night, when the insolent princes had gone to bed, the queen carefully unraveled the work they had seen her do by day.

For three long years did Penelope mock her suitors in this way, but when the fourth year came, and the robe was still incomplete, one of the queen's serving-maids betrayed her secret to the princes.

Then the queen could no longer refuse to wed, yet still she tried to put off the day as long as might be. So she promised to marry him who could most easily bend the great bow of Odysseus, and hit the mark on which she should decide. There was now but a little while until the day would dawn on which the trial of strength and skill was to take place.

Telemachus meanwhile had grown into a tall lad, and, guided by Athene, he left the palace where the princes wasted his wealth to go in search of his father. It might be that Odysseus was a captive in some distant land.

But Odysseus was on his way to Ithaca, sailing in the ship of a king who had befriended him.

As the vessel glided into the harbour of the little island, Odysseus lay asleep on the deck. So the sailors lifted him in a rug on which he lay and put him down in his own kingdom by the side of the road.

When he awoke Odysseus did not at first know where he was, for Athene had covered the land with a thick mist.

"O woe is me now, unto what mortals' land am I now come?" cried the king, well-nigh in tears with desire for his own country.

Even as he spoke, Athene stood by his side disguised as a young man.

"What land is this?" asked Odysseus, not yet knowing that it was the goddess to whom he spoke, but thinking that it was one of the country folk.

"Thou art witless, stranger, or thou art come from afar, if indeed thou askest of this land," said Athene. "Verily it is rough and not fit for the driving of horses, yet is it not a very sorry isle, though narrow withal. For herein is corn past telling, and herein, too, wine is found, and the rain is on it evermore and the fresh dew. And it is good for feeding goats and feeding kine; all manner of wood is here, and watering-places unfailing are herein. Wherefore stranger, the name of Ithaca hath reached even unto Troyland."

Then Odysseus knew that it was the grey-eyed goddess Athene who spoke to him, and he answered, "Methinks that thou speakest thus to mock me and beguile my mind. Tell me whether, in very deed, I am come to mine own country?"

The goddess did not answer, but silently she scattered the mist that the king might see that he was indeed in his own kingdom.

Then Odysseus was glad and stooped to kiss the earth, knowing that at last his weary wanderings were at an end.

CHAPTER XIX

ARGUS THE HOUND DIES

ATHENE knew that if Odysseus went to the palace, the princes would pretend that he was not the king, and would perhaps even slay him. So she bade him go, not to the palace, but to the hut of his swineherd Eumaeus, who had remained loyal to him and to his house.

That no one, not even the swineherd, might recognise the king, Athene changed him into an old beggar man, with dirty, tattered garments.

In this miserable guise Odysseus reached the hut of Eumaeus. Now Eumaeus believed that strangers were sent by Zeus, so he welcomed the beggar and gave him food.

As he ate, the swineherd sat beside him, bewailing the absence of his king, who had never returned from the Trojan War.

"His name," said Eumaeus, "even though he is not here, it shameth me to speak, for he loved me exceedingly, and cared for me at heart; nay I call him 'worshipful,' albeit he is far from hence."

Much, too, did the swineherd tell of Penelope, of Telemachus, and of how the insolent suitors lived at the palace and wasted the king's goods. As Odysseus listened, he longed to go at once to the palace to avenge his wrongs.

That night the king spent in the hut of his swineherd, lying before the fire, while over him the swineherd flung a covering of goatskins. But Eumaeus did not sleep. He cast over his shoulders a rough mantle, and taking with him a sharp sword he went out to guard his herd of swine. And the king was glad when he saw how well the swineherd cared for the flocks of his absent lord.

In the morning, as Eumaeus kindled a fire and prepared breakfast for the stranger, footsteps were heard without. Telemachus had returned to Ithaca, having sought for his father in vain.

Eumaeus hastened to welcome his master's son and "kissed him all over as one escaped from death." Then he set before the prince the best that his hut could provide.

When Telemachus had eaten and had drunk sweet wine out of a wooden goblet, he bade Eumaeus hasten to the palace to tell his mother that he had come safely home. So the swineherd took his sandals, bound them on his feet and set out for the city. Odysseus and Telemachus were left alone.

Then Athene came to the hut unseen, and changed Odysseus into his own goodly form, bidding him tell Telemachus who he was.

At first the prince could not believe that this stranger, so strong, so fair, was Odysseus. But when at length he knew that it was indeed his father he embraced him, while tears of joy fell down his cheeks.

Then Athene bade them determine how the king should make himself known to Penelope, and how the greedy and insolent suitors should be punished.

The father and son talked long together and they agreed that on the morrow Telemachus should go to the palace, but to none, no, not even to Penelope, was he to tell that Odysseus had returned.

The arms that hung in the hall of the palace the prince was to hide in his own room, so that when the time for the king's revenge should come the suitors might find neither sword nor shield with which to defend themselves. Odysseus was to follow his son to the palace when a few hours had passed, disguised once more as a beggar.

So, on the morrow, Telemachus set out for the palace. As he entered the hall the first to see him was his father's old nurse Eurycleia. She was busy spreading the skins upon the oaken chairs, but she left her work and ran to greet the prince, "kissing him lovingly on the head and shoulders."

ARGUS THE HOUND DIES

Penelope, too, coming from her chamber, saw him, and cast her arms about her dear son and fell a-weeping, and kissed his face and both his beautiful eyes. "Thou art come, Telemachus," she said, "a sweet light in the dark. Methought I should never see thee again."

While Telemachus was still telling his lady-mother all that had befallen him in his search for his father, the beggar with Eumaeus by his side, entered the court of the palace.

In the court lay Argus, the great hound that Odysseus himself had trained ere he went to Troy. Old was he now and despised, for no longer could he run in the hunt, swift as the wind. The princes had banished him from the hall, while by the servants he was spurned.

As the beggar drew near, Argus raised his head, looked at the stranger, and began to wag his tail to show his joy. For rags could not hide his master from the faithful hound.

Odysseus turned his head away, that Eumaeus might not see his tears.

"Surely a hound so noble as this should not lie thus neglected in the yard," he said to the swineherd.

"In very truth," answered Eumaeus, "this is the dog of a man that has died in a far land. If he were what once he was in limb and in the feats of the chase, when Odysseus left him to go to Troy, soon wouldst thou marvel at the sight of his swiftness and his strength. There was no beast that could flee from him in the deep places of the wood when he was in pursuit of prey."

As the king and the swineherd passed on into the palace, Argus fell back content to die, for after watching and waiting for twenty years he had seen his master once again.

CHAPTER XX

THE BOW OF ODYSSEUS

In the hall of the palace the suitors sat feasting, as was their custom. When Eumaeus entered, followed by the beggar, they no sooner caught sight of him than they began to mock at his rags. But Telemachus took a loaf and gave it to the stranger, bidding him go to each prince and beg for himself, for said he, "Shame is an ill mate of a needy man."

One haughty suitor, named Antinous, rebuked Eumaeus for bringing a beggar to the palace. "Have we not here vagrants enough," he said in angry tones, "killjoys of the feast?" And he seized a footstool and struck Odysseus on the shoulder.

Penelope heard how Antinous had treated the stranger in her halls and she was angry. Turning to her old nurse Eurycleia she said, "Nurse, they are all enemies, for they all devise evil continually, but of them all Antinous is the most like to black fate. Some hapless stranger is roaming about the house, begging alms of the men as his needs bid him; all the others filled his wallet and gave him somewhat, but

Antinous smote him at the base of the right shoulder with a stool."

Then she summoned Eumaeus and bade him send the stranger to her, for she wished to know if he had heard aught of Odysseus as he wandered from place to place.

So when evening came the old nurse brought a settle, spread over it a fleece, and placed it near to Penelope. Then the beggar was brought to the queen's room, and, sitting on the settle, he told to her many a tale, and some were true and some were false, for he would not yet have her know that he himself was her lord Odysseus.

Penelope wept as she listened to the stories the stranger told. For he had seen Odysseus, and she thought that her husband might yet return in time to save her from the suitors whom she despised.

But at length the queen dried her tears and called to Eurycleia to come wash the feet of the stranger, who was of the same age as her master.

The old woman answered, "Gladly will I wash his feet, for many strangers travel-worn have ere now come hither, but I say that I have never seen any so like another as this stranger is like Odysseus, in fashion, in voice, and in feet."

Then the king feared lest his old nurse should know him, and he turned his face from the hearth. But she, as she tended him, saw a scar on the spot where a boar had wounded him long years before, and she knew her master had come home.

"Yea, verily, thou art Odysseus"

Tears well-nigh choked her, yet she touched his chin lightly and said, "Yea, verily, thou art Odysseus, my dear child."

But when she would have told the queen, Odysseus bade her be silent, until he had taken revenge on the princes who were feasting in his palace.

As she dismissed the stranger, Penelope told him that on the morrow the suitors held a feast, when they were to contend for her hand. "Him who shall most easily bend the bow of Odysseus I have promised to wed," she said. "Then will I go and forsake this house, this house of my wedlock, so fair and filled with all livelihood, which methinks I shall yet remember, aye, in a dream."

Then Odysseus answered, "Wife revered of Odysseus, no longer delay this contest in thy halls; for lo, Odysseus will be here before these men, for all their handling of this polished bow, shall have strung it and shot the arrow to the mark."

Penelope scarce heard the stranger's words, so troubled were her thoughts. She bade him farewell, then went to her room to weep for her absent lord until "grey-eyed Athene cast sweet sleep upon her eyelids."

On the morrow Odysseus awoke early, and as he thought of all that he hoped to do that day, he lifted up his hands to Zeus.

"O Father Zeus," he cried, "if thou hast led me to mine own country of good will, then give me

THE BOW OF ODYSSEUS

a sign." And in answer the god thundered from Olympus, and Odysseus knew the voice of the god and was glad.

Penelope too arose early on this fateful day, and when she had put on her royal robes she came down the wide staircase from her chamber, carrying in her hand the strong key of her lord's treasure-chest.

She unlocked the chest, and taking from it the great bow in its case she laid it upon her knees and wept over it. Then, drawing the bow from its case, she carried it into the hall where the suitors were feasting.

"Ye suitors," she said, as she laid down before them the bow and quiver of arrows, "Ye suitors, who devour this house, making pretence that ye wish to wed me, lo! here is a proof of your skill. Here is the bow of the great Odysseus. Whoso shall bend it easiest in his hands and shoot an arrow nearest to the mark I set, him will I follow, leaving this house of my wedlock, so fair which methinks I shall yet remember, aye, in a dream."

Then each suitor in turn tried to bend the mighty bow, but each tried in vain.

"Give the bow to me," cried the beggar, as he saw that the suitors had failed to bend the mighty bow, "give it to me that I may prove that my hands are strong."

The princes laughed at the words of the stranger. How should the old man bend the bow which they in their youthful strength were unable to move?

But Telemachus gave the bow into the stranger's hands, for, said he, "I would fain see if the wanderer can bend the bow of Odysseus." Then turning to his mother, the prince besought her to go to her daily tasks until the contest was over, for not for her eyes was the dread revenge of Odysseus. So Penelope with her maidens went to her room, and as she spun she mourned for her absent lord.

In the hall Odysseus stood with his beloved bow in his hand. Carefully he tested it lest harm had befallen it in his absence. Then taking an arrow from the quiver he placed it on the bow and drew the string, and lo! it sped to its mark and reached the wall beyond.

At once Telemachus, his sharp sword in his hand, sprang to his father's side, while Eumaeus, to whom the beggar's secret had been told, followed him fast.

The suitors leaped to their feet in dismay as the arrows of Odysseus fell swiftly among them. Then they turned to the walls to seek the arms which usually hung there, but Telemachus had carried them away.

Not until the proud suitors were slain did Odysseus cease to bend his mighty bow. But at length all was over and none were left to mock at the stranger.

Then Odysseus bade Eurycleia go tell Penelope that her lord had returned and awaited her in the hall.

The queen lay on her bed fast asleep when the old nurse broke into her room, and, all tremulous with joy, told her that Odysseus had come and slain the suitors. Too good were the tidings for Penelope to believe.

"Dear nurse," she cried, "be not foolish. Why dost thou mock my sorrow? It may be that one of the gods hath slain the suitors, but Odysseus hath perished in a strange land."

"Nay, I mock thee not, dear child," answered Eurycleia. "The stranger with whom thou didst talk yesterday is Odysseus."

Yet Penelope could not believe that her lord had returned. She spoke sadly to the old nurse, telling her that she was deceived and did not understand the ways of the gods. "None the less," she added, "let us go to my child, that I may see the suitors dead, and him that slew them."

Down in the hall Odysseus, clothed no longer in rags, but in bright apparel, awaited his wife.

Then Penelope as she gazed upon him knew that it was indeed Odysseus, and she threw her arms around him and kissed him, saying "Be not angry with me, Odysseus, that I did not know thee when I first saw thee. For ever I feared lest another than thou should deceive me, saying he was my husband, but now I know that thou art indeed he." So welcome to her was the sight of her lord, that "her white arm she would never quite let go from his neck."

Thus after twenty years did Odysseus come back to Ithaca.

CHAPTER XXI

THE LAND OF HELLAS

THE stories of gods and heroes are not pure history. They are myths or legends which have grown with the ages, until sometimes they are told as though they were true.

Although the tales I have been telling you of the early days of Greece are myths, yet the Greeks who lived in later times would often speak of them as though they had actually happened.

I am going to tell you now, not of gods or heroes, but of the true deeds of mortal men. And first of all you will wish to hear a little about the land in which the ancient Greeks lived.

It was named, as you already know, Hellas, while the inhabitants were called Hellenes.

But Hellas and her people had another name given to them by the Romans, who called Hellas Graecia, and the Hellenes Graeci, from a tribe that dwelt in a part of the country known as Epirus. Epirus was not a very important region, but it was well known to the Romans who dwelt in the south of Italy. We have altered these Roman names a little and call Hellas Greece, the Hellenes Greeks.

If you open your atlas at the map of Europe, you will find in the south the little country of Greece, which although it is so small has yet flung its influence over all the wide world.

On three sides Greece is bounded by the Mediterranean Sea, and the country is now usually known as the Balkan Peninsula.

Greece is a land of great mountains. Of its loftiest summit, Olympus, which in ancient days was the abode of the gods, you have already read.

The coast-line is broken up much as is the coast of Scotland, by arms of the sea which run far inland, so far inland that it is easy to reach the water from any part of the country.

Close to the shores of Greece lie the islands of the Ægean Sea. In these islands many Greeks settled, so that they became an important part of Greece. The Ægean Sea we now call the Archipelago.

In the time of Homer all Greeks were called Achaeans. But in later days, only those Greeks were called Achaeans who lived in the narrow strip of land in northern Peloponnesus called Achaea.

The ancient Achaeans dwelt in the valleys, which were cut off from one another by great spurs of mountains. They were united by an ancient league, and quarrelled less with one another than did the other peoples of Greece.

Besides the Achaeans there were three other great races in Greece.

The Dorians came from a little country called Doris, near the famous Pass of Thermopylae, of which you have still to hear. The Ionians dwelt on the east side of the Ægean Sea, that is, they lived on the coast of Asia, while the Æolians were scattered here and there throughout Greece.

All these different tribes were Greeks, and they were proud of their name, counting all other peoples barbarians, and despising them because they were not Greeks. Many of them were traders or adventurers from Asia, and they entered the new country from the north-east, through Thessaly, and that was not a difficult journey.

Others crossed over from Asia by sea to search for a new home. But their galleys were rough, uncomfortable vessels, in which there was little room for the many who embarked. When storms arose they suffered great misery, huddled closely together on their small and unseaworthy boats. Fear, too, took hold of them and the horror of death.

So the wanderers were glad when they saw the many little islands that were studded here and there over the Ægean Sea. Some of these islands, it is true, were mere rocks, desolate and without water. But there were others where people had already settled and made a home. On these the strangers landed to fight with the inhabitants, until, by the help of the gods, they had conquered and taken possession of them. Here they feasted, glad of heart that the perils of the sea were now at an end.

In the Heroic Age the kings of the different tribes were believed to have descended from the gods, and each country or state had its own king. And so it was when the Heroic Age had passed away. Each tribe or little nation, living in its own valley or plain, still had its own separate sovereign, and each soon built for itself a city. The city might be small, but it was always surrounded by a wall, which was built for defence. If there was no wall it was not a city but a village, however large it might be.

In those days kings were not ashamed to work. They were often to be seen in the fields at harvest time, not looking idly on, but toiling side by side with their people.

Odysseus, King of Ithaca, is said to have built his own bedroom as well as his own boats. He claimed too to be a skilful ploughman and reaper. And still, for many years after the age of Odysseus, kings worked as hard as he had done.

The queens and princesses were as diligent as the kings. Often they were to be found, like Penelope, sitting at a loom weaving or working beautiful embroideries. They even went to the well themselves to fetch water, and were sometimes to be seen by the riverside, where they helped to wash the linen of the household.

In battle the king was always on the field, riding before his army in a war chariot.

When peace reigned he often sat in the market-place to judge his people. Each suppliant told his own tale and brought his own witnesses. The elders of the city then gave their judgment of the case, after which the king, taking his sceptre in his hand, stood up to pronounce sentence.

But above all else the king was the chief priest of his people, offering sacrifices for them, while they, with due reverence, looked upon him as a god.

CHAPTER XXII

LYCURGUS AND HIS LITTLE NEPHEW

THE Dorians were a brave and sturdy race, braver, perhaps, than any other of the Greek tribes. Apollo, the Sun-God, one of the noblest of the Olympians, was the god they held in greatest reverence.

A band of these Dorians came from the north and settled in the valley of Laconia, through which flows the river Eurotas. Here they built villages and called themselves Lacedaemonians.

Before long five of these villages joined together to form a city, which was named Sparta. Sparta became the capital or chief city in Laconia.

At first the new city was weak, scarcely able to hold her own against the neighbouring tribes, and much less able to add to her dominion. She was indeed hardly able to keep order within her own borders.

Sparta was ruled not by one king but by two, and so you might perhaps think that she would be governed better than any other city or state, but this was not so.

The first kings were twin brothers, for an oracle had bidden the Spartans "to take both as kings, but to give greater honour to the elder."

Instead of helping each other to improve their country, the two kings often disagreed, and then spent their days in quarrelling. The people were content that they should do so, for while the kings quarrelled they had no time to frame stricter laws or to punish those who disturbed the peace of the city.

It soon became clear that if Sparta was to grow great and prosperous a strong man must be found to guide the kings as well as the people. This strong man was found in Lycurgus the famous lawgiver.

History tells little about the life of the lawgiver, but many legends cluster around his name. It is told that Lycurgus belonged to one of the royal houses, and that when his elder brother died he became for a short time one of the kings of Sparta.

The queen-mother was an ambitious woman, and she wished still to sit on the throne as she had done while her husband was alive. So she said to Lycurgus that she would kill her tiny baby boy who would one day be king, if he would marry her. But the lawgiver was angry, and rebuked the queen-mother for wishing to do such a wicked deed.

One night as he sat at supper with the chief men of Sparta, Lycurgus ordered his little nephew to be brought to him.

When the child was carried into the room he took him in his arms and holding him up for all to see, he cried, "Men of Sparta, here is a king born unto us." Before them all he placed the babe on the throne, and as the child had not yet been named, he called him Charilaus, the joy of the people.

From that time Lycurgus became the guardian of his little nephew and the regent of the kingdom. So upright were his ways, so honest his words, that he was reverenced by the people as greatly as when he was king.

Meanwhile the queen-mother had not forgiven Lycurgus for thwarting her ambition, and she determined to punish him. So she spread a report among the people that Lycurgus meant to put his nephew to death that he might again become king.

Before long the rumour spread by the queen-mother reached the ears of Lycurgus, and he at once made up his mind to leave Sparta until Charilaus was old enough to reign. As he journeyed from place to place Lycurgus studied the laws and manners of the different countries, so that when he returned to Sparta he might be able to improve the laws of his own land.

In Ionia he is said not only to have read the works of Homer, but to have met the poet himself. So wise were many of the customs described in the poet's books that he set to work to reframe those that he thought would be of most use in his own country.

Some stories tell that Lycurgus made a copy of part of the poet's works, for it is thought that the Greeks at this time (about 800 or 900 B.C.) already knew how to write. It was thus Lycurgus who made the works of Homer well known to his countrymen.

But in all his travels what interested Lycurgus most was the way the soldiers were trained in Egypt. In other countries he had seen men who ploughed their fields or plied their trade, leave their work to fight when war broke out, but the Egyptian soldiers were soldiers and nothing else all the year round.

Lycurgus determined that he would train the youths of Sparta as strictly as the soldiers in Egypt were trained. They should be neither ploughmen nor merchants, but the best soldiers the world had ever seen.

CHAPTER XXIII

LYCURGUS RETURNS TO SPARTA

While Lycurgus was journeying from country to country, Sparta was ruled more badly than before. The laws were not obeyed, and no one punished those who disobeyed them.

The citizens who cared for the welfare of the State longed for the return of Lycurgus and even sent messengers to bid him come home.

"Kings, indeed, we have," they said, "who wear the marks and assume the titles of royalty, but as for the qualities of their minds they have nothing by which they are to be distinguished from their subjects. You alone have a nature made to rule and a genius to gain obedience."

Lycurgus was at length persuaded to return to Sparta, but before he would attempt to reform the laws of his country he went to Delphi to ask the help and advice of Apollo.

LYCURGUS RETURNS TO SPARTA

The oracle encouraged the future lawgiver, for it told him that he was beloved of the gods, who heard his prayers, and that his laws would make Sparta the most famous kingdom in the world.

Then Lycurgus hesitated no more. He went back to Sparta determined to spend his life for the good of his country.

His first act was to call together thirty of the chief men of Sparta and tell them his plans. When they had promised to support him he bade them assemble armed, at the market-place at break of day, for he wished to strike terror into the hearts of those who were ready to resist any change in the laws of the land.

On the day appointed, the market-place was crowded with the followers of Lycurgus and the mob who had come to see what was going to be done.

King Charilaus hearing the tramp of armed men was so frightened that he fled to the temple of Athene for sanctuary, or, as we should say, for safety. He believed that a plot had been formed against him and that his life was in danger.

But Lycurgus soon allayed the king's fears, sending a messenger to tell him that all he wished to do was to give better laws to the State, so that it might grow strong and prosperous.

King Charilaus was a kind and gentle prince. His brother-king, who knew him well, said, "Who can say he is anything but good. He is so even to the bad."

When he had been reassured by his uncle, Charilaus left the temple of Athene, and going to the market-place he joined Lycurgus and his thirty followers.

Lycurgus began his reforms by limiting the power of the kings, for he decreed that on all important matters of State they should consult the Senate or Council of Elders.

The plans of the Senate were laid before the assembly of the people, the members saying, "Yes" if they agreed to them, "No" if they disagreed. Nor were they allowed to talk together over the matter before they gave their answer.

Long after the death of the lawgiver, five new rulers, called ephors or overseers, were chosen from the people.

At first the ephors shared their power with the kings, but little by little they succeeded in getting more power into their own hands. They began their duties with this strange order to the people, "Shave your upper lip and obey the laws."

Although the kings lost some of their power through the laws that were made by Lycurgus, yet they kept their right as priests to offer each month solemn sacrifices to Apollo for the safety of the city. Before the army marched to battle it was usual, too, for the kings to pray to the gods to give them victory. But there were other priests in Sparta as well as those who belonged to the royal houses.

The supreme command of the army belonged to the kings, who might go to war with any country as they pleased. If a noble or one of the people tried to interfere with their decision, he was punished. A bodyguard of a hundred always attended the royal commanders.

But as the years passed, a new law was made declaring that only one of the kings should go to battle at the head of the army, and that one was forced to account to the people for the way in which he carried on the war.

In still later times the power of the king on the battlefield was checked by the presence of two ephors. Sometimes a king was glad of their presence, and would even appeal to them to make the soldiers obey the royal commands.

When a king died, no public work was done until ten days after the funeral. Herodotus, a great Greek historian, tells us how the news of the royal death was made known. "Horsemen carry round the tidings of the event throughout Laconia, and in the city women go about beating a caldron. And at this sign, two free persons of each house, a man and a woman, must put on mourning garb (that is sackcloth and ashes), and if any fail to do this great pains are imposed."

Lycurgus not only made laws to lessen the power of the kings. He tried also to alter the extravagant customs of the people. Gold and silver money was banished from the country, and large bars of iron were used in its place. These bars were so heavy, and took up so much room, that it was impossible to hoard them.

CHAPTER XXIV

THE TRAINING OF THE SPARTANS

LYCURGUS had seen the severe discipline which soldiers in Egypt were forced to undergo. He had made up his mind that his own countrymen should be trained as thoroughly.

The Spartans at this time were poor and their numbers were small, perhaps about ten thousand were fit to bear arms. They were surrounded by enemies whose attacks they found hard to repulse.

But Lycurgus thought that if each citizen became a soldier, and that if each soldier was trained from his childhood to fight and to endure hardship, Sparta would soon have an army that no other power could conquer.

So as soon as a baby boy was born in Sparta he was taken to the Council of Elders that they might decide if he should live or die. If the child was strong and healthy he was given back to his parents, if he was weak and ailing he was left alone on a hillside to die from cold and hunger.

When he was seven years old, the Spartan boy was taken from his home to a public training-house. Here the strict discipline commanded by Lycurgus was begun.

Shoes and stockings were never worn by the little lads of Sparta, although the hills and countryside were rough for unshod feet. In winter they were clad in one garment, just as in summer.

Their beds were made of rushes, which they had themselves gathered from the banks of the river Eurotas. This was a hard task, for they were not allowed to cut them with a knife, but must break them with their hands. In winter the boys used to scatter thistle-down on the rushes to give a little warmth to their hard couch.

Each child, from the age of seven, cooked his own food, which was scanty and plain. If after their meals the boys were still hungry, so much the better, said Lycurgus. It would teach them to hunt the more keenly, that they might add to their daily portion of food. It would teach them to steal from the neighbouring farm-yards or gardens without being found out.

So a hungry Spartan boy would climb into a garden undiscovered, or even slip into a stranger's larder in search of fruit and food.

THE TRAINING OF THE SPARTANS

If the boys were caught, they were punished, not, I am sorry to tell you, for stealing, but for being so clumsy as to be found out.

Once a Spartan boy stole a young fox and hid it under his coat. It soon began to scratch with its claws, to bite with its teeth, until the lad was in terrible pain, yet he would have died rather than tell what he was suffering. Such was the endurance taught to the lads of Sparta.

If a boy shirked any hardship or flagged at his gymnastic exercises he was flogged, perhaps even tortured. One test of his endurance was a terrible scourging, under which he would die rather than utter a cry of pain.

In public the boys were trained to be silent, or if they were spoken to, to answer as shortly as possible. Their short, abrupt way of talking was called laconic, because the name of their country was Laconia. We still use the word laconic when we hear anyone speak in as brief a way as possible.

Hard as the Spartan training was, cruel as it sometimes became, it yet made boys into strong and hardy soldiers.

Girls, too, were trained, although not so severely as boys. They ran, they wrestled, they boxed with one another, while boys and girls marched together in religious processions and danced on the solemn feast days.

When they were twenty years of age, the girls usually married. They had been taught, as had the boys, that they belonged to the State, and that they must love their country and serve her with all their strength. So when Spartan mothers sent their sons forth to war, they handed them their shields saying, "Return either with your shield or upon it," for they feared death less than disgrace or defeat.

The children were taught to sing in chorus as part of their drill. At some of the festivals three choirs took part, one of old men, one of young men, and one of boys.

When the old men sang a song beginning, "We once were young and brave and strong," the young men answered, "And we're so now, come on and try," while the boys' voices rang out bravely when their turn came, "But we'll be strongest by-and-by."

The Spartan lads were twenty years old before they left the training-house to which they had been sent when they were seven. They were then fully-trained soldiers and left the training-house for the barracks.

After they married, the men still had to take their meals in the barracks with their fellow-soldiers. Not until they were sixty years of age were the Spartans allowed to live and take their meals in their own house. In this way almost the whole of a Spartan's life was given to the State.

When war actually came and the Spartans were on the field, they were treated with more kindness than in time of peace. Their food was more plentiful and pleasant, their discipline less strict. This

THE TRAINING OF THE SPARTANS

was done to make the soldiers look forward to war, and to desire it rather than peace.

The younger soldiers, too, were allowed to curl their hair before the battle began, to wear gayer clothes, and to carry more costly arms. It is said that Lycurgus thought that "a large head of hair added beauty to a good face and terror to an ugly one."

So famous became the bravery and the endurance of the Spartans, that even now we call one who suffers hardships without complaint "a Spartan."

CHAPTER XXV

THE HELOTS

When Lycurgus made a law compelling soldiers to eat their meals in the barracks, some of the wealthier citizens were indignant.

They did not wish to sit at table with their fellow-soldiers in batches of fifteen; they would rather have gone to their homes and taken their meals with their families.

Nor did they enjoy the plain fare on which Lycurgus insisted, a share of which each citizen was forced to send to the mess table month by month.

The most usual food in Laconia was black broth, which was not a palatable soup. When someone ventured to grumble at the broth, the cook answered, "It is nothing without the seasoning of fatigue and hunger." This black broth, with barley meal, cheese, and figs, was the Spartan's daily fare. Meat was a luxury which they enjoyed only on special occasions.

THE HELOTS

So great was the indignation against Lycurgus that a crowd assembled in the market-place to complain of his laws, and to speak harshly of his conduct.

When they saw the great lawgiver coming toward the market-place they were so angry that they picked up stones to throw at him, and he was forced to fly for his life.

His enemies followed him, but he outstripped them all save one, named Alexander. As he turned to see who pursued him so closely, Alexander struck his face with a stick and put out one of his eyes.

As others hastened up, Lycurgus showed them what Alexander had done, and they, ashamed of his violence, told the lawgiver to take the rash youth and punish him as he would. They then went with him to his house, to show that they were sorry for what had happened.

When they reached the door Lycurgus sent them all away save his prisoner. Then going into his dining-room, he dismissed his attendants and bade Alexander wait upon him. During the meal he uttered no word of reproach, although the boy had done him so great an injury.

Alexander lived with Lycurgus until he learned not only to admire but to imitate the industry and the gentleness of his host. And so Lycurgus had the pleasure of seeing a rash and wilful lad become a grave and sensible citizen.

Each Spartan had a portion or "lot" of land given to him, on the produce of which he and his family had to live. But citizen soldiers had no time to dig the ground, to sow, to reap, for all the days were spent in drill and military exercises. So their land was cultivated for them by the Helots, who had owned Laconia before the Spartans conquered them and took possession of their land.

The Helots were treated very much as slaves, although they had no taskmasters to drive them to their work. They were even allowed to own property. But they had many hardships to endure, and were always ready to rebel against their masters.

One of their greatest hardships was that their lives were never safe. For while the Spartans were being trained, they were often sent into the country with orders to kill any Helot who was suspected of wishing to rebel.

In time of war the Helots fought as light-armed troops. If they showed themselves brave and loyal in the service of the State, they were sometimes rewarded by being made free.

Once during the great Peloponnesian War between Sparta and Athens, of which you will read in this story, the Spartans believed that the Helots had plotted to rise against them. They determined that the rising should never take place, and to prevent it they did a cruel deed. For they chose two thousand of the bravest Helots, set them free, and gave them a great feast to celebrate the event. Then when the feast was over and the Helots had gone away to their homes, suspecting nothing, the Spartans ordered each of the two thousand freed men to be put to death. When the bravest were killed the others were not likely to rebel.

The Spartan army became strong as Lycurgus had foreseen it would, if it were trained according to his strict methods. It conquered Peloponnesus, and for a time Sparta was the chief city in that land.

But there was one strange thing about these soldiers. Well as they had been trained, they could never learn how to attack or to take a town that was fortified. "Wall-fighting," as the Greeks called it, was beyond their power. Even an ordinary wall or fence would stop them in their victorious course. At sea too they were not nearly so successful as on land.

Sparta itself was not, like other Greek cities, surrounded by a wall. For when the citizens once sent to ask Lycurgus if it were necessary to enclose their city with a wall, his answer was, "The city is well fortified which hath a wall of men instead of brick."

When, after many years, Lycurgus had finished his code of laws, he called the people together and told them that he was going to Delphi to consult the oracle on an important matter which concerned the State.

Before he set out he begged them, and also the two kings and the Senate, to take an oath to keep his laws unaltered until his return. This they gladly promised to do.

Then Lycurgus journeyed to Delphi, and after offering sacrifices to Apollo, he asked the god if the laws he had made for his country were good laws.

The oracle answered that the laws were good, and that as long as the people kept them their fame would endure.

Lycurgus sent this answer in writing to Sparta. Then, that the Spartans might not be set free from their oath he determined never to go back to the city. Yet it seemed that he could not live away from her, and so, for the welfare of the State, as he believed, the lawgiver starved himself to death.

The Spartans kept the oath that they had taken, and when they died their sons and their sons' sons observed it. For five hundred years, during the reigns of fourteen kings, the laws of Lycurgus were unaltered and strictly followed.

After his death Lycurgus was worshipped as a god, and a temple was built for him in Sparta, where sacrifices were offered to him every year.

CHAPTER XXVI

ARISTOMENES AND THE FOX

THE Spartans were eager to fight and to add to their dominions. So they determined to attack the Messenians, whose country lay west of Laconia, close to their own borders.

One day, while the Messenians were feasting and offering sacrifices to their gods, the Spartans sent three youths disguised as maidens across the borderland. Beneath their robes the young soldiers carried arms. They stole quietly in among the Messenians and attacked them in the midst of their feast.

But although the Messenians were unarmed they soon captured the three Spartan lads. They then advanced against the Spartans, and in the tumult that followed, one of the kings of Sparta was slain.

The war, which was thus begun in 743 B.C., lasted for many years, and was known as the First Messenian War.

No great battle was fought until four years had passed. Even then neither side could claim a victory, but so many Messenians had fallen that Aristodemus, their chief, withdrew, with those of his followers who were left, to a mountain fortress called Ithomé.

Then, as was their custom, when it was difficult to know what to do next, the Messenians sent to consult the oracle. The answer filled them with dismay, for the oracle declared that not until a maiden belonging to one of their ancient houses was sacrificed to the gods need they hope to conquer the Spartans. But Aristodemus loved his country so dearly that he did not hesitate to sacrifice his own daughter to the gods.

When the Spartans heard what the brave chief had done, they hastened to make peace with the Messenians. They could not hope to conquer those for whom the gods would now fight.

A few years passed, and then the Spartans determined to attack the Messenians once again, and to drive them from Ithomé their mountain fortress.

Again a great battle was fought, and again neither side could claim the victory. But the king of the Messenians was killed, and Aristodemus was chosen to rule in his place. In the fifth year of his reign he defeated the Spartans and drove them from his dominions.

The victory brought no happiness to the king, for omens of evil seemed to pursue him.

ARISTOMENES AND THE FOX

In the temple a brazen shield fell from the hand of the statue of Artemis the goddess. The daughter of Aristodemus appeared to her father and bade him lay aside his armour. He obeyed, and she then placed on his head a crown of gold and clad him in a white robe. These things meant that the death of the king was near.

Aristodemus believed that not only he but his country was doomed, and deeming that he had sacrificed his daughter in vain, he slew himself in his despair on her tomb.

For twenty years the war still dragged on, and only then were the Spartans able to drive the Messenians from Ithomé and raze the fortress to the ground.

Many of the conquered people fled, while those who remained were treated more harshly than were the Helots. For they were compelled to pay as tribute to the Spartans half the produce of their lands. This was the end of the First Messenian War.

For almost thirty years the conquered people bore their cruel lot, then in 685 B.C. they rebelled, and the Second Messenian War was begun.

Aristomenes, the leader of the rebels, was a bold and daring foe. To show how little he feared the Spartans, he secretly crossed the borderland into the enemy's country, and one night he succeeded in entering the city of Sparta itself. He made his way to the temple of Athene, and walking in boldly he hung up his shield beside the statue of the goddess, with these words tied to it: "Dedicated by Aristomenes to the goddess from the Spartan spoils."

With a band of his bravest followers, the chief made more than one successful raid into the heart of the enemy's country, and plundered two of their cities.

As in the first war, so in this second war, no decisive victory was gained at first by either side. But legend tells that Aristomenes did many valiant deeds.

Three times he offered a strange sacrifice to the king of the gods, which one who had slain in battle a hundred of the foe was alone permitted to do. The sacrifice was named the Hekatomphonia.

The Spartans, alarmed at the daring of Aristomenes, sent to consult the oracle at Delphi. They were told to send to the famous city of Athens for a leader. Now the Spartans did not wish to do this, for they were not on good terms with the Athenians. Still, as they dared not disregard the oracle, they did as they were bid.

The Athenians did not wish to help the Spartans any more than they wished to ask for help, yet they too knew they could not ignore the oracle. So they got out of the difficulty, as they thought, by sending a lame schoolmaster, named Tyrtaeus. He would not be likely to lead an army far.

But although Tyrtaeus was a lame man, he was also a poet. His war-songs roused the Spartans, and inspired them to fight more bravely than ever. When they marched again to battle they were singing the songs of Tyrtaeus and marching to victory. Aristomenes was forced to retreat to the mountains to a fortress called Ira.

For eleven years the war lingered on. The Spartans often encamped at the foot of Ira to keep the enemy in check. But again and again Aristomenes broke out of the fortress, and with a band of followers crossed the border and laid waste Laconia. Twice he was taken prisoner and twice he escaped, but the third time he was captured he was carried in triumph to the city of Sparta. With fifty of his countrymen he was flung from Mount Taygetus into a great chasm in the rock below.

The fifty followers of Aristomenes were killed by the fall, but Aristomenes was saved by the gods. For, so the legend tells, an eagle with wings outspread carried him unhurt to the bottom of the pit.

For three days Aristomenes lay in the cavern surrounded by the dead bodies of his comrades. To escape seemed impossible. But when no hope was left in the heart of the brave man, he noticed something move at the foot of the cave. At once he roused himself to look more closely at the moving object; it was a fox, prowling about in search of food.

In an instant hope was alive in the heart of Aristomenes. If an animal had got into the cave, it was possible for him to get out of it.

Weak though he was for want of food, Aristomenes managed to seize the tail of the fox, and to hold it fast when the animal tried to escape.

Onward the fox struggled, until it reached a narrow hole in the rock. Then Aristomenes let his deliverer go, while he began at once to enlarge the hole.

The next day, to the joy of his countrymen and to the alarm of his enemies, Aristomenes was again in the Messenian fortress.

But there was a traitor in the camp of the Messenians, and one night, soon after the return of their leader, the mountain fortress at Ira was betrayed into the hands of the Spartans.

In the battle that followed, Aristomenes was wounded, but gathering together the bravest of his followers, he made a desperate charge through the lines of the enemy and escaped. Some time after he died in Rome, but it is told that two hundred and fifty years later, he was seen on a battlefield fighting against the Spartans.

The Second Messenian War ended, as had the first, in the triumph of the Spartans, who again treated their prisoners as slaves. In 464 B.C. war again broke out between the Messenians and Sparta. The Spartans were victorious, and the conquered people were driven from Peloponnesus. But in 369 B.C. a great Theban leader called Epaminondas restored freedom to the Messenians, and brought them back again to their own country.

The history of the Messenian War was written by the poet Tyrtaeus, whose songs were sung for many years by the Spartans as they marched to battle.

Some of these songs we can still read for ourselves.

CHAPTER XXVII

THE OLYMPIAN GAMES

GREECE was made up of many separate States, each independent of the other. But there were several bonds which united the States. They spoke the same language, they worshipped the same gods, they kept the same great festivals.

The festivals, held by a council called the Amphictyonic Council, were honoured by all the States. The council was made up of men chosen from twelve of the most ancient Greek tribes and met twice each year.

The temple of Apollo at Delphi was under the care of the Amphictyonic Council, and it was at Delphi that the spring-tide festival was held. Another great festival of the Amphictyonic Council was celebrated in the temple dedicated to Demeter at Thermopylae.

The Amphictyons, as the members of the council were called, did not govern Greece as a parliament governs a country. But they often talked of

THE OLYMPIAN GAMES

what could be done for the good of the States, and of how their interests could be united more closely.

Of more power to weld the States together than the council, were the national games, where members of all the different countries of Greece met together.

The chief of these games was the Olympian Games, which were believed to have begun far back in the shadowy past, and to have been revived by Lycurgus the lawgiver in 776 B.C.

Olympia, where the games were held, was in the country of Elis in Peloponnesus. The King of Elis helped Lycurgus to renew the interest of the Greeks in the ancient games.

It is said that when Apollo first saw the beautiful valley of Olympia he exclaimed, "Here will I make me a fair temple to be an oracle for men."

The ancient Stadium, or race-course, was erected in the valley, as well as a temple to Zeus, in which the victors of the games were given wreaths of wild olive. These wreaths were valued more than any other prize or distinction in Greece. Indeed at Olympia no other reward was given save the simple wild olive branches, which were plucked from the sacred grove in the Olympian plain, and twined into a wreath.

But when the victor returned to his own country, he was loaded with gifts and honours, for he had gained for his State and for his relations a glory which all longed to possess.

In the Olympian temple, in later days, there was a marvellous statue of Zeus in gold and ivory, wrought by the genius of Pheidias, the greatest sculptor of Greece.

The games were open to all, and spectators as well as competitors flocked to Olympia from every state in Greece. To the Greeks these games were part of their religion; they were rites pleasing, so they believed, to the gods.

Should there be war between any of the Greek States at the time of the games, all hostile acts were forbidden in Olympia. Until the festival was over, those who had been in arms, one against another, might meet in safety and in peace. Twice or thrice an armed force made its way into the sacred territory of Elis to interfere with the games. This to the Greeks was sacrilege.

In the earliest times the games lasted only for one day, and a simple foot-race was the only event. But soon the festival came to last five days, for there were now, not only foot-races, but wrestling, boxing, racing in armour, and above all else chariot races. In these races it was not the driver who, if successful, won the wreath of olive, but the owner of the chariot.

On the first day of the games, sacrifices were offered to the gods, on the following three days the races were held, while on the last day people marched in procession to the temple and again offered sacrifices and feasted.

THE OLYMPIAN GAMES

In the earliest times a simple foot-race was the only event

At the end of every four years the games were celebrated; the time between the games being called an Olympiad. The year 776 B.C. was counted as the first Olympiad, the second began in 772 B.C. In ancient times the Greeks reckoned their dates by the Olympiads, thus an event was said to take place in a certain year of a certain Olympiad.

Games were held at many other places as well as at Olympia, but the three most important celebrations, after the Olympian, were the Isthmian, the Pythian and the Nemean.

To these festivals came the poets of Greece, prepared to celebrate in song the skill of the victors. During the intervals between the games, great numbers of the people assembled in a hall to listen to the poets while they recited their poems.

As the years passed the great Greek dramas or plays came to be acted also at these festivals. At first the stage was a simple wooden platform in the open air, but soon wooden buildings were erected. Plays were performed at Athens in a splendid theatre which was hewn out of the solid rock of the Acropolis or citadel of the city. Tier after tier was cut, until the theatre could hold thirty thousand spectators.

CHAPTER XXVIII

THE LAST KING OF ATHENS

You remember how Cecrops came to Attica and built a city so beautiful that the gods marvelled, and how Athene made the first olive-tree and was therefore awarded the honour of naming the city and becoming its patron. The olive-tree was now said to grow on a rock in the stronghold or Acropolis of the city.

In ancient days Sparta was a more important city than the beautiful one built by Cecrops, but little by little, as the years passed, Athens became supreme in Greece and the most glorious city of the world.

At first Athens, like Sparta and the other States, was governed by kings. But while Sparta continued to be a monarchy, Athens became an oligarchy—that is, she was governed by a few, and these few were nobles.

When Codrus, the last king of Athens, was on the throne, the State was invaded by the Dorians. An oracle had declared that unless the Athenian king was slain in the camp of the enemy, Athens would be taken.

Codrus loved his city and determined to save it from the enemy. So he disguised himself as a peasant and went to the camp of the Dorians, where he killed the first soldier he met. The comrades of the dead man at once fell upon Codrus and, as he had hoped, he was speedily slain. Then as the oracle had foretold Athens was saved from the enemy.

The Athenians resolved that they would no longer have kings to rule over them, because they were sure that they could never find any worthy to follow Codrus who had died for the sake of his country. This seems a strange reason for which to overturn the monarchy. In most countries it is the bad conduct of their kings which makes the people wish to get rid of them.

As Athens would not have another king, the son of Codrus was given neither the power nor the title of royalty. He was named merely archon, or ruler. An archon ruled only for ten years.

Soon the Athenians determined to choose nine archons each year, for they thought it would be well to divide the power among these men rather than entrust it to one ruler.

The archons were obliged to consult a council of nobles before they made a new law, while the council had to lay their plans before the assembly of the people.

THE LAST KING OF ATHENS

In this way Athens became before long an oligarchy governed by a few nobles. The nobles often proved harsh rulers, taking from the people the rights that had been theirs when Athens was a monarchy.

At length the people grew so angry that they determined to destroy the nobles who treated them so cruelly. But as they were helpless without a leader, they were glad to follow any ambitious noble who would place himself at their head and lead them to fight against their oppressors. Too often the deliverer seized the supreme power himself and oppressed the people more than had the oligarch.

The usurper was called by the Greeks a tyrant. But the word tyrant did not mean to them, as it means to us, a cruel man. It meant simply one who had seized a power to which he had no real right.

Some of the tyrants were cruel, but others used the power which they had seized for the good of the State.

The years 700 B.C. to 500 B.C. are known as the Age of the Tyrants, because there were few States, save Sparta, which did not fall under the power of a tyrant during those years.

Often the people learned to hate a tyrant as greatly as they had hated the nobles under whose harsh treatment they had groaned. But it was not easy to get rid of him, for he usually had hired soldiers to help him keep the citizens from rebelling. One of the wisest and best of the tyrants was named

Pisistratus, and he was a cousin of Solon, the greatest lawgiver of Athens.

Solon was not a tyrant, although had he wished he might have become one.

CHAPTER XXIX

CYLON FAILS TO MAKE HIMSELF TYRANT

THE people of Attica were divided into three classes. There were the men of the Plain, who owned land and were wealthy; the men of the Shore, who were fisher-folk and traders; the men of the Hill or Uplanders, who were shepherds and herdsmen.

These three parties, the Plain, the Shore, the Hill, as they were often called, were dissatisfied with the way in which they were treated by the nobles. For, little by little, they were taking possession of the land and making free men slaves.

When the harvest failed, or when trade was bad, the poor were forced to borrow from the rich. And if a poor man could not pay his debt when it became due, his land and his goods were seized by the rich man. Nor was that the worst, for if the land and goods were not enough to cover the debt, then the poor man himself was taken to be used or sold as a slave.

So great was the discontent of the people, that in 632 B.C. a noble named Cylon determined to put himself at their head, overthrow those who were in power, and make himself tyrant. But Cylon did not trouble to gain the goodwill of the people. He succeeded in seizing the Acropolis, but it was by the aid of soldiers whom he had hired from the neighbouring city of Megara, not by the help of the people of Athens. The Athenians were indignant when they saw Megarian soldiers in their capital, and they looked on coldly and struck no blow for Cylon when the archons besieged the rebel noble in the citadel.

Cylon did not stay to see his plans destroyed; he escaped from the city by night, but his followers held the Acropolis until famine stared them in the face. Then they gathered for sanctuary around the altar of Athene and threw open the gates of the citadel.

Megacles, the chief archon, promised that the lives of the defenders should be spared, but no sooner had they left the altar than he ordered that they should be put to death.

The Athenians punished Megacles for this treacherous deed, for he and the family to which he belonged were banished from Athens, while their property was seized by the State. It is told that the city lay under a curse after the treacherous deed of Megacles, nor was she freed from it until a priest purified her with solemn religious rites.

Cylon had neither gained his own ends nor had he helped the people by his rebellion.

CYLON FAILS TO MAKE HIMSELF TYRANT

Poverty and debt were hard to bear, yet these the citizens might now have suffered in silence, but injustice drove them to demand that the laws should be reformed. For the archons punished as they pleased those who disobeyed the law, and at courts, sentence was often passed in favour of those who had bribed or befriended the judge.

When the people rose in 621 B.C. demanding that justice should be done in the land, the task of reforming the laws was entrusted to one of the archons named Draco.

Until now the laws had not been written, and so many of them were unknown to the people. Draco ordered that the laws should be inscribed on tablets that they might be read by the people. Sometimes he was blamed for the severity of these laws, although all he had done was to make them known.

But the code of laws which Draco drew up was so severe that in later days, as the Athenians read them, they exclaimed in horror, "The laws of Draco seem to have been written in blood rather than with ink." And indeed there was cause for dismay when the theft of a cabbage was punished with death. Draco was thus of little real help to the poor people of Athens.

CHAPTER XXX

SOLON FREES THE SLAVES

SOLON, the wise lawgiver of Athens, was a descendant of King Codrus. His father had given away most of his wealth to help his city or his countrymen, so Solon became a merchant, as the sons of noblemen often did in these days of long ago. To increase his business, Solon journeyed through many of the states of Greece as well as to Asia. Wherever he went he studied the laws and manners of the people, just as Lycurgus the lawgiver of Sparta had done.

Solon was not only a merchant, he was also a poet, and because he was both wise and learned he was counted one of the seven sages of Greece.

When Solon returned from one of his journeys about 593 B.C., he was made an archon and asked to reform the laws.

His first act was a great and unexpected one, for he proclaimed that henceforth no one might be made a slave because he was unable to pay his debts.

And more than that, he said that those who were already slaves were at once to be set free.

Hundreds of men were thus delivered from slavery, many hundreds more were freed from the fear of becoming slaves. As these men ploughed their own lands and reaped their own harvests they were full of gratitude to Solon. For this law alone the name of Solon might well be held in reverence.

So great was the joy of the people that the day the law was passed was kept each year as a festival. But the rich nobles were not pleased with Solon's act, for they lost many of their slaves and found it less easy to add to their wealth.

The lawgiver also declared that if there was war or strife in the State, each citizen must take one side or the other. No one was to be allowed to look on idly, or side now with one party, now with another.

Solon restored to the assembly of the people the rights that had been wrested from it, and he did all he could to add to its powers.

In these ways Solon made Greece less and less of an Oligarchy and more and more of a Democracy. That is to say, Greece began to be governed by the many rather than by the few.

The laws made by Solon, and there were many of which I have not told, were written on tables of wood and placed in frames that revolved. These were called axones and were numbered.

Solon, the wise lawgiver of Athens

SOLON FREES THE SLAVES

When the laws had been written on the tables of wood they were placed in the public hall that they might be read by all. Other copies were made on stone pillars and kept in the portico of the king. Each citizen took an oath that he would keep these laws, which were to remain unaltered for a hundred years.

Solon had enemies, as reformers in all ages have had. Some people complained because his laws were not bold enough, others because they were too bold.

Once when he was asked if he believed that he had given to the Athenians the best possible laws, he answered, "The best they could receive."

The complaints of his enemies did not greatly disturb him. He declared that neither friend nor foe influenced him as he worked. "I threw my stout shield over both parties," he said, and steadfastly refused to alter his code.

When he ceased to be archon he left Athens and spent ten years seeing many strange people and many new places. It is said that during his absence he met Croesus, King of Lydia, the richest man in the world. As Solon and Croesus did not live at the same time, it is not possible that the wise lawgiver and the rich king could have met, but this is the story that is told.

When Solon reached Lydia, he went to the court of Croesus. The nobles were clad in such rich garments and were attended by so many guards and pages that the Athenian thought that one of them must be the king himself. But when he actually stood in the presence of the monarch he must have smiled at his mistake, so gorgeously was the king arrayed in gold and purple, so plentifully was he bedecked with sparkling jewels.

Croesus thought that Solon would be filled with awe at the sight of his grandeur, but he soon found that purple cloth and rare stones had no great interest for the Athenian.

There were still his treasure-houses! These could not fail to impress the stranger. So the king led Solon through gallery after gallery that he might see his pictures, his statues, and all the wonderful things that his wealth had brought to him. Then in a glow of pride he turned to his guest, asking if he did not think that Croesus was the happiest man in the world.

"Nay, O king," answered Solon, "Tellus, one of my own countrymen, was happier than thou, for he died bravely on the battlefield in defence of his country."

Croesus thought Solon was foolish not to count that man happiest who owned the most gold. But he only said, "After Tellus, dost thou count me the happiest man in the world?"

"Nay," again answered the wise man, "but two sons who loved their mother well, and served her with their strength."

Then the king was angry and he said, "Dost thou not count me a happy man?"

"Call no man happy until he dies," replied the wise man, "for who knows what pains the gods may yet have in store for him while he lives."

Croesus was yet to learn the truth of what Solon said. For in days to come Cyrus, King of Persia, seized his city, took him prisoner, and condemned him to be burned to death.

As he was being bound to the pyre, Croesus remembered the words of the Athenian, and he cried aloud three times, "O Solon, Solon, Solon."

The King of Persia had never heard of Solon, and he asked on what strange god his prisoner was calling.

"On no god," answered the miserable man, "but on one whom I would that all tyrants might meet and converse with." He then told Cyrus how Solon had said no one need count himself happy while he lived, as he could not know what misfortunes the gods had yet in store for him.

Already the pyre had been set alight, but Cyrus, struck by the words he had heard and thinking that he did not know what fate might yet befall himself, ordered Croesus to be set free.

But the flames had blazed up fiercely, and no one could quench the fire. Then Croesus besought Apollo to help him, and lo! the sky which had been clear grew dark, and a heavy downfall of rain soon extinguished the flames.

"Thus," says Plutarch, who tells this story, "Solon had the glory by the same saying to save one king and instruct another."

CHAPTER XXXI

THE ATHENIANS TAKE SALAMIS

SALAMIS, an island lying about a mile from both Athens and Megara, was in the hands of the Megarians. Its position between the two States made it an important one. So the Athenians determined to proclaim war against the Megarians and try to win Salamis for themselves.

But the war dragged on so long that the Athenians grew weary, and although the Megarians still held the island they longed for the war to end. The poor soldiers wished to go home to plough their fields, the rich wished to escape from the hardships of the camp to their own comfortable homes.

So at length peace was made, and a law was passed by the Athenians forbidding any one either to say or to write, upon pain of death, that Athens ought still to try to win Salamis.

There were many citizens both indignant and ashamed that such a law had been passed, yet lest they should be put to death they did not dare to say what they thought.

Solon was away from Athens when this law was passed, and when he came back from his journey and found that peace had been made while Salamis was still in the hands of the Megarians, he was much displeased.

Some time had passed since peace had been made, and Solon knew that the Megarians were not now as strong as they had been when the Athenians gave up fighting. So he determined that he would rouse his countrymen to try again to capture the island. Yet what could he do? He would be put to death if he defied the law, which said that no one must say or write that Athens ought still to try to win Salamis.

At length he hit on a strange plan. He pretended that he was mad, and persuaded his own family to spread the report that this terrible fate had befallen him. He then wrote some verses, learned them by heart, and ran toward the market-place, a cap upon his head. In those days a cap was worn by a man if he were ill.

Solon soon attracted as much attention as he had hoped to do by his strange gestures and by the words he shouted.

As the people crowded round him he jumped on to the platform from which heralds were used to announce important tidings, and began to recite the verses he had written.

THE ATHENIANS TAKE SALAMIS

"I came myself as a herald from lovely Salamis, but with song on my lips instead of common speech," so began the poem. It then went on to blame those who wished no longer to fight, and bade them "Arise and come to Salamis to win that fair island and undo our shame."

As the people listened they forgot that they believed Solon was mad, and their hearts were stirred by his words.

From that day so strong became the desire of the people to blot out their disgrace and win Salamis, that the law which had so displeased Solon was repealed. No one had thought of punishing the man who had broken it.

The Athenian forces were again mustered; Solon himself being made commander of the troops. His cousin Pisistratus went with him to battle, and it was he who succeeded in taking the port of Salamis.

In those days Athens had no fleet. Solon sailed toward Salamis in a ship, but his army followed him in a number of fishing-boats.

When the Megarians caught sight of the Athenian ship, they sent one of their own vessels to find out the strength of the enemy's fleet.

Solon managed to capture this ship, and all on board were taken prisoners. The captured vessel was then manned with Athenians, and the men were ordered to sail slowly and quietly to the island.

Solon meanwhile reached the shore and, landing with his army, at once attacked the Megarians.

While the fight still raged, the ship manned by Athenians sailed unnoticed to the port. The soldiers leaped to the ground, sped swiftly to the city, and took it almost before the citizens were aware of the presence of the enemy.

The island was soon in the hands of the triumphant Athenians, by whom it was held for many long years, until indeed Philip of Macedon conquered Greece.

To celebrate the victory in after years, an Athenian ship used to sail to the island just as the victorious one had done on the actual battle day. When it reached the shore, a soldier, armed as though for battle, jumped to the ground, and with a loud shout ran toward the city, where he was met and welcomed by his countrymen.

Close to the spot where Solon won this victory a temple was built and dedicated to the god of battle.

CHAPTER XXXII

PISISTRATUS BECOMES TYRANT

SOLON did not expect the laws he made to please each of the three parties in Attica. So he was not greatly surprised that while the Plain and the Coast were more or less content, the Hill was dissatisfied and even rebellious.

Pisistratus wished to help the Hill folk, who were shepherds and herdsmen, and he hoped at the same time to fulfil his own ambition, which was to become tyrant of Athens.

Solon did not think that it was good for the State to have a tyrant at its head. He warned the people again and again that Pisistratus would take away their freedom. But it was in vain that he spoke, no one would listen to him.

One day as Pisistratus drove in a chariot to the market-place, the citizens saw to their horror that he had been wounded. They crowded round his chariot begging to be told what had happened. This was what Pisistratus wished. He pointed to his wounds, telling them that the men of the Plain had attacked him, because he was defending the rights of the poor Hill folk. But Pisistratus was deceiving the people, for he had given himself these wounds that he might gain the sympathy of the people and be voted a bodyguard.

Lest he should be killed outright by his enemies, the citizens agreed that he should have a guard of fifty clubsmen.

At first Pisistratus seemed content with his guard, but after a time he began to add to its number now one, then another, until he knew that he was strong enough to defy his enemies. He then seized the Acropolis and soon made himself master of the State.

The leaders of the Plain and the Shore were forced to flee, and the people, in spite of the warnings of Solon, were amazed at the cunning and the boldness Pisistratus had shown.

Solon himself felt that all he had done for the State was undone when a tyrant ruled at Athens.

Old as he now was, he was brave enough to go to the market-place to upbraid the citizens for their folly in having allowed Pisistratus to deceive them, and to beg them not to lose their freedom without a struggle. "You might with ease," he said, "have crushed the tyrant in the bud; but nothing now remains but to pluck him up by the roots."

PISISTRATUS BECOMES TYRANT

It is said that he even begged the people to take up arms against Pisistratus, but they were not bold enough to defy the tyrant.

So Solon went home sadly, gathered together his arms and laid them on the threshold of his house, saying, "I have done my part to maintain my country and my laws, and I appeal to others to do likewise."

Here is a verse from one of the poems which he wrote at this time—

"If now you suffer do not blame the Powers,
For they are good and all the fault is ours.
All the strongholds you put into his hands,
And now his slaves must do what he commands."

His friends feared that Pisistratus would punish Solon for his bold words and actions, perhaps even take his life, so they begged him to leave the country, but he refused to go.

When they asked him why he was not afraid, and to what he trusted to save him from the anger of the tyrant, he answered simply, "To my old age."

And his trust was well founded, for Pisistratus treated Solon with kindness and with respect. He even asked his advice in matters of State.

But the overthrow of his reforms was more than the old lawgiver could bear, and two years later, when he was eighty years of age, he died. It is said that by his own wish his ashes were scattered on Salamis, the island which he had won for Athens.

Pisistratus was a good tyrant. For five years he ruled, doing all that he could for the welfare of the State. But his enemies, although they saw that Athens grew more prosperous under his control, were ever plotting to get rid of him. At the end of five years the Plain and the Coast joined together and succeeded in driving Pisistratus from the city.

But Megacles, the leader of the Coast, quarrelled with the Plain, and he then offered to help Pisistratus to return to Athens.

It was by a strange trick that the Athenians were persuaded once more to allow the tyrant to rule.

In one of the villages of Attica, Megacles knew of a woman named Phya, who was taller and more stately than most Greek women. He ordered Phya to be clad in armour, such as was worn by the goddess Athene, and then seating her in his chariot he drove to Athens. Before the chariot went a herald to proclaim that the goddess Athene was herself coming to bid them open their gates to Pisistratus and to restore him to power.

The story tells that the Athenians believed that Phya was indeed the goddess, and they hastened to obey her behests. Pisistratus was allowed to enter the city and rule it as before.

PISISTRATUS BECOMES TYRANT

For six years all went well, then the tyrant quarrelled with Megacles, who again joined the Plain, and Pisistratus was expelled for the second time.

But the tyrant was a patient and a persistent man. For ten years he lived in a province called Thrace, keeping in touch all the time with the Hill. In 535 B.C. he was back again in Attica, with no goddess to help him, but with a band of hired soldiers to strengthen his party.

The Athenian army was sent against the invaders, but Pisistratus pretended that he did not mean to fight. So the Athenians, thinking themselves safe, sat down to their midday meal. Then, while they were eating and drinking, the tyrant fell upon them, scattering them with but little loss on either side. As the Athenians fled, the sons of Pisistratus, Hippias and Hipparchus, rode after them, crying aloud that all who went quietly home would be pardoned. The citizens saw that it was useless to resist, so Pisistratus entered Athens as tyrant for the third time.

During the next eight years Pisistratus devoted himself to making Athens the most beautiful city of the world. He ordered that a new feast should be held in honour of the gods, and he began to build a magnificent temple to Zeus, which he did not live to finish. Many learned men were invited to Athens, and poets and historians were encouraged to write and to read their works to the people. It is even said that Pisistratus collected a library, which he urged the citizens to use, but of this we cannot be sure.

Then, thinking perhaps that Athens was strong enough to defy her enemies, the tyrant ordered the walls of the city to be pulled down. So that for half a century Athens, like Sparta, was an unwalled town.

In many of the States where tyrants ruled, Pisistratus had formed allies, and he even offered his friendship to Sparta, the State that despised tyrants and would not allow them to rule in Peloponnesus.

Pisistratus died in 527 B.C., and was succeeded by his two sons, Hippias and Hipparchus.

CHAPTER XXXIII

HARMODIUS AND ARISTOGITON

HIPPIAS and Hipparchus were as eager as their father Pisistratus had been to govern Athens well. Nor did they quarrel as to the way in which they could best do this, as brother-tyrants might have done.

But one day Hipparchus quarrelled with a citizen named Harmodius, and to quarrel with Harmodius meant to make an enemy of his great friend Aristogiton.

Harmodius showed that he was angry with Hipparchus, who then used his power as tyrant to punish the citizen. This was unfair, as the quarrel was a private one.

The tyrant even refused to allow the sister of Harmodius to carry a basket in the procession of the gods, an insult which the citizen could ill brook. He therefore resolved to revenge himself, and together with Aristogiton he made a plot to slay not only Hipparchus but his brother Hippias as well. Only a few friends were told of the plot, which they hoped to carry out on the day of the procession. As it was usual to carry arms at the festival, it would arouse no suspicion if the friends were seen to carry theirs.

When the day arrived, Harmodius and Aristogiton appeared at the festival bearing lances, as did the other citizens. But to be the more certain of carrying out their plan, they also carried daggers concealed beneath their cloaks.

The conspirators wished to kill Hippias outside the city gates, while he was arranging the order of the procession. But when they approached the tyrant he chanced to be talking to one of those who knew of the plot, and the conspirators fled, thinking that Hippias had learned their secret.

Hippias was saved, but rushing to the market-place the two friends fell upon Hipparchus and killed him.

The conspirators expected the citizens to rally round them, but they stood aloof, while Harmodius was seized by the guards and put to death. Aristogiton was tortured to make him betray the names of those who knew of the plot, but he too died, steadfastly refusing to speak.

Although at first the Athenians paid little attention to what Harmodius and Aristogiton had done and had suffered, they began ere long to think of them as heroes who had freed Athens from the rule of one of the tyrants. Perhaps this was because Hippias, frightened by his brother's death, brought hired soldiers into the city, raised the taxes that he

HARMODIUS AND ARISTOGITON

might have money with which to pay his mercenaries, and began to oppress the citizens in many other ways.

The discontent of the people encouraged Cleisthenes, the son of Megacles, to put himself at their head and lead them against Hippias, but they were soon crushed by the hired soldiers of the tyrant.

Cleisthenes then tried to do by a trick what he had been unable to do by force. He knew that he was liked by the priests at Delphi, for he had given munificent gifts to the temple. So he begged them if a Spartan came to consult the oracle, no matter about what, to answer always, "Athens must be set free." This the priests promised should be done.

The Spartans had been friendly with Pisistratus, and they did not wish to harm his son. But when the oracle's one answer to all their requests was "Athens must be set free," they knew that they must march against the tyrant if they wished their own affairs to prosper. At first they were defeated by the mercenaries of Hippias, but one of their kings then took command of the army and defeated the tyrant, who took refuge in the Acropolis.

The citadel would stand a long siege, as Hippias was well aware. But he was soon forced to surrender, for his children whom he was sending secretly out of the country were captured by the Spartans. On condition that their lives should be spared, Hippias promised to leave the state within five days.

So the children were released and sailed with Hippias, under a safe conduct, to Asia, where they lived in a small town which had belonged to Pisistratus.

CHAPTER XXXIV

THE LAW OF OSTRACISM

AFTER Cleisthenes had set Athens free from the rule of Hippias, he began to reform the laws and to make Athens a more democratic State than she had yet been.

Until now the Athenians had been divided into four tribes; Cleisthenes split up the four tribes into ten. Each of the ten tribes he then arranged in ten parishes or "demes."

In each tribe there were demes made up of the Plain, the Shore, and the Hill. As these demes had to fight together in time of war, the three different parties grew to be friends instead of enemies. And that was why Cleisthenes had arranged the tribes in this way, instead of making one tribe consist of ten demes of Hill men and another of ten demes of Plain or Coast men.

Members from the new tribes were sent to the assembly of the people, and to the assembly Cleisthenes gave new powers. It could choose its own rulers, and punish those who ruled unjustly. It could impose taxes, make war, and settle terms of peace.

But of all the laws which Cleisthenes made, the one which will interest you most is the one that was called the law of Ostracism. The word ostracism comes from the Greek *ostrakon*, a shell.

In Athens there were often two leaders opposed to one another, but each as powerful as the other.

Cleisthenes thought that it would be a good plan to be able to get rid of one of these leaders for a time and so save the city from civil war, which often threatened to overtake it. So he said that when it was necessary to banish one of these leaders, the citizens should meet together, each being given an oyster-shell on which to write the name of the man of whom he disapproved.

If six thousand votes were given against one leader he was said to be ostracised, and was compelled to leave the city within ten days for five or perhaps even for ten years. His exile was not a disgrace, it was enforced only for the good of the State. When the five or ten years had passed, the leader returned to Athens to hold as high a position as he had held before and to take possession of his property.

The reforms of Cleisthenes displeased the nobles who wished Athens to be an oligarchy, and they were angry that so much power had been given to the assembly of the people. They said the city would soon be ruined, for how could the people who were unaccustomed to so much power use it well and wisely. But the fears of the nobles were groundless, for from this time Athens grew more prosperous as well as more powerful. She soon had a stronger army, a better fleet, and, as you shall hear, was victorious over her enemies both by land and by sea.

Great writers and sculptors too added to the glory of Athens and made her the most famous city of Greece.

CHAPTER XXXV

THE BRIDGE OF BOATS

ALONG the western shore of Asia Minor there were many Greek colonies. One of these was called Ionia, and the chief city of the Ionian state was Miletus.

The Greeks who lived in these colonies owned, often against their will, the King of Persia as their overlord. In time of war they were forced to fight for him.

In 521 B.C. a great monarch, named Darius, became King of Persia. He added many kingdoms to his dominions during the first nine years of his reign. In 512 B.C. he determined to conquer Greece and add it also to his possessions.

So he assembled a great army and crossed the Bosphorus, but instead of going west to Thessaly which lies in the north-east of Greece, Darius turned first toward the north, and crossing the Balkans, he reached the river Danube. Beyond the river lay a wild and desolate country, the home of the

THE BRIDGE OF BOATS

Scythians, who wandered up and down the land, settling now here, now there, as their fancy pleased.

The "great king," as the Persian monarchs were often called, bade the Ionian Greeks, who formed part of his army, throw a bridge of boats across the river. When this was done he bade them stay to guard the bridge, while he marched with the main body of his men into the wild Scythian country. Should he not return in sixty days, Darius told the Ionians that they might break up the bridge and go back to their homes.

No sooner had the great king crossed the bridge and marched into Scythia, than his difficulties began.

The foe he had come to seek was not to be found. Knowing that they were not strong enough to face Darius in battle, the Scythians had driven their herds far into the desert, while they themselves, like shadows, dogged the steps of the Persian army.

Two months passed, and still the king had not been able to make the enemy fight. Their shadowy forms were sometimes seen, but they were never near enough to be attacked.

Darius was unwilling to own that his expedition had been useless. Yet his men were sick from cold, and their provisions were nearly at an end, so he had almost made up his mind to order the retreat. But while he still hesitated, the story tells that the Scythians sent one of their number to the great king, carrying with him as gifts a bird, a mouse, a frog, and five arrows.

The Persians demanded the meaning of these strange gifts, but the messenger had no answer to give. He had been but bidden to give them to the great king and return to his people.

Then Darius called together his council to consider what the offering might betoken.

The king himself thought that the presents were to show that the Scythians were ready to surrender their land, for on it the mouse found its home; their water, for in it dwelt the frog. The bird was a symbol of their war-steeds, and with the arrows showed that they were willing to lay down their arms. Darius was satisfied with his own explanation, but one of his councillors thought that the gifts had quite a different meaning.

"O Persians," he cried, "listen to my words and be wise. For unless ye become as birds and fly up into heaven, or go down like mice beneath the earth, or, becoming frogs, leap into the lake, ye will not escape being shot by these arrows."

As he listened to these alarming words, the king thought that after all perhaps this was the true meaning of the gifts, so he determined to return to the Danube. But the sick men and beasts of burden were left behind when the army set out, for they could not march as quickly as Darius wished. The groanings of these miserable men and the cries of the animals were heard by the Scythians, who soon discovered what had happened and set out in pursuit of Darius and his army.

THE BRIDGE OF BOATS

Now the Ionians in charge of the bridge had long been tired of waiting for the return of the great king. He had perished, they said one to the other, and it would be well for them to break up the bridge and return to their homes.

Those who longed most to throw off their allegiance to the Persians muttered that even if the king had not already perished, he would soon do so, if he reached the Danube without provisions, to find the bridge was no longer there.

Miltiades, an Athenian, was strongly in favour of withdrawing, but Histiaeus, tyrant of Miletus, begged the Ionians to remain, for Darius would come back, of that he felt certain. Then turning to the other tyrants, he cried, "O ye tyrants, be sure of this, that if we leave the Persians to perish, the men of our cities will rise up against us, because it is the king who strengthens us in our power; and if he die, neither shall I be able to rule in Miletus, nor you in those cities of which ye are tyrants." Then the other tyrants agreed with Histiaeus that it would be for their own good to wait for the king.

CHAPTER XXXVI

DARIUS REWARDS HISTIAEUS

MEANWHILE a band of Scythians had reached the banks of the Danube. The Ionians had already loosed some of the boats on the farther side, that the enemy might think that the bridge was useless. And they, seeing this, and thinking that it would be impossible for Darius to cross the river, turned back to meet him.

But that same night, after a terrible march, the great king reached the river unnoticed by the Scythians. He saw at once that there were no boats on his side of the river. Had the Ionians gone home and left him to fall into the hands of his enemy?

Then he bade one of his men who was noted for the strength of his voice to call aloud for Histiaeus of Miletus. No sooner was this done than an answering shout was heard, and Histiaeus sent in haste to restore the bridge of boats. When the boats were secure, Darius with his weary army crossed to the other side, and was greeted with every token of loyalty by the Greeks.

DARIUS REWARDS HISTIAEUS

The king was grateful to Histiaeus when he heard that it was he who had persuaded the other tyrants to await his return, after the sixty days had passed, and he bade him ask for whatever he wished.

Now the tyrant longed to build a strong city far from the control of the Persian power. So he asked for land in the country called Thrace, which stretches north of Macedon to the river Danube, and Darius granted his request.

But Megabazus, the general of the great king, did not trust Histiaeus, and when he came to Sardis, where the king's court was, he said to Darius, "O king, what hast thou done? Thou hast given to a Greek who is wise and crafty a city in Thrace, where there is much timber for building ships and blades for oars, and mines of silver, and round it there are many people, both Greek and barbarian, who will take him for a chief and do his will by night and by day. See then that he make not war against thee in time to come."

Darius feared lest Megabazus was right, and he determined to send for Histiaeus and keep him at his own court. Yet as Megabazus might have made a mistake, the message the king sent to the Greek was a kind one.

"O Histiaeus," said the king, "I have pondered it well, and I find none who is better minded to me and to my kingdom than thou art. This I know, for I have learnt it, not by words but in deed. And now I purpose to do great things. Come therefore to me in any wise, that I may entrust them to thee."

These words pleased Histiaeus. It seemed to him that the great king was treating him even as one of his counsellors. But when he reached the king's court and was told what the commands of Darius were, he was not so well content.

"O Histiaeus," said the king, "there is nothing more precious than a wise and kind friend, and I knew that this thou art to me. So now thou must leave Miletus and the new city which thou has built, and come with me to my court at Susa."

The Greek found it hard to hide his anger and disappointment. Rather would he be tyrant at Miletus, or ruler in his new city, than a favoured courtier at Susa.

Aristagoras, the brother-in-law of Histiaeus, was now made tyrant of Miletus, while Darius appointed his own brother Artaphernes to be ruler of Sardis.

CHAPTER XXXVII

HISTIAEUS SHAVES THE HEAD OF HIS SLAVE

FOR a few years after Histiaeus was summoned to Susa, the Greek cities in Asia showed no disloyalty.

But about 500 B.C. the people of Naxos, an island in the Ægean Sea, rose and expelled the nobles from their city. This was the beginning of a war between Greece and Asia, known as the Ionian revolt.

The nobles, when they were turned out of Naxos, went to Aristagoras, tyrant of Miletus, to beg him to help them to punish the rebels and to gain possession of the island.

Aristagoras knew that alone he was not strong enough to regain Naxos for the nobles, but he said that he would ask Artaphernes, the Persian ruler in Sardis, to help him.

So Aristagoras went to Sardis and begged Artaphernes to give him a hundred ships to sail against Naxos, promising if he would do so to reward him with money and with gifts.

Artaphernes offered, if Darius would consent, to give not only a hundred, but two hundred ships. The great king bade his brother do as he thought well, so two hundred ships, under the command of Megabates, were sent from Sardis to join Aristagoras in his expedition against Naxos.

The two leaders, Aristagoras and Megabates, had not sailed far together when they quarrelled, and it was because of this quarrel that the plans of Aristagoras went awry.

One night Megabates found that no watch had been set on one of the ships belonging to Aristagoras. He was so angry with the captain for being careless that he ordered his head to be placed in one of the oarholes in the side of the vessel. When this was done the unhappy man could do nothing to set himself free, but with hanging head he was forced to gaze into the water.

When Aristagoras found what Megabates had done he went at once to ask him to set the culprit free. This Megabates refused to do, and the tyrant himself released the captain.

To have his authority flouted in this way made Megabates angry, but when he would have spoken, Aristagoras proudly bade him be silent, saying, "Did not Artaphernes send you to serve under me?"

Perhaps it would have been wiser to allow the Persian to speak, for now his anger smouldered in his heart, and he resolved to be revenged on Aristagoras. So he sent a messenger to Naxos to warn the citizens that an enemy was at hand.

The Naxians at once strengthened their walls and brought provisions into their city, so that when Aristagoras arrived, he found to his astonishment that the citizens had been warned and were ready to resist an attack.

For four months the Greeks and Persians besieged Naxos, but all their efforts to take the city were vain. Then, their money and their provisions having come to an end, Aristagoras was forced to order the fleets to withdraw.

The tyrant was now in great trouble. He had neither gold nor gifts to give to Artaphernes as he had promised. He had wasted Persian money on a useless expedition, and he had made Megabates his enemy. What would Darius say when he heard these things? Aristagoras was afraid that the king would no longer allow him to be tyrant of Miletus.

It seemed to Aristagoras that the only way to save himself from disgrace was to persuade the Greeks in Asia Minor to revolt against Darius and himself to become their leader.

Now just at this time Histiaeus was more than ever determined to escape from the court of Susa. He thought if Aristagoras would but incite the Greeks to rebel, Darius would send him back to Miletus to restore order to the city.

So while Aristagoras was still hesitating about rousing the citizens, a slave was shown into his presence. He came from Histiaeus, and said that his master had bidden him tell Aristagoras to shave off his hair and look at the message that was branded on his head.

This was a strange way to send a message! But Histiaeus had been unable to think of any other way to tell Aristagoras what he wished him to do. So he had himself first shaved the head of his slave, and branded on it certain signs which meant that the tyrant was to revolt against the Persians. He had waited only until the slave's hair had grown again, when he had at once sent him to Miletus.

When Aristagoras looked at the slave's head and learned that Histiaeus encouraged him to revolt, he hesitated no longer. He determined to rouse the Ionian Greeks, and he began with his own city Miletus. When he had assembled the citizens he told them that the time had come to throw off the Persian yoke. He then gave up his position as tyrant that Miletus might be made into a democracy. The example of Miletus was quickly followed by many other cities, and the Greeks were soon in open rebellion against Darius.

CHAPTER XXXVIII

SARDIS IS DESTROYED

The Ionians knew that they would not be able to throw off the Persian yoke without help from their kinsfolk in Greece. So Aristagoras was appointed to go to Sparta to beg king Cleomenes to help the Ionians, who were of the same race as were he and his people.

When Aristagoras reached Sparta he tried to tempt the king to help the Ionians by telling him of the wealth he might gain for himself. After Artaphernes was conquered at Sardis it would, he said, be an easy matter to go to Susa and seize the treasures of the great king. He then showed Cleomenes a thing he had never seen before—a map engraved in bronze. Aristagoras pointed out to him all the countries he might make his own if he would aid the Ionians in their revolt.

The king listened and looked, then he dismissed the Greek, promising to think over the matter. In three days he sent for Aristagoras and asked him how long it took to journey from Ionia to Susa.

"Three months," answered the messenger.

"O stranger," then said Cleomenes, "depart from Sparta before the sun goes down; thou art no friend to the Lacedaemonians when thou seekest to lead them three months' journey from the sea."

In spite of the king's command, Aristagoras still tarried in Sparta. He had made up his mind that he would see Cleomenes once again ere he left the country.

So one day, taking an olive branch in his hand as a sign of peace, he went to the king's house. He found Cleomenes alone with his little daughter Gorgo, a child about eight years old.

Aristagoras begged the king to send his daughter away, but Cleomenes said, "Pay no heed to the child."

Then the Greek tried to bribe the king to send help to Ionia. Ten talents he offered, twenty, thirty, but in vain. Forty, fifty! Surely, thought Aristagoras, the king would be won by fifty talents.

But at that moment little Gorgo interfered. "Father," she said, "the stranger will corrupt you unless you rise up and go."

Cleomenes listened to the child's words and knew that they were wise. He rose and left the room, and Aristagoras knew that he had been beaten by the little princess.

SARDIS IS DESTROYED

But although Sparta would not help, Athens might. So Aristagoras went to the beautiful city and found that the Athenians were willing to send twenty ships to the aid of the Ionians. "These ships," said Herodotus, "were the beginnings of evil both to the Greeks and to the barbarians."

In 498 B.C. the Athenian fleet was ready. It sailed across the Ægean and the troops landed at Ephesus, where they were joined by the Ionians. Together they marched upon Sardis.

Artaphernes saw that he could not hope to hold the town against the force that was approaching. So he left the city to be plundered, while he with a small band of soldiers took refuge in the Acropolis.

As they met with little resistance, the Athenians at once began to pillage the town. One of the soldiers set fire to a house, and as many of them were made of wickerwork, while all the roofs were thatched, the flames spread quickly through the city until Sardis was destroyed. Then the Greeks, loaded with plunder, began to march back to Ephesus, but on the way they were met by a troop of Persians and defeated. The Athenians now determined to go home. Aristagoras begged them to stay, but they paid no heed to his request, and hastening to the shore they embarked and set sail for Athens. Nor did the Athenians take any further share in the Ionic revolt.

But they had already done enough to rouse the anger of Darius. The great king knew that it would be easy to punish Aristagoras and the Ionians.

As for the strangers who had burned Sardis, one of his capital towns, they, whoever they were, should suffer most heavily. He was told that the strangers were the Athenians.

"The Athenians—who are they?" he demanded haughtily. And when he had been told he sent for a bow and shot an arrow high into the air, saying as he did so, "O Zeus, suffer me to avenge myself on the Athenians." He then bade one of his slaves say to him three times each day as he sat at dinner, "O king, remember the Athenians."

Meanwhile Aristagoras saw that there was little chance of the revolt being successful against the forces of Darius. So, like a coward rather than like a brave leader, he deserted those whom he had encouraged to rebel and fled to Thrace. Here, while besieging a town, he was slain.

CHAPTER XXXIX

THE SANDAL SEWN BY HISTIAEUS

Now when Darius heard that Sardis had been destroyed, he sent for Histiaeus and said to him, "O Histiaeus, I hear that the man to whom thou hast given thy city has been doing strange things. He has brought over men from Europe to help the Ionians whom I shall punish.... How can all this seem good to thee? And without thy counsel how could such a thing be done? See that thou bring not thyself into blame afresh."

Histiaeus tried not to think of the slave whose head he had shaved and whom he had sent to Aristagoras, as he told the king that he had had nothing to do with the revolt in Ionia. He begged to be allowed to go to help Artaphernes to put down the rebellion. He would do even more to show his loyalty; he would seize the rich island of Sardinia to add to the possessions of the great king.

"Yea, I swear by the gods whom the king worshippeth," he cried, "that I will not put off the tunic in which I shall go down to Ionia, before I bring under thy power the mighty island of Sardinia."

It was not difficult to persuade Darius that Histiaeus was innocent, for since the Greek had tarried for him at the bridge of boats the king was ever ready to believe in his loyalty. So to his great delight, Histiaeus was bidden to go to Sardis and help Artaphernes to put down the revolt.

But Artaphernes was less easily deceived than the great king. No sooner had Histiaeus arrived at Sardis than the Persian accused him of treachery.

"Why did the Ionians rebel against the king?" he asked the Greek in a stern voice.

"I cannot tell," answered Histiaeus. "I have marvelled at all the things which have happened."

"O Histiaeus," said Artaphernes, "thou hast thus much to do with these matters. Thou didst sew this sandal and Aristagoras hath put it on."

Then at length Histiaeus was afraid lest his deceit had been discovered, and lest he should be punished. So when night came he stole out of the city and went as speedily as might be to the sea. From that time he became a sea-robber or pirate, seizing any vessel from which he could hope to get booty, whether it belonged to Greek or to barbarian.

After a long time he was take prisoner by the Persians. Artaphernes ordered that he should be crucified and that his head should be sent to Darius.

THE SANDAL SEWN BY HISTIAEUS

But the great king was displeased that his general had not sent the Greek to him alive.

"If Histiaeus had been sent away alive to King Darius," says Herodotus, "he would not, I think, have suffered any harm, but his trespass would have been forgiven him."

Even as it was, Darius was determined to show what honour was yet possible to his faithless servant. For he ordered his slaves to "wash the head and adorn it well, and to bury it as the head of one who had done much good to himself and to the Persians."

In 494 B.C., four years after the Athenians had sailed to the help of the Ionians, the revolt was crushed. Miletus, where the rebellion had begun, was punished more severely than the other rebellious cities.

CHAPTER XL

DARIUS DEMANDS EARTH AND WATER

THE Ionian revolt was ended, but Darius had yet to punish the Athenians for burning the city of Sardis. Eight years had now passed since she had been destroyed, yet his anger against the Greeks was as fierce as ever.

Daily during all these years a slave had said to him as he sat at dinner, "Sire, remember the Athenians." And now, at length, his vengeance was at hand.

Mardonius, one of the king's generals, was ordered to invade Greece and to bring back with him to Susa the Athenians who had dared to destroy Sardis.

So Mardonius crossed the Hellespont, and began to march through Thrace and Macedonia. His fleet, with part of his army, was to meet him later, beyond the perilous promontory of Mount Athos.

The country through which Mardonius marched was wild, and inhabited by rough and savage tribes. These tribes attacked the Persian troops so fiercely that more than half of them were slain. Meanwhile the fleet had encountered a terrible storm, and three hundred ships were dashed to pieces upon the rocks near Mount Athos, while twenty thousand were drowned.

When Mardonius heard of this terrible disaster he knew that his troops would not now be strong enough to invade Greece. So he went back to Persia.

But Darius was as determined as ever to punish the Athenians. He spent two years in preparations, and then, before he set out for Greece, he sent heralds to the different states, demanding from each earth and water. To give earth to the great king was to acknowledge him as ruler of their land, to give water was to own that he was monarch of the sea.

Many of the states were afraid to refuse, and sent the earth and water which Darius demanded, but among these was neither Athens nor Sparta.

So indignant were these two cities that a barbarian, as they called Darius, should send such a demand to the free States of Greece, that they treated his heralds with scant courtesy. The Athenians flung the messenger who came to their city into a deep pit, while he who went to Sparta was tossed into a well and told that there he would find the earth and water that his king desired.

In the spring of 490 B.C. Darius sent the army and fleet that he had assembled, across the Ægean Sea to the island of Euboea. Here there was a city named Eretria, whose inhabitants had shared in the destruction of Sardis. The Persians plundered the city and took its chief citizens prisoners, loading them with chains.

Flushed with victory, the army then crossed over to Attica and landed near the plain of Marathon. There where

> "The mountains look on Marathon,
> And Marathon looks on the sea,"

a great battle was fought between the Greeks and the Persians.

Hippias, the tyrant who had fled from Athens many years before, had been living under the protection of Darius and was now with the Persian army. It is said that it was he who had advised the enemy to land at Marathon.

The army of Darius was much larger than that of the Athenians, for it was one hundred thousand strong, while the Greeks numbered only about ten thousand trained soldiers.

The Greeks were commanded by ten generals. If they did not agree how to attack the enemy or how to defend themselves, they consulted one of the archons called the polemarch, or commander-in-chief. The polemarch at this time was Callimachus. But the glory of the victory of Marathon belongs not to Callimachus but to the general Miltiades.

It was Miltiades who had urged the Greeks to break up the bridge of boats at the Danube and to

DARIUS DEMANDS EARTH AND WATER

leave Darius to his fate, and he had ever rebelled against the lordship of the Persian king. He had done all he could to encourage the Ionian revolt, and when it was crushed he fled to Athens, to which city he belonged.

When the Persians landed at Marathon the ten Greek generals met together to decide how best they might defend their country. Five of them, among whom Miltiades was the most urgent, wished to march at once to Marathon to attack the enemy. But the other five were more timid, and said that it would be better to wait until they were joined by the other Greek States before they risked a battle.

Then Miltiades rose in the council of war to beg Callimachus to give his vote for war without delay. So sure was he of success that his eagerness decided the polemarch to give his vote as Miltiades wished. Thus it was settled that the army should march to Marathon without delay.

At this time an army was usually drawn up for battle in three divisions—the right wing, the left wing, and the centre.

On the field of Marathon, Miltiades made his wings as deep as possible, but as his army was small, this left his centre less strong than that of the enemy.

CHAPTER XLI

THE BATTLE OF MARATHON

WHILE the council of war was being held, a youth named Philippides was on his way to Sparta to beg the citizens to hasten to the help of their country. Philippides was sometimes called by his friends Pheidippides.

As Philippides sped on his errand a strange adventure befell him, for it is told that he met the great god Pan:

"There, in the cool of a cleft, sat he—majestical Pan.
Ivy drooped wanton, kissed his head, moss cushioned his hoof,
All the great God was good in the eyes grave-kindly—the curl
Carved on the bearded cheek, amused at a mortal's awe,
As under the human trunk, the goat thighs grand I saw.
'Halt, Pheidippides!' halt I did, my brain in a whirl;
'Hither to me; why pale in my presence?' he gracious began."

The young Athenian was too amazed to answer, he but gazed at the god in silence. Then Pan asked why he was no longer worshipped in Athens,

THE BATTLE OF MARATHON

and promised that he would fight among the ranks of the Athenians against Persia, so that henceforth they would worship him in gratitude for his help.

> "Test Pan, trust me!
> Go bid Athens take heart, laugh Persia to scorn; have faith
> In the temples and tombs. Go say to Athens, 'The Goat-God saith;
> When Persia—so much as strews not the soil—is flung under the sea,
> Then praise Pan who fought in the ranks with your most and least,
> Goat-thigh to greaved-thigh, made one cause with the free and the bold.'"

As a pledge the god then gave to Philippides a handful of a herb called fennel.

The youth then sped on as before until he reached Sparta. But although the Spartans said they were willing to fight, they could not march until the moon was full, for their religious rites forbade that they should.

So Philippides, having done his errand, hastened back to Athens and told the citizens all that had befallen him.

Glad that the god had promised his aid the Athenians at once set out on their march to Marathon. Here they were joined by a force of one thousand men from the little town of Plataea. They came to show their gratitude to the Athenians who had sent help to them when they were attacked by their enemies.

From their camp on a hill above the plain of Marathon, the Greeks looked down upon the vast army of the Persians. For several days no battle was fought, the Persians being unable to attack the Athenians without danger as they were on the hill.

At length Miltiades, whom the other nine generals were willing to follow, resolved to wait no longer. He ordered his men to advance at a sharp run down the hill and to charge the enemy.

When they had started, the soldiers could not stop themselves. Quicker and quicker they ran, until, when they reached the plain, they crashed into the Persian army with tremendous force.

The shock was so great that the enemy gave way before it and was driven by the Athenians toward the sea or toward a small marsh that lay at one end of the plain.

But while both wings of the Greek army were victorious, the centre, which was weak, would have been beaten, had not Miltiades seen the danger and called back those who were pursuing the scattered Persian wings. Only after a fierce struggle was the centre of the Persian army also driven to the shore in utter confusion.

Those who escaped the sword of the Athenians tried to reach their ships, but seven of the vessels had been seized by the victors. In the struggle on the shore, Callimachus the polemarch was slain.

The battle of Marathon was won, and the glory of the victory was due to the prowess and skill of Miltiades.

THE BATTLE OF MARATHON

They crashed into the Persian army with tremendous force

No sooner was the victory certain, than the whole army cried that Philippides should race once again, but this time to the Acropolis, to tell Athens that by the help of Pan she was indeed saved.

"So Pheidippides flung down his shield,
  Ran like fire once more; and the space 'twixt the Fennel-field
  And Athens was stubble again, a field which a fire runs through,
  Till in he broke; 'Rejoice, we conquer.' Like wine through clay
  Joy in his blood bursting his heart, he died—the bliss! . . .
  So is Pheidippides happy for ever, the noble, strong man
  Who could race like a god, bear the face of a god, whom a god
      loved so well.
  He saw the land saved he had helped to save and was suffered to tell
  Such tidings, yet never decline, but gloriously as he began
  So to end gloriously—once to shout, thereafter be mute:
  'Athens is saved!' Pheidippides dies in the shout for his meed."

CHAPTER XLII

MILTIADES SAILS TO THE ISLAND OF PAROS

UNTIL the Greeks won their great victory at Marathon, in 490 B.C., they had always feared the Persians. Now their fear was forgotten. They had still a long struggle before the Persians were banished from their land, but, inspired by the memory of Marathon, the Greeks fought bravely and were sure always that they would be the victors. "It was as though on the day of Marathon the gods had said to the Athenians, 'Go on and prosper.'"

Among those who fought on this famous field was Themistocles. He was young then and fought in the ranks, but he was yet to become one of the greatest men that Athens ever knew. Aristides too was there, of whom as of Themistocles there are many things to tell; Æschylus, the great tragic poet, also bore arms at Marathon.

When the battle was over, it was found that the Athenians had lost only one hundred and ninety-two men, while of the Persians six thousand four hundred lay dead upon the field. In spite of this the army of the Persians was still large enough to attack the unwalled city of Athens.

Soon after the battle a bright shield was hung on one of the heights of the city, and it was said that a traitor had signalled to the enemy that now was the time to attack her. But Miltiades saw the light as well as the Persians, and guessing what it meant, he took his army back to Athens by a forced march. He arrived in time to see the fleet of the enemy as it approached the harbour.

But when the Persian general saw that he need not hope to take the city unawares, he did not venture to risk another battle. An army already flushed with victory would soon scatter his dejected troops. So he ordered the fleet to sail for Asia.

While Miltiades was making a forced march back to Athens, Aristides was left at Marathon with a band of soldiers to guard the prisoners and the plunder, for his honesty was already well known.

Neither he himself touched any of the treasures of the Persian camp, nor did he allow his followers to plunder. Callias, the torchbearer, "most cruel and impious of men," did, it is true, seize a treasure, but he did so unknown to Aristides. For one of the Persians, thinking Callias was of noble rank and hoping to win his favour, fell at his feet, and then, rising, took his hand and led him to a ditch in which a large quantity of gold had been hidden.

Callias seized the treasure, then lest the Persian should tell what had happened, he slew him.

MILTIADES SAILS TO THE ISLAND OF PAROS

The Spartans who had promised to help to fight against their country's foe did not forget to march to Marathon when the moon was full. They even marched one hundred and fifty miles in three days, but in spite of this they reached the battlefield too late to share in the victory.

A mound was raised over the Athenians who had perished, about half a mile from the sea. If you go to where

"The mountains look on Marathon,
And Marathon looks on the sea,"

you may see it still.

After the victory, Miltiades was the hero of Athens. He knew that the citizens would grant what he chose to ask, so he begged for a fleet of seventy ships. He knew of a land where gold and treasures were to be had in abundance. Thither would he sail and return to enrich the city.

The fleet was entrusted to him, but Miltiades did not sail to the wonderful land of which he had told, but, so it is said, to the island of Paros. Here in the capital city, which was also called Paros, dwelt a citizen with whom the Athenian had a quarrel. To punish him, Miltiades laid siege to the town, but again and again his attacks were repulsed. Then one day as he was on his way to the temple of Demeter, Miltiades was seized with sudden panic. In his haste to leave the sacred grove he leaped over a fence, and in doing so he hurt his thigh.

When he returned to Athens he was no longer in favour with the people whom he had deceived. Wounded as he was, he was carried into court on a couch and was condemned to pay a heavy fine. But he died before he had collected the money.

Meanwhile Darius heard how his army had been defeated at Marathon. In his wrath he vowed that he would never rest until he had conquered Greece.

Three years he spent, preparing once again to invade Europe. His heralds were sent all over his wide dominions to gather together a great army. Horses and corn too the king demanded should be sent "much more than before."

But the great king never carried out his plan of again attacking Greece, for he died in 485 B.C., after having reigned for thirty-six years. His son Xerxes succeeded to the throne of Persia.

CHAPTER XLIII
ARISTIDES IS OSTRACISED

FOUR years after the battle of Marathon, Themistocles and Aristides were the two chief citizens in Athens.

Themistocles wished to make Athens a great sea-power, for he was sure that some day the Persians would return. He believed that if the Athenians were able to destroy the Persian fleet, all would be well. The land forces of the enemy would be powerless to conquer Greece.

But if Athens was to have a better fleet, Themistocles knew that she must first have a better harbour. The one that the Athenians used was at Phalerum, where the sea almost reached the city. It was only an open roadstead, a place where ships might ride at anchor, which would be of little use to protect vessels from an enemy.

Themistocles knew a better site than Phalerum, where a strong harbour might be built.

This was the rocky peninsula of Piraeus, which was about four miles from Athens.

By his advice three harbours were made here, into which the largest vessels could enter. Yet the opening to all three was such that it could be closed easily with chains and logs, so as to prevent the entrance of an enemy. The Piraeus soon grew into a large town, for those who did not own land flocked to the port in the hope of finding work.

Not only did Themistocles persuade the Athenians to fortify the Piraeus, but he also made Athens a great sea-power.

At this time there was money to spare in the public treasury, for a rich bed of silver had been discovered in an old mine. This money was to be divided among the Athenians. Themistocles was brave enough to risk the anger of the people by proposing that it should not be given to them, but should be used to build ships.

The Athenians were eager to conquer the people of Ægina who for years had harried their coasts, and they agreed to his proposal more readily than Themistocles had dared to hope. With the money the State built two hundred ships, so the people were able to conquer their enemy and were well content. But it was Themistocles alone who wished to prepare Greece for a great Persian invasion. Of this the Athenians had no fear.

When the ships were ready, Themistocles saw that the soldiers must be trained to manage the vessels, to become indeed good sailors.

ARISTIDES IS OSTRACISED

A wise Greek named Plato tells us that Themistocles "from steady soldiers turned the Greeks into mariners and seamen, tossed about the sea, and gave occasion for the reproach against him, that he took away from the Athenians the spear and the shield, and bound them to the bench and the oar."

Aristides and Themistocles were rivals. They were brought up together, and when they were boys they usually took different sides, just as they continued to do when they were men.

If you could have watched the boys in school or in the playground you would have seen at once how different they were. Themistocles was impetuous and bold, artful too, if by being so he could gain his own ends. Aristides was gentle and retiring, honest as the day, in work as in play.

Themistocles was not fond of lessons nor yet of games. But he knew a great deal even as a boy of what was going on in the city and in the State, and he was eager to know more.

While Aristides and his comrades were laughing and shouting over their game of quoits, Themistocles was walking up and down alone in a quiet corner of the playground. He was rehearsing a speech, which he would soon begin to recite aloud.

Sometimes, in more friendly mood, he called his play-fellows together and delivered his speech to the crowd of little critics. It was usually about the affairs of the State—about politics, as we would say.

His schoolmaster saw that although the lad did not love lessons, he could be an earnest student if he were interested in a subject. One day he said to him, "You, my boy, will be nothing small, but great, one way or other, for good or else for bad."

From his boyhood Themistocles was ambitious, and when he grew up he accepted bribes, if by doing so he thought he could reach a higher position in the State.

When he became a judge he showed favour to his friends, even though to do so was unjust. One of them once said to him that he would be a good judge, if he would give sentence "without respect of persons." But in no way abashed, Themistocles answered, "May I never sit upon the seat of judgment where my friends shall not receive more favour from me than strangers."

Aristides was in this, as in other things, the opposite of his rival, for he was an honourable and upright judge. He was ever ready to please or to help a friend, but to do so he would stoop to no act of injustice. Once he accused one of his enemies of a crime, and the people, with whom Aristides was at that time a favourite, wished to condemn the man without listening to his defence. But this Aristides would not allow.

When he himself was judge, two people came before him, one of whom was an enemy of his own. The other, knowing this, felt sure that he would win his suit, and instead of telling of what he accused the man, he began to remind Aristides that it was an enemy of his own who stood before him. But Aristides bade him be silent. "Tell me not," he said, "what injury he has done to me, but what harm you have suffered from him, for I am trying your cause and not my own."

Themistocles not only took bribes, but he often tried to make others accept them. Many of the Greeks did so, for they could not easily resist gold, but Aristides was never one of those who took money from Themistocles, or indeed from anyone.

When Themistocles urged the Athenians to increase their fleet, Aristides opposed him with all his strength. And he did this, not because he disliked his rival, but because he believed that it would be better for the State to increase her army rather than to have a powerful navy.

About this, as about other important affairs, the two great men disagreed so often and so long, that the people thought the city would be governed better if one of the leaders was ostracised.

So they assembled in the market-place, where each was given an oyster-shell on which to write the name of the man he wished to be banished from Athens.

As the citizens were busy writing on their shells, a rough country fellow who could not write came up to Aristides and, handing him his shell, asked him to put down the name of Aristides. The countryman did not know that he was speaking to Aristides himself.

"Has Aristides done you an injury?" asked the Athenian, as he took the shell.

"None at all," answered the fellow, "neither know I the man, but I am tired of everywhere hearing him called the Just." Aristides did not answer the ignorant countryman, but he quietly wrote his own name upon the shell and handed it back to its owner.

The necessary number of votes being recorded against him he was ostracised. As he left the city he lifted up his hands to heaven and prayed that the Athenians "might never have any occasion which should constrain them to remember Aristides." And this he did although it was a bitter thing to him to leave the city that he loved so well. In his absence he knew that Themistocles would be able to carry out his plans unopposed, and this added to his pain.

But Themistocles was wiser than Aristides when he urged the Athenians to increase their fleet. For although the great king Darius was dead, Xerxes his son was preparing to invade Greece as his father had hoped to do. And without a large and well-equipped fleet, the Athenians would have been unable to meet the Persians at sea.

CHAPTER XLIV

THE DREAM OF XERXES

XERXES, the new ruler of Persia, looked every inch a king. He was tall and handsome, standing head and shoulders above the great warriors he led to battle. But although he looked a king among men, in character he was most unkingly, for he was both weak and foolish. It is true that he was sometimes good-natured, but it was not wise for his people to trust his temper, for he was often seized by sudden fits of rage, when he would do deeds of terrible cruelty.

In 483 B.C. Xerxes put down a revolt in Egypt. Then his captain and kinsman, Mardonius, begged the king to go to Greece to avenge the Persian defeat at Marathon.

"O king," said Mardonius, "it is not seemly that the Athenians, who have done much wrong to the Persians, should not suffer for their doings. . . . And now, will any one dare to face thee, O king, with thy great army from Asia and all thy ships? Sure I am that the Greeks are not so desperate. But if I am wrong and in their rash folly they come out to battle, they will find that of all men we are the bravest."

To tempt Xerxes yet further to do as he wished, Mardonius told him how fair a country Europe was, how rich in fruit and trees. "Such a country," said the subtle flatterer, "should belong to none save to thee, O king." Mardonius hoped that if Greece was made a province of Persia, he himself would become her ruler.

But while Mardonius urged one thing, Artabanus the king's uncle urged another.

"Thou, O king," said Artabanus, "art going against men ... who are said to be most brave and strong both by sea and land. And it is right I should say why we ought to fear them. Thou sayest that thou wilt make a bridge over the Hellespont and carry thine army through Europe against Hellas: and so we may be beaten either by land or by sea or by both; for the men are said to be strong, and it would seem that they are, if by themselves alone the Athenians destroyed the great host that landed at Marathon."

Now Xerxes was, as I told you, a timid king. So as he listened now to one, now to another of his counsellors, he did not know what to do. First he thought that he would go to Greece, then he thought that he would not go. One night, while he still hesitated, the king had a strange dream. In his dream a man fair and tall stood over him, who said, "Dost thou repent, O Persian, from leading an army against Hellas, when thou hast charged thy people to

THE DREAM OF XERXES

gather their hosts together? Thou doest not well in thy change of counsel, neither is there any one who will forgive thee. Go thou on the road in which thou didst purpose to walk on the day that is past."

When Xerxes awoke he tried to thrust away the memory of his dream, for he now wished to follow the advice of Artabanus and stay at home.

But the next night, as he slept, he saw the same fair, tall man, who chided him for putting aside his words, "as though they had never been spoken." "But be thou sure," he said, "that if thou set not out forthwith, as thou hast become great and mighty in a little while, so in a little while shalt thou be made low."

The king awoke from this second dream in sudden fear, and springing from his bed, he bade his servants bring Artabanus to him without delay.

When his uncle stood before him, Xerxes told his vision in feverish haste.

"Now if it be a god who sends it," said the king, "and if it must be that an army go against Hellas, then the same vision will come to thee."

The foolish king then begged Artabanus to put on his clothes, to sit upon his throne, and afterwards to lie down upon his bed.

At first Artabanus refused to do as the king wished. For he said, "If the vision must come, it ought to come to me no more if I put on thy dress than if I wear my own, and if I rest on thy couch than if I sleep on my own. For that which comes to thee in thy sleep, whatever it be, is surely not so silly as to think on seeing me that it looks upon thee, judging by thy vesture."

But at length Artabanus was persuaded to do as the king wished, and lo! when he had lain down on the royal couch, "the dream of Xerxes came and stood over him, saying 'Neither now nor hereafter shalt thou go unscathed, if thou seekest to turn aside that which must be.' " Then the dream appeared as though it were about to sear out his eyes with hot irons.

Artabanus awoke in great fear, and leaping from the couch he told Xerxes what he had seen and heard. From that night Artabanus was as ready as Mardonius to urge the king to invade Greece.

CHAPTER XLV

XERXES ORDERS THE HELLESPONT TO BE SCOURGED

IN the autumn of 481 B.C. Xerxes led his vast hosts to Sardis. His warriors were of many different races, and each was clad in the dress of the country from which he came. Each, too, was armed with his own weapon, and each talked his own language. So you can picture to yourself with what a strange army Xerxes set out to conquer Greece.

From Sardis he sent heralds, with an interpreter, into Greece, to demand from the people earth and water, the signs of their subjection to the great king of Persia.

Themistocles was so angry with the interpreter, who was a barbarian, for daring to utter the demands of Xerxes in the Greek language, that he ordered him to be put to death.

Another messenger was then sent by Xerxes, and he brought with him gold to bribe the Athenians to join the Persians. Him also Themistocles punished.

Now that danger was near, the Athenians recalled Aristides from exile. They were afraid lest he should join the Persians, for they knew that if he did so, many of his friends would go over to the enemy with him. But it was a needless fear, and the citizens might well have trusted the exile not to betray his country. Even before he knew that his banishment was over, Aristides had begun to stir up the Greeks that were with him to fight against the Persians.

Themistocles, too, was using all his influence to persuade the different States to lay aside the quarrels they had with one another and to fight together against the force that was coming to invade their land.

Meanwhile Xerxes, to avoid sailing across the Hellespont with his vast army, ordered a bridge to be built across it. But soon after the bridge was finished, a violent storm dashed it into fragments.

When Xerxes heard of the disaster, his cruel and childish temper was roused. He ordered the engineers who had planned the bridge to be beheaded, and that was a cruel act. He also commanded that the Hellespont should be scourged with three hundred stripes and that a pair of fetters should be cast into the sea, and these were foolish acts. "He sent branders, too, as some say, to brand the Hellespont; and he charged them to rebuke the water and cry unto it, 'O bitter water, thus doth the

THE HELLESPONT TO BE SCOURGED

king punish thee, because without wrong from him thou has done him harm.'"

Before long a new bridge was built, with hedges planted on either side, so that the horses as they passed across might not be frightened by seeing the water.

First of the great host came a thousand gallant Persian troops, followed by a thousand spearmen. The points of their lances were turned downward; on the handles, which were held aloft, shone golden pomegranates.

Ten sacred horses, with splendid trappings, stepped behind the spearmen, while after the horses came a chariot, dedicated to Zeus, and drawn by eight white horses. No driver was allowed to mount the sacred chariot, he might only walk behind, holding the reins in his hands.

Xerxes himself was in another chariot, surrounded by a thousand guards, bearing spears, upon which glistened apples of gold. Ten thousand of the king's own bodyguard were named the Immortals, for, if one of their number was slain or if one died, his place was at once filled, so that the number of the Immortals might never become less.

As I told you, the Persian army was made up of many different tribes.

"Æthiopians from beyond Egypt were there, clad in leopard skins, and carrying bows made of the central rib of the palm leaf, while their arrows were reeds tipped with sharp fragments of stone. They carried as well spears, pointed with gazelles' horns or knotted clubs. Half their body they painted white and half red before going into battle." Some had no arms but only a lasso and a long knife; others bore staves that had had their points hardened in the fire.

From Caucasus came wild tribes that had no armour to protect their bodies, and only wooden hats to guard their heads.

Xerxes's army was indeed vast, but with so many half-clad and but poorly armed barbarians in his ranks, he would, had he been wise, have feared to face the small but well-armed and well-trained forces of the Greeks.

On the shore of the Hellespont a throne of white stone or marble was placed, and here Xerxes took his seat to watch his army cross the bridge which led from Asia into Europe.

But before the vast host began to move "Xerxes poured wine from a golden cup into the sea and prayed to the Sun that no harm might happen to him, which might prevent him from conquering all Europe. Then he threw the cup into the Hellespont with a golden goblet and a Persian dagger."

It is said that the king called himself a happy man as he watched the countless numbers of his troops crossing the bridge. But soon after Artabanus was amazed to see him burst into tears.

"O king," he said, "thou doest strange things; even now thou didst call thyself happy and yet thou weepest."

"Thought came upon me and sorrow for the shortness of the life of man," answered Xerxes, "because after a hundred years, of all this great host not one shall remain alive."

When the army had crossed the bridge, it marched on toward the plain of Thessaly, while the fleet, sailing round the south-east point of the same country, anchored near the promontory of Magnesia. Here it was as near to the army as it was possible for it to be. Not long after the fleet had anchored, a sudden storm arose, and for three days did much damage to the ships.

The Greeks meanwhile had been preparing to fight the invaders. They had sent spies to Sardis to find out, not only the numbers of the Persian host, but its mettle.

As it chanced, the spies were captured and were on the point of being put to death, when Xerxes ordered them to be brought before him.

When they stood in his presence, he demanded why they had ventured into the camp of the enemy. On hearing the reason he bade an officer show them the strength of his army and then send them back unharmed to their own country. "For," said the king, "if the spies had been killed, the Greeks could not have heard beforehand of all my great might, yet it would do them but little hurt to slay three men. But now will I have no trouble by marching against them, when the spies have already told of my mighty army."

So confident was the king that he would conquer the enemy without difficulty, that when vessels filled with corn sailed past his fleet on the way to Athens, he would not allow any of his ships to pursue them.

"Whither are they sailing?" asked Xerxes when the corn ships were pointed out to him.

"To thy enemies, O king, laden with corn," answered his anxious councillors.

"Why, we are going thither also," said the king. "What harm do they do by taking corn for me?"

Now that the Persians were actually at hand the Spartans and Athenians summoned the Greek states to a council of war to be held at the Isthmus of Corinth. But some of the states were afraid, and instead of attending the council they sent earth and water to Xerxes.

Thessaly, in the north, would be the first to suffer from the invading army. So a Greek force was sent to the Pass of Tempe, between Mount Olympus and Mount Ossa, to try to stop the advance of the Persians.

But there were other ways by which the enemy could slip past the Greeks, so after a time, they determined to withdraw from Thessaly. The northern people, being thus left defenceless, hastened to submit to Xerxes while there was still time.

CHAPTER XLVI

"THE BRAVEST MEN OF ALL HELLAS"

THROUGH the Pass of Thermopylae lay the entrance from the north to the south of Greece. It was this pass that the Greeks determined to hold against the Persians when they withdrew from the Pass of Tempe.

The Pass of Thermopylae was about a mile long and the narrow road ran between the mountains and the sea. At each end of the pass the mountains were sheer cliffs, descending so close to the sea that the only pathway was a mere strip of sand.

To enter the pass, at either end, it was necessary to go through a narrow entrance called Pylae or the Gates. In the road between the Pylae or Gates there were hot springs. The Greek word for hot is thermos, and that is how the pass came to be named Thermopylae or Hot-Gates.

At the narrowest part of the pass stood an old broken-down wall, and this wall was repaired by the order of Leonidas, King of Sparta, that it might form a defence against the enemy.

A short distance from the mainland lay the island of Euboea, the strait between being at one place only two and a half miles in breadth. Here the Greek fleet took up its position under the command of the Spartan Eurybiades, Themistocles being second in command. Themistocles would have held the chief command had not some of the States refused to serve under an Athenian admiral.

The land army was led by Leonidas, one of the kings of Sparta. But because this was now the month of June 480 B.C., the time when the Olympic games were held, many of the Spartans did not march with Leonidas to Thermopylae. For although the country was in danger, the games, being also religious rites, must be held as usual, and numbers of brave soldiers stayed at home to take part in the festival.

When Leonidas set out on his march to defend the entrance to the south of Greece, he had with him only three hundred Spartans. On the way to Thermopylae he was joined by troops from other States, so that when he reached the pass he was at the head of seven thousand men.

Now there was only one narrow hill track by which the enemy could reach the rear of the Spartans, and strangers to the country were little likely to find it. Yet Leonidas bade the Phocians,

"THE BRAVEST MEN OF ALL HELLAS"

who lived in the district, guard well this narrow footpath. He would leave nothing to chance.

When Xerxes with his great army reached Thermopylae, he was told that it was in the hands of a small band of Spartans, under king Leonidas. The tidings did not disturb the Persian monarch, he was sure that the Spartans would soon leave their post, when they saw his great army.

But the Spartans did not retreat, although they could see plainly the vast hordes that had come against them.

By and by Xerxes grew impatient and sent a horseman to reconnoitre. The horseman could not see the Spartan camp, for it was hidden by the old wall that had been repaired, but he could see the men themselves without the wall. Their arms were piled up against it in stacks, as though no enemy was near. Some of the soldiers were wrestling with each other, others were combing their hair, as if they were getting ready for a festival rather than for a battle.

The Persian was astonished at what he saw. As the Spartans took no notice of him, he stayed to count their number, and then rode quietly back to tell Xerxes all that he had seen.

Xerxes, too, was amazed. Why should soldiers trouble to comb their hair before fighting? Why should they wrestle with one another as though no danger lay before them? He thought that they were doing "childish and silly things," for he did not understand that this was the Spartans' way of getting ready either to die or to slay their enemies.

In the Persian camp was an exiled King of Sparta, named Demaratus. Xerxes sent for him to ask why his countrymen wasted their time, wrestling and combing their long curls.

"These men," answered Demaratus, "are here to fight for the pass; and when they have to face a mortal danger, their custom is to comb and deck out their hair. Be sure then, that if thou canst conquer these and all the rest who remain behind in Sparta, there is no other nation which shall dare to raise a hand against thee, for now art thou face to face with the bravest men of all Hellas."

But Xerxes laughed at the thought of a small band of men like the Spartans daring to fight against his great army. He dismissed Demaratus and sent to demand that the Spartans should give up their arms. But the only answer that Leonidas sent back was to bid the king "to come and take them." It was plain that the Spartans did not fear the enemy. When one of them was told that the Persian host was so numerous that "the flight of their arrows would darken the light of the sun," he answered carelessly, "So much the better, we shall fight in the shade."

For four days Xerxes waited, expecting the Spartans to flee, but on the fifth day they were still there, wrestling and combing their hair as before.

Then the king sent a band of soldiers to the enemy's camp, bidding it take these bold Spartans alive and bring them bound into his presence.

But the Persians could not push their way through the narrow gates which were guarded by the enemy. They were not only kept at bay, they were thrust back again and again, and many of their number were slain by the long spears of the Spartans.

CHAPTER XLVII

THE BATTLE OF THERMOPYLAE

XERXES looked on while his soldiers fought at the entrance to the pass. And they did their best, for they were unwilling that their king should see them beaten back by men who had spent their days in games or in bedecking their hair. But they could not stand against the fierce attacks of the Spartans, and at length, when many of their number had been slain, they withdrew.

The king then ordered his own chosen bodyguard, the ten thousand famous Immortals, to advance against the gallant defenders of the pass.

Even at the approach of these renowned warriors, the Spartans did not waver. They pretended to flee, only to turn and slay the barbarians who had followed them into the pass. At length after a furious conflict, the Immortals were forced to give way and return to their camp.

THE BATTLE OF THERMOPYLAE

Three times as he watched the Immortals, Xerxes sprang from his throne, thinking that all was lost. But the next day he sent them against the foe once more, for now he believed that the Spartans would be too weary to fight.

But Leonidas was careful of the little band he commanded. It was easy to hold the pass with only a small number of men. As each company grew tired, the king ordered it to withdraw and sent a fresh one to take its place. Soon the entrance to the pass was choked with the dead bodies of the barbarians.

Some of the most valiant of Xerxes' warriors were next sent against the enemy. But they were cowed by the bravery of the Spartans, and as they saw their comrades falling around them, they turned to flee. Then their officers drove them back with lashes.

For two days, the terrible slaughter never ceased, and Xerxes was almost ready to leave the pass to its brave defenders, so hopeless seemed the task of taking it.

But that night, a Greek named Ephialtes came to the great king, and for a large sum of money, he offered to show the Persians a path which led over the hill down to the pass of Thermopylae. The path was the tiny track that was guarded by the Phocians.

The offer of the traitor was at once accepted, and at midnight Xerxes sent his officer Hydarmes, at the head of his Immortals, to follow Ephialtes.

"All night long they followed the path with the mountains on the right and on the left. The day was dawning when they reached the peak of the mountain, and there the thousand Phocians were keeping watch and guarding the pathway. While the Persians were climbing the hill, the Phocians knew not of their coming, for the whole hill was covered with oak trees, but they knew what had happened when the Persians reached the summit. Not a breath of wind was stirring, and they heard the trampling of their feet as they trod on the fallen oak leaves."

No sooner had they heard than the arrows of the Immortals were pouring in upon them. They fell back, leaving the pathway free, while they hastily put on their armour and prepared to fight to the death. They did not dream that the Immortals had no wish to fight with them. But so it was, for the Persians took no more notice of them, but finding the hill path free, they sped downward to the pass to take the Spartans in the rear. The Phocians were left along on the heights almost before they were aware.

Leonidas had heard of the treachery of Ephialtes soon after the traitor left the Persian king. He knew that to try to hold the pass now that he would be attacked in the rear was certain death. Yet the brave king did not hesitate, for his orders had been to hold the pass at all costs.

Nor did he waver as he remembered the ominous words of the oracle, "Sparta must be overthrown or one of her kings must perish." It

THE BATTLE OF THERMOPYLAE

seemed that he was the king who was doomed to die, but what of that if his country was saved?

He resolved that to Sparta alone should belong the glory of the defence of Thermopylae. So while there was still time, he sent away all his allies, keeping with him only his three hundred Spartans, seven hundred Thespians who refused to leave him, and four hundred Boeotians, lest they should join the enemy.

Then "when the sun arose, Xerxes poured out wine to the gods and the barbarians arose for the onset, and the men of Leonidas knew now that they must die." But they would die fighting, and before they were attacked in the rear they would do great deeds.

Fierce and desperate was their defence, and before the fury of their blows the barbarians fell in heaps. Once again, the Persian officers, armed with whips, had to drive their men forward to face the small but undaunted band.

In the confusion many of the great host of Xerxes were pushed into the sea while many more were trampled to death by their comrades.

So furious was the struggle, that at length the spears of the Spartans were broken in their hands. In a moment, they had seized their swords and hundreds of the Persians fell before their terrible thrusts.

But now the worst that could befall the Spartans happened. Leonidas, their brave king Leonidas, was slain where he fought in the forefront of the battle. A terrible struggle at once began for the body of the king.

Four times the Spartans drove back the Persians, and then with one tremendous effort they carried away the body of their king.

It was at this moment that the Immortals, led by the traitor, Ephialtes, reached the pass. The Spartans hastily withdrew behind the wall, which had been repaired by the order of their king. Here, on a hillock, "they defended themselves to the last, such as had swords using them, and the others resisting with their hands and teeth; till the barbarians, who had in part pulled down the wall and attacked them in front, in part had gone round and now encircled them upon every side, overwhelmed and buried the remnant which was left, beneath showers of missile weapons."

As you read the story of the brave defence of Thermopylae, you do not wonder that Leonidas and his three hundred Spartans have won for themselves immortal fame.

On the hillock where the little band took their last stand, a stone lion was placed in honour of king Leonidas, while in the pass itself a pillar was erected on which were written these words:—

> "Go, tell the Spartans, thou that passest by,
> That here obedient to their laws we lie."

When the battle was over, Xerxes ordered his men to search for the body of Leonidas. When it was found he ordered the head to be cut off and the body to be hung upon a cross.

It was the custom of the Persians to honour the bodies of those who had fallen fighting bravely against them. This unusual and cruel treatment was but a proof of the fear the brave Spartan had inspired in the heart of Xerxes. Nor could the king forget that he had been on the point of leaving the pass in the hands of its brave defenders.

Demaratus could not look at the slaughter of his countrymen unmoved. He had seemed to be a friend of the great king, yet now he longed to warn the Spartans who had stayed at home that the Persians were ready to march against them.

But how could he send a message unknown to the Persians. He soon thought of a strange and less cruel way than had Histiaeus, who, you remember, branded his secret on the head of his slave.

The exiled king took a writing tablet and scraped away the wax on which letters were usually engraved. On the wood beneath he scratched the message he wished to send. He then poured melted wax on the top of what he had written, and the tablet looked as any other tablet looked.

When it reached Sparta, the people studied it with amazement. There was a tablet, but where was the message? They turned it this way and that, they peered at it now on one side, now on another— nothing was to be seen.

Then Gorgo, whom you heard of last as a little maiden of eight years old, gave the people advice as wise as she had given to her royal father long before. She was grown up since those days and had been married to brave king Leonidas.

"Scrape off the wax," she said to the people, "and see if the message lies on the wood beneath."

And when this was done, there stood the warning words of Demaratus, so that all might read.

CHAPTER XLVIII

THE BATTLE OF ARTEMISIUM

WHILE Leonidas was fighting so bravely on land, Themistocles was with the fleet at Artemisium. If the Persians passed this point and entered the Malian Gulf, they would be able to land troops behind Leonidas and secure the pass of Thermopylae without difficulty.

But before the Persian fleet reached Artemisium, a sudden storm arose and dashed some of the ships upon the rocks, some against each other. For three days the tempest raged, and when at length the sea grew calm, four hundred ships had been destroyed.

In spite of this disaster, the Persian fleet was still large enough to alarm the Greeks. When they saw it sailing off the north of the island of Euboea, Eurybiades, the Greek admiral, wished to sail away.

But the inhabitants of the island went to Themistocles to beg him not to let the fleet desert them. So fearful were they, that they offered him thirty talents (about £5800) if he would use his influence to persuade the other admirals to stay and protect their island.

Themistocles readily took the money, and sent eight talents (about £1552) to Eurybiades and his colleagues to bribe them to remain at Euboea.

The next night another storm arose, and again many of the Persian ships were scattered or dashed to pieces on the rocks. But when the wind fell the ships were repaired and the two fleets met in battle.

The struggle was fierce and long, but though the Persians lost a greater number of ships than did the Greeks, yet the fleet under Eurybiades was so heavily damaged that even Themistocles saw that safety lay in retreat. At the same time tidings reached him of the defeat of Thermopylae, and he knew that Xerxes would soon be marching to the south. The fleet must hasten home to protect her own coasts.

So the Greek fleet set sail down the long Euboean strait and did not stop until it reached the island of Salamis. But as they sailed, Themistocles bade the captains of the Athenian fleets send some of their ships to the rocks where the Persians would search for water.

On these rocks Themistocles ordered to be cut in large letters these words, "Ye do wrong, O Ionians, by going against your fathers and bringing Hellas into slavery. If ye can, take our side; if ye cannot, then fight for neither. But if this also is impossible, at least in the battle be slack and lazy, remembering that ye are sprung from us and that we are fighting in a quarrel which ye began."

By these words Themistocles hoped to win the Ionians to his side; or, if that might not be, he hoped at least to make Xerxes so suspicious of them that he would be afraid to let them take part in the battles which had yet to be fought.

CHAPTER XLIX

THEMISTOCLES URGES EURYBIADES TO STAY AT SALAMIS

AFTER Xerxes had secured the pass of Thermopylae, a march of six days would bring him to Athens. There was no army in his way, for the Spartans and other tribes in Peloponnesus were now fortifying the Isthmus of Corinth, so as to protect their cities from the foe.

If the Athenians wished to save themselves they would have to desert their city and seek refuge elsewhere, for it was impossible to hold Athens against the great army that was marching towards her. Yet even to save their lives how hard it was to leave their homes, their temples, their gods!

The oracle at Delphi was consulted, and told them that "when all was lost a wooden wall should still shelter the Athenians." Some there were who believed that the oracle meant that if the Acropolis were fortified with timber it would not be taken by the Persians, and they shut themselves up in the citadel and refused to leave the city.

But Themistocles knew that the only way to save the people was to get them away from Athens, and he used all his eloquence to make them willing to go. When it seemed that he had failed, he tried another way—he began to work upon their superstitious fears. He told them that Athene, their own goddess, had already deserted the city, and taking with her her pet snake had gone to the sea. He assured them that the "walls of wood," of which the oracle had spoken, were the good ships that were at Salamis, waiting to defeat the Persians and put their fleet to flight.

At length his words prevailed, and the old men, women, and children were sent to the island of Salamis, while the fighting men joined the fleet.

In the confusion, many faithful animals were forgotten. These ran along the shore, while the ships carrying the fugitives sailed away. One faithful dog leaped into the water and followed his master's ship until it reached Salamis. But when he had dragged himself out of the water the poor creature was so exhausted that he lay down on the shore and died.

Meanwhile Xerxes was marching toward Athens. On the way he ordered a large company to break off to the west to seize Delphi and the sanctuary of the oracle, in which, as the king knew, vast treasures were kept. No Greek would have dared to rob the sacred temple.

When the Delphians heard that the Persians were approaching, they fled to Parnassus, leaving only sixty men and the priest to defend the sanctuary. They did not think that the treasures would be stolen, for the gods would protect their own.

And as soon as the barbarians were close to the city, strange things are said to have taken place. The sacred arms, which none might touch, were mysteriously carried out and placed in front of the temple. The sky was ablaze with brilliant flashes of lightning, while two great crags were wrenched from the heights of Mount Parnassus and fell with a loud crash upon the enemy. At the same time, from the temple of Athene a shout as of a mighty warrior was heard.

The barbarians were stricken with terror at these strange sights and sounds, and they fled, pursued, so they declared, by two Greeks, each taller and more fearful than any mortal they had ever seen.

Xerxes had now reached Athens, to find the city deserted, save for the few who had taken refuge in the citadel. These defended themselves bravely, and as it was difficult to scale the height on which the Acropolis stood, they were able for a time to keep the enemy at bay.

But at length the wooden defences, in which the people had put their trust, were set on fire by the burning brands of the enemy. At the same time a band of Persian soldiers discovered a secret path on the north side of the citadel. Although it was steep, they at once began to climb, and before long they

EURYBIADES STAYS AT SALAMIS

reached the summit and entered the citadel. The defenders were slain; the temples were plundered and burned.

As the Greek fleet lay in the narrow strait between Salamis and the Attic coast, the Athenians saw smoke and flames rising from the burning city. They were filled with grief as they gazed upon the destruction of their homes and their temples, while their wrath burned hot against the destroyers.

Themistocles and the Athenians wished to stay where they were to await the enemy. But the other admirals were anxious to sail to the Isthmus of Corinth, where they would be within reach of the Peloponnesian army.

A council of war was called, at which Themistocles urged that they should stay where they were to fight and to conquer the Persian fleet. He reminded the other admirals that in the narrow strait of Salamis the big and heavy ships of the Persians would have no room to move and would be captured without great difficulty. But no one agreed with the Athenian general, and the council broke up, after having agreed that the fleet should sail to the Isthmus of Corinth on the following day.

Themistocles was so sure that it was a mistake to move, that he went alone to Eurybiades and earnestly begged him not to withdraw. His gravity impressed the commander, and he promised to recall the council to discuss the matter once more.

No sooner had the admirals again assembled than Themistocles rose, without waiting until the council was opened in the usual way, and again explained the urgent reasons why the fleet should stay to fight at Salamis.

The Corinthian admiral was angry already because the council had been reopened; he was angrier still as he listened to the words of Themistocles.

At length he could keep silent no longer, and he interrupted the orator, saying in a harsh voice, "Themistocles, at the games they who start too soon are scourged."

"True," answered the Athenian, "but they who loiter are not crowned."

Even Eurybiades lost his temper as Themistocles urged his wish more and more vehemently, and at length he raised his staff as though he would strike the persistent orator.

Themistocles looked calmly at the admiral and said, "Strike if you will, but at least hear me." His self-control pleased the Spartan commander. He let his arms drop to his side and listened until Themistocles had ended his speech.

But although Eurybiades said nothing, an officer began to taunt Themistocles, saying that he was the last man who should urge them to stay at Salamis, for he had no city to defend, as Athens was in the hands of the barbarians.

"A base fellow art thou to use such a taunt," answered Themistocles. "True it is that we have left our houses and our walls, for we will not endure to be made slaves for such things. But in these two hundred ships here ready to defend you all, we still possess the fairest city in Greece."

Then turning to Eurybiades he said, "By remaining here, thou wilt show thyself a brave man. By going away, thou wilt destroy all Hellas, for with the war on land the Athenians have nothing more to do. If thou wilt not stay, we will sail away with our two hundred ships and build a city in the west, where the Persians will not trouble us."

Then Eurybiades grew afraid, for he knew that without the help of the Athenians the Greeks need not hope to conquer the enemy, so he agreed to stay to fight at Salamis.

CHAPTER L

THEMISTOCLES TRICKS THE ADMIRALS

EURYBIADES had determined that the fleet should stay at Salamis. But the other admirals were dissatisfied. When great numbers of the Persian ships were sighted, and when at the same times Xerxes was seen marching with his vast land forces toward the shore, they were more than dissatisfied; they were afraid.

So they called a secret council at which they resolved to retreat to Corinth, as they had wished to do from the first. To settle the matter they bade the pilots get ready to sail.

Themistocles soon heard what had been done, but he was determined to thwart the plans of his adversaries. He would force them to fight in the narrow strait of Salamis.

So he sent a message to the King of Persia, and pretending to be his friend, he warned him that the Greek fleet had determined to escape. "If you wish to win a great victory, O king," ran the message, "seize each end of the strait before the Greek fleet sails away."

Xerxes was overjoyed when he heard that the Greeks wished to escape, for it seemed to him that they must be cowards whom it would be easy to beat.

So while Themistocles called together a last council of war and did all that he could to delay the fleet, Xerxes was busy securing the strait as Themistocles had bidden him do.

The pilots were on board the Greek ships, impatient to sail, the admirals were listening to Themistocles with but scant courtesy, when the messenger the Athenian was so anxiously awaiting arrived.

Themistocles hastened from the council to find that it was Aristides, his old rival, who had brought the tidings, that the Greek fleet was shut in by the Persian ships. Flight was no longer possible.

Then Themistocles told Aristides the trick he had played on the Persian king, and how he had at the same time duped the other admirals.

Whether Aristides approved or disapproved of what his old rival had done, he believed that it was well that the battle should be fought in the straits, and he determined to support Themistocles. He himself hastened to the council, to tell the admirals that they were surrounded by the enemy.

At first the admirals refused to believe such evil news. They did not guess the truth, but they came so near to it that they said Themistocles had probably started the rumour, so as to delay their flight.

While they still talked, some sailors who had deserted from the Persians brought the same tale. The Greek admirals were at last convinced that a battle was inevitable.

CHAPTER LI

THE BATTLE OF SALAMIS

ON the morning of the battle, Xerxes ascended a golden throne which had been placed for him upon a rock that overlooked the sea. Around him sat scribes ready to record the events of the battle. That they would all be to the honour of his fleet Xerxes never doubted.

Themistocles saw with pleasure that the wind was rising, making it difficult for the Persians to manage their unwieldy vessels. As he watched their efforts he urged the Greeks to attack them at once.

The narrowness of the strait, as well as the force of the wind, added to the confusion of the enemy and made the number of its ships of little use. Yet the Persians fought bravely, remembering that the eyes of the great king were upon them.

One of the ships was commanded by a queen named Artemisia. She was fighting fiercely when her ship was attacked by an Athenian vessel at close quarters.

Artemisia tried to escape, but as her ship sailed away it was followed by the enemy. Straight in her path lay one of Xerxes' vessels. The queen did not try to avoid it, but pursuing her course struck the ship, so that her own countrymen who were on board were sent to the bottom.

When the Athenian captain saw what the queen had done, he thought, as perhaps she meant him to do, that she had deserted her own side and was now fighting for the Greeks, so he turned back and followed her no more.

From his golden throne, Xerxes too saw what Artemisia had done, and he supposed it was a Greek vessel that she had run down. In his delight he exclaimed, "My men are become women, my women men." This was a hard thing to say of his soldiers who were fighting gallantly for their king.

Meantime the Persian ships were driven into the narrow strait. Ship dashed against ship till the Persian dead strewed the deep "like flowers." When evening fell, two hundred Persian ships had been destroyed and the Greeks had won the great sea-battle of Salamis. The glory of the victory was due to Themistocles. There might indeed have been no battle at Salamis had he not tricked both the Persian king and the Greek admirals.

The Athenian was proud of his success, and he now determined by another crafty message to Xerxes to drive him out of Greece.

But first he sent for Aristides, and to test his wisdom he told him that he thought they should sail

THE BATTLE OF SALAMIS

Ship dashed against ship, till the Persian dead
strewed the deep "like flowers"

to the Hellespont to destroy the bridge by which Xerxes had crossed into Europe and by which he could return to Asia.

"Rather than break down the bridge," answered Aristides, "we should build another, if by so doing we may hasten his departure."

Now this was what Themistocles himself really wished—to hasten the king's retreat. So although he did not mean to destroy the bridge, he sent once again to Xerxes, and this is what he said: "O king, the Greeks are hastening to the Hellespont to destroy the bridge by which alone thou canst return to Asia. Hasten then to reach the bridge, while I delay the Greek fleet, lest evil overtake thee."

Once more the king fell into the trap Themistocles had prepared for him. For he set out in haste with the main body of his army for the Hellespont, leaving Mardonius with a large force to carry on the war as well as he could.

The march to the Hellespont was a terrible one, for Xerxes had himself laid waste the land when he advanced upon Athens, and now there was neither food nor shelter for his army. The soldiers who were starving ate plants, grass, the bark of trees—anything to satisfy their hunger.

In their weakness they were attacked by plague, and hundreds perished long before the Hellespont was in sight. Even when at length the gleam of water gladdened the hearts of the soldiers, they were soon stricken again with fear, for where was the bridge?

THE BATTLE OF SALAMIS

The Greeks had not outstripped them, so this was not their doing. A storm had destroyed the bridge. Weak and hungry as they were, the soldiers had to rebuild it before they could cross over to Asia, where food and shelter awaited them.

When the Greeks saw that the Persians were marching to the Hellespont, they were eager to follow them. But Themistocles persuaded them to go back to Athens to rebuild the city.

Then he sent yet another message to Xerxes, saying, "Themistocles, the leader of the Athenians and the best and wisest of the Greeks, has out of goodwill to thee held back the allies from chasing thy ships and breaking up the bridge at the Hellespont. So go thy way in peace."

Although Themistocles sent these proud words to the great king, he really believed it was wiser for the Greeks not to pursue the retreating army. But he also wished to make Xerxes his friend, so that if at any time he was ostracized by the Athenians, he would find a welcome at the Persian court.

Greece was full of rejoicing when she heard of the victory of Salamis. The generals of the different states met at Corinth to propose a reward for the bravest and wisest among themselves.

Each general wrote on a tablet the names of two whom he believed to be worthy of a prize. They were not very modest, these brave soldiers of Greece, for each general wrote his own name first, though nearly all added beneath, the name of Themistocles.

The Spartans gave their meed of honour to the great Athenian, for a crown of olive was placed upon his head and he was presented with the most magnificent chariot that Sparta had ever produced.

Æschylus, one of the great Greek poets, wrote a tragedy on the fall of Xerxes, called *The Persians*, which was acted in 472 B.C., eight years after the battle of Salamis. Sculptors too wrought statues to commemorate the war, which were placed in the temple of Athene.

CHAPTER LII

THE BATTLE OF PLATAEA

MARDONIUS stayed with his troops in Thessaly during the winter months. But in the spring of 479 B.C. he determined to win Athens from the league which she had formed with the other Greek states, or if he failed to do this, to drive the citizens once again away from their city and occupy it himself.

So he sent an ambassador to the Athenians to offer, in the name of Xerxes, not only to repair all the harm that the Persians had done to Athens and to the country round about the city, but to give them new lands and to treat them as independent allies, if they would make a treaty with the great king.

The Spartans were afraid that the Athenians would accept so generous an offer, and they knew that alone they could not hope to conquer the large Persian army which Mardonius commanded. So they sent to the Athenians to beg them to be true to the league, promising that if they were so, Spartan soldiers would be sent to help them against the attacks of the enemy.

But the Athenians did not need to be entreated to refuse the offer of the great king, for they loved their city and their liberty.

"Tell Mardonius," they said to the ambassador whom the Persian general had sent, "so long as the sun moves in his present course we will never come to terms with Xerxes."

After receiving this defiant message, Mardonius marched with his army against Athens. The Spartans, in spite of their promises, sent no troops to defend the city, and the Athenians were forced once again to take refuge at Salamis.

Then they reproached the Spartans, and in bitter anger they declared that if an army was not sent at once to Attica to attack Mardonius, they would be forced to make an alliance with the enemy.

Again the Spartans grew alarmed for their own safety. Without further delay they sent a force of five thousand citizens, each attended by seven helots. Other troops soon followed, and all were under the command of Pausanias, who was a relation of Leonidas, the hero of Thermopylae.

The Persians had reached the province of Boeotia and were encamped on the plain of Plataea, while the Athenians and the Spartans set up their camp on a hill above the enemy.

Masistius, the favourite and most famous officer of the Persians, led his cavalry against the cavalry of the enemy and soon a fierce conflict was raging. Only after their leader fell wounded from his horse and was slain, were the Persians repulsed. The armour of Masistius could not be pierced by any weapon, but a spear which was thrust into his eye caused his death. In vain the soldiers tried to recover the body of their general, again and again they were driven back.

"Then there was a great mourning throughout the army of the Persians, for all lamented for Masistius, shaving themselves and their horses, and their beasts of burden. And there was a great cry through all the host, and the sound of it went through all Boeotia, as for the death of one who next to Mardonius was of most note among the Persians and with the king."

As for the Greeks, after having driven the Persian cavalry from the field, they "became much more bold and cheerful, and putting the dead body of Masistius on a car, they drew it along their ranks; and so wonderful was it for its stature and its beauty, that the men left their places and came forward to look upon Masistius."

Pausanias now determined to lead his troops down to the plain. Here he encamped, opposite the Persians, with only the little river Asopus between the two armies.

The oracles had foretold that the side which began the attack would be conquered; so day after day passed, neither army daring to move.

But although the Persians dared not attack the Greeks, they did them all the harm that they could, for they filled up the springs to which the enemy went for water, and cut off several convoys with provisions.

Pausanias was in despair when the water supply was stopped, and he determined to withdraw and take up a position nearer to Plataea, where both food and water would be secure.

Discipline had grown slack in the Greek camp, and the retreat, which began at night, was carried out in a disorderly manner.

One company set off in haste, but did not halt where Pausanias had arranged that it should. The Spartans refused to move at all. One of their captains, "lifting a piece of rock with both hands and flinging it at the feet of Pausanias, cried, 'Thus do I cast my vote against the counsel of flying from strangers.'" Only when the retreat was nearly ended did the Spartans tardily obey the order to withdraw. This was how it happened that, when morning dawned, the Persians found that the enemy had disappeared, all but the Spartans, whose captain had delayed to follow the orders of Pausanias.

When Mardonius caught sight of the loiterers he ordered his men to set out in pursuit of them, and before the Spartans could get into position the Persians were upon them. But Pausanias soon learned what was taking place in his rear, and he hastened back with the troops that were with him to aid the disobedient Spartans.

The Persians had thrust their shields into the ground to form a rough barrier between them and the Spartans, while they sent shower after shower of

THE BATTLE OF PLATAEA

arrows upon the loiterers. The Spartans soon tore down the breastwork of shields, and with their swords in their hands advanced upon the enemy.

Mardonius did all he could to encourage his men, but they had no armour to protect them from the blows of the Spartans, and they were forced back toward the river, throwing into confusion those of their own army who were still advancing.

In the thick of the battle Mardonius rode on a white horse, surrounded by ten thousand chosen Persians. He was easily known by his white charger, and many were the spears that were aimed at him by the angry Spartans. At length one smote him so that he fell dead to the ground. "Thus," says Herodotus, "Mardonius paid the recompence for the murder of Leonidas."

No sooner was their leader slain than the Persians fled in utter confusion, all but forty thousand who were led off the field by one of the generals, and these marching north reached the Hellespont and crossed over to Asia in safety.

Those who fled from the field took refuge in their camp, where the Spartans attacked them. But the barricades were strong, and the camp was not taken until the Athenians had returned and joined in the assault.

As the Greeks swarmed into the camp they slaughtered the enemy without mercy. So severe was the defeat of Plataea that the Persians were utterly crushed.

The spoil in the camp was enormous. Gold and silver dishes were there in abundance, rich carpets too, and weapons inlaid with precious stones. Horses, camels, mules were captured in great numbers.

It is told that the great king had left his own magnificent war camp for Mardonius to use.

When Pausanias saw it "all blazing with gold and silver and embroidered hangings, he commanded the cooks and bakers to make ready for him a banquet, as they had been used to do for Mardonius.

When all was ready, he saw couches and tables of gold and silver, all fairly spread and a banquet splendidly set forth; and then, marvelling at this magnificence and glory, he charged his own servants, by way of mockery, to prepare a Spartan feast.

So the meal was made ready, but it looked not much like the other, and Pausanias laughed, and sending for the generals of the Greeks, pointed to the two banquets, saying, "Men of Hellas, I have brought you together that ye may see the madness of the Medes, who faring thus sumptuously came to rob us of our sorry food."

While the battle of Plataea was being fought, the Greek fleet was lying at Delos, an island in the Ægean Sea. The Persian fleet was near Samos, which is not far from the coast of Africa, while close at hand, at Cape Mycale, the Persian land forces were encamped.

THE BATTLE OF PLATAEA

The Samians were afraid when they saw the Persian army, and begged the Greeks to come to their aid. This they readily agreed to do, and sailing to Cape Mycale they landed and attacked and burned the Persian camp. The victory would have been harder to win had not the Ionian Greeks who were with the Persians deserted and fought with those of their own race.

Both the victory of Plataea and that of Mycale were said to have been gained on the same day in August 479 B.C.

Bands of Persians had still to be driven from some of the islands of the Ægean and from some of the Greek cities in Asia. But the victory of Mycale freed the Ionians from the rule of the great king, ended the Persian war, and laid the foundations of the Athenian Empire.

CHAPTER LIII

THE DELIAN LEAGUE

For at least forty years Sparta was the chief city in Greece, and she was the head of the league which bound the cities of Peloponnesus together. It was her brave king Leonidas who had fallen gloriously at Thermopylae, it was her admirals who had been the chief commanders at Salamis and at Mycale. The decisive victory of Plataea had been won by the Spartan Pausanias.

But after the Persian war was ended, the power of Sparta grew less and less, while that of Athens increased by leaps and bounds, until it was she who held the first place among the cities of Greece.

One reason for this was that Athens, owing to the foresight of Themistocles, owned a well-equipped navy and could therefore rule the islands of the Ægean which had been wrested from the Persians.

THE DELIAN LEAGUE

Sparta had no navy, nor had she any great statesman to tell her that she must become a great sea-power if she wished still to hold the chief place among the cities of Greece. Sparta was content to drill her soldiers as she had been taught to do by Lycurgus, and she looked with contempt or with suspicion on what was new or unusual. It was only after Athens had far surpassed her in glory and in empire that her ambition was at length aroused, and she determined to win fame for herself by destroying her rival. Of Sparta's efforts to conquer Greece you will read when I tell you about the Peloponnesian wars.

After the battle of Plataea, Sparta soon lost the command of the allied fleet, through the folly and treachery of Pausanias.

The admiral was sent to drive the Persians from some of the Greek cities in the east. His success at Plataea had made him haughty and proud, and he treated his officers with contempt. He flogged his men for small offences or made them stand with an anchor on their shoulders. If food or water were scarce, he forbade them to help themselves until his own Spartan troops had been fed.

Aristides and another admiral named Cimon, who treated their officers with courtesy and their men with kindness, went to Pausanias to beg him to behave more justly. But the Spartan would not listen to the remonstrances of the Athenians. "I have no time to hear complaints," was his sorry excuse.

When Pausanias succeeded in taking Byzantium, which we now know as Constantinople, his pride and ambition increased, and he determined to play into the hands of the Persian king.

So he sent for some of the prisoners, and, setting them free, he bade them carry letters to Xerxes their king. In these letters he offered, as only a traitor could do, to subdue Sparta and the other states of Greece, and to hold them for the Persian monarch. He asked Xerxes to grant him money to carry on the war, and as a reward for his services he requested the hand of his daughter. Pausanias hoped in this way to gain his great ambition and become tyrant of all Greece.

Xerxes was pleased with the Spartan's letter, nor did he stay to wonder if so disloyal a citizen would be a faithful ally. He sent a letter to bid the traitor "work on night and day to accomplish his purpose, without letting himself be held back by lack of gold or silver, or want of troops, for all should be at his command."

When Pausanias held the king's letter in his hand, and saw the king's money at his disposal, he began to behave as though he was already the son-in-law of the great king. He clad himself as a Persian prince, he journeyed from place to place in royal state, attended by Persian guards. The Spartan simplicity in which he had been trained was forgotten, and he lived in as great luxury as did his new friends.

Rumours of the strange way in which Pausanias was behaving soon reached Sparta. When

THE DELIAN LEAGUE

it was found that the rumours were true, Pausanias was ordered to come home, and another commander, named Dorcis, was sent to take his place.

But before Dorcis reached Byzantium, the fleet had refused to obey Pausanias and had placed itself under Aristides, the admiral of the Athenian ships.

A league, called the Delian League, was then formed, to enable Greece to carry on the war against Persia. It was named the Delian League because its treasures were kept in the temple of Apollo, on the sacred island of Delos.

Athens became the head of the league, Aristides its leader, and so greatly was he trusted that he was asked to arrange the sum of money or the number of ships which each city belonging to the league should provide.

Most of the Greek cities in the Ægean islands joined the Delian League, as well as those on the north and east coasts of the Ægean Sea. Those who joined took solemn oaths to be true to the demands of the league, and their oaths were ratified by sinking masses of iron in the sea. Not until these reappeared might the people be set free from the vows which they had taken.

Pausanias had now returned to Sparta, where he was thrown into prison. But though there was abundant proof of his foolish conduct there was none of his treachery, and he was soon set free.

The traitor continued to send letters to Xerxes by his slaves, and those who carried them never returned, for Pausanias feared lest they should betray him.

One of his slaves noticed that those who carried letters to the great king never came back. He made up his mind that when his turn came to go to Xerxes, he would find out what was in the letter he carried before he delivered it.

So when one day he was bidden to hasten with a letter to the Persian king, he no sooner left the presence of his master than he broke the seal, opened the letter, and found among other things an order for his death. This was what he expected, and he at once carried the letter to the ephors. It contained proof of the traitor's guilt.

But, so it is told, the ephors wished to hear that Pausanias was guilty from his own lips, so they laid a trap for him.

The slave was sent to take refuge in a hut that stood in a sacred grove. Pausanias soon heard of the strange conduct of his slave, and, as the ephors had foreseen, he at once hastened to the hut to demand why his servant had not sped on his master's errand.

Two of the ephors were hidden behind the hut and could hear all that Pausanias said to his slave.

In his anger the admiral forgot to be prudent, and exclaimed that he meant to subdue Greece and deliver her into the hands of Xerxes. The ephors had heard what they wished. They hastened home and at once ordered that the traitor should be seized.

But either Pausanias was warned or he was filled with sudden foreboding, for he fled to the temple of Athene for sanctuary. It was forbidden to drag a fugitive out of the temple, so the ephors ordered that the door should be built up, that he might starve to death.

His mother, in bitter anger because her son had wished to betray his country, herself placed the first stone at the door of the temple.

When hunger had all but done its work, Pausanias was carried out of the sacred place to breathe his last, lest the temple should be polluted by the death of a traitor.

CHAPTER LIV

THEMISTOCLES DECEIVES THE SPARTANS

AFTER the battle of Plataea, the Athenians brought their wives and children back to the city, which the Persians had again left in ruins. Not only were the temples and the houses burned, but of the city wall scarce a trace was to be found.

Themistocles encouraged the citizens to rebuild the city, and this they did with good will. More beautiful temples, better houses, soon sprang up under the eager hands of the citizens.

The wall they determined to make so strong and so high that they would be able to defend their city against any attack rather than be compelled again to forsake her.

But Sparta was alarmed at her neighbour's industry; she was more than alarmed, she was suspicious and angry. Athens was making herself too strong, the Spartans murmured in ungenerous mood.

THEMISTOCLES DECEIVES THE SPARTANS

The wall had risen but a little way from the ground when the Spartans sent to ask the Athenians not to go on with their work. The reason they gave was a selfish one, for they said, "If the Persians return and take a strongly walled town so near to Peloponnesus, our cities will not be safe." They then promised to offer shelter to the Athenians, should they again be forced to leave their city, but only on condition that they would stop building a wall around Athens. They even asked the Athenians to help them to destroy the walls that already surrounded the other cities of Greece.

The Athenians were in a dilemma. They were determined to finish the wall, yet they dared not anger the Spartans, lest they attacked their city while the wall was still unfinished.

In their perplexity they turned to Themistocles, who had before now saved them by craft when open defiance threatened to ruin them.

Themistocles was not long in solving the difficulty. He said that he would go as an ambassador to Sparta to talk over the matter. Other ambassadors were to follow him only when the walls were nearly complete, and meanwhile men, women and children, all must work day and night, so that the wall might grow apace.

When Themistocles reached Sparta, he at once said to the council that he could do nothing until his fellow ambassadors arrived, and he pretended that he expected them every day.

He refused to attend the council alone, and when the Spartans grumbled, he assured them that the Athenians were not going on with the wall. When they grew impatient he amused them so well by his clever speeches that they forgot for a little while to be angry with him.

But when day after day passed and still the other ambassadors did not come, the Spartans did not hide their suspicion that they were being deceived. When a rumour reached them that the Athenians had never ceased to build the wall, which was now nearly complete, they were angry indeed, and going to Themistocles they demanded that he should tell them the truth.

He still denied that the citizens had been building the wall in his absence, but if they doubted his word, he bade them send ambassadors to Athens, that they might see for themselves whether he was deceiving them or not.

So the Spartans sent ambassadors to Athens, and then Themistocles bade his colleagues join him, for he knew that now both he and they would be safe. The Spartan ambassadors would be hostages for their lives.

The first thing the Spartans saw as they approached Athens was a high, strong wall. Then they knew that they had been deceived, and they sent a messenger to tell their countrymen that Themistocles had played them false.

Themistocles was no coward. He went into the council and boldly told the Spartans that it was true he had deceived them, so that the walls of Athens might be built before they could interfere.

Indignant as the Spartans were and ashamed of their own folly in being deceived by the crafty Athenian, they dared not harm the ambassadors lest their own messengers should not return in safety.

So they sent them away, and Themistocles and his fellows returned in triumph to Athens.

Soon after this the city wall was finished, and Themistocles then urged the people to build another great wall round the Piraeus. When this was done, Athens had the largest and safest harbour in Greece.

The other states now appointed her to be the head of the allied fleet, and no one was more proud of this than Themistocles. For it was he who had first persuaded the Athenians to make themselves into a great sea-power.

CHAPTER LV

THEMISTOCLES IS OSTRACISED

FOR many years Themistocles had been a favourite with the Athenians. But soon after the walls of the city were complete he began to grow less popular.

Perhaps this was his own fault, for he tired the people by boasting continually of the good he had done to the city. It was known too that he did not hesitate to take bribes, and the citizens were indignant that he should have grown rich in this dishonourable way.

One day, as he was talking in public with Aristides, he said, "The chief excellence of a statesman is to be able to prove and frustrate the designs of public enemies." Aristides answered, "Another very excellent and necessary quality in a statesman is to have clean hands." And those who listened applauded Aristides the Just, for they knew well that he had never soiled his hands with the gold of his country's foes.

THEMISTOCLES IS OSTRACISED

In 471 B.C., the people determined to ostracise Themistocles, so weary had they grown of the claims he made upon their gratitude. At the time of Pausanias' death he was living at Argos, which city lies south of Corinth. When the papers of the traitor were read it was found that Themistocles had written to him. There was nothing in his letters to show that he had meant to help Pausanias to betray his country, yet he was accused of treason.

When he heard of the charge that was brought against him, he wrote to the council at Athens, "I, Themistocles, who was born to command and not to serve others, could not sell myself, and Greece with me, into servitude to the enemy."

These proud words only angered the Athenians the more, and the council sent men to arrest him. But Themistocles did not wait to be captured. He fled from Greece to Epirus, where he hoped that King Admetus, whom he had once befriended, would shelter him from his foes.

Admetus was not at home when the exile reached the palace, so he threw himself upon the mercy of the queen.

She bade him take her little son in his arms and go sit by the hearth until her lord returned.

Then, when the king arrived, Themistocles arose, and begged Admetus to protect him, while the little prince stretched out suppliant arms to his royal father.

This was the most sacred way to proffer a request, and according to the custom of his country the king was pleased to do as Themistocles asked. He refused to give him up to the Athenians, and sent him in safety to the Persian court, where Artaxerxes now reigned.

Themistocles begged one of the officers to take him to Artaxerxes, saying that he was a Greek who had come to see the king on important matters.

"If you will promise to prostrate yourself before the monarch, as is the custom in my country, I will do as you wish," answered the Persian.

Some Greeks would have refused to prostrate themselves before any king, but it was easy for Themistocles to conform to the customs of the country in which he found himself.

"I that come hither," he said, "to increase the power and glory of the king, will not only submit myself to his laws but will also cause many more to be worshippers and adorers of the king."

"Who shall we tell him you are?" asked the officer, "for your words signify you to be no ordinary person."

"No man," replied Themistocles, "must be informed of this before the king himself."

So at length the Athenian was brought into the presence of Artaxerxes, and after having prostrated himself he stood silent before the king.

"Who art thou?" asked Artaxerxes.

THEMISTOCLES IS OSTRACISED

He stood silent before the king

"O king," answered the exile, "I am Themistocles the Athenian, driven into banishment by the Greeks. I come with a mind suited to my present calamities; prepared alike for favours and for anger. If you save me you will save your suppliant; if otherwise, you will destroy an enemy of the Greeks."

Artaxerxes liked the courage the exile showed, but he gave him no answer that day. At night, in his sleep, he was heard to cry aloud for joy three times, "I have Themistocles the Athenian."

In the morning he commanded his courtiers and captains to assemble in the hall, while the stranger was brought before him.

As the Athenian passed close to the captains, one of them whispered to him. "You subtle Greek serpent, the king's good genius hath brought thee hither."

Themistocles thought these were ominous words, but to his surprise the king greeted him kindly.

A reward had been offered to whoever should bring the famous Athenian to the court of the great king. This reward Artaxerxes now declared should be given to Themistocles himself.

The Greek besought the king to grant him a year in which to learn the Persian language. He promised that when he could speak without an interpreter he would tell Artaxerxes the best way to subdue Greece.

Artaxerxes not only granted his request, but showed him great kindness. For he gave to him three cities, and ordered the inhabitants to supply him with bread, meat, wine and whatever else he might need for himself and his family.

In Magnesia, one of these cities, the Athenian lived content for many years. But at length Artaxerxes assembled an army to invade Greece, and he sent for the Greek to come to lead it into his own country.

But whatever promises he had made to ensure his own safety, Themistocles had never really meant to harm the land he loved so well.

So when the message of Artaxerxes reached him, the Athenian invited his friends to a feast, and after bidding them farewell he offered sacrifices to the gods. He then took poison and soon after died.

Artaxerxes respected the Athenian, because he had died rather than betray his country, and he ordered his family to be treated with kindness.

Themistocles was buried without the walls of Magnesia, and the Magnesians erected a statue to him in their market place, because he had been the "Saviour of Greece."

In 464 B.C., three years after the death of Themistocles, Aristides died. The Athenians, both rich and poor, mourned for his loss, because his rare justice, his true patriotism, had made him to be loved and honoured by all who knew him.

CHAPTER LVI

THE ELOQUENCE OF PERICLES

AFTER the death of Aristides, Cimon became commander-in-chief of the allied fleet.

Cimon was beloved by the Athenians, for he showed them great kindness. Every day he invited some of the poorer citizens to supper. When he walked through the city he ordered several well-dressed slaves to follow him. Then, if he met a citizen clad in shabby or threadbare garments, he would order one of his slaves to exchange clothes with him.

The allied fleet gained many victories while Cimon was at its head.

In 470 B.C., he sailed to an island named Scyrus, in which dwelt a race of pirates, who had for many years fallen upon and captured the merchant vessels of Greece. The island of Scyrus lay between Athens and Thrace.

The Greek traders were pleased when Cimon banished the pirates, as he was soon able to do. A number of Athenians were sent to settle in Scyrus, which from that time belonged to Attica.

Now there was a legend which said that in this island there was a grave where lay the bones of Theseus, one of the old heroes of Hellas.

It may be that Cimon ordered his men to search for the spot where the hero was said to be buried; in any case a grave was found in which lay the body of a giant warrior. No one doubted that this was the body of Theseus, and, as the oracle had commanded, the bones were brought to Athens and placed in a temple which was henceforth called Theseum. The Athenians were loud in the praise of Cimon because he had obeyed the commands of the oracle, and had brought the bones of the hero to Attica.

Four years later Cimon gained two great victories over the Persians, by which those Greek cities which had been left under the yoke of the great king were set free. They then hastened to join the Delian League.

Cimon was now at the height of his power, but his friendship with Sparta, on which the Athenians had always looked with dislike, soon led to his downfall.

In 464 B.C. there was an earthquake in Peloponnesus. Chasms yawned in the valleys, landslips changed the face of the mountains. The loss of life in Sparta itself was terrible, while both houses and temples were destroyed. The Helots, who were always ready to revolt, did so now that their masters were overwhelmed by this great calamity.

Cimon begged the Athenians to forget their old grudge against the Spartans and to send to her help, remembering only how they had shared in the glory of the Persian war.

"Do not let Greece be lamed of one foot," he urged, "and Athens herself be left to draw without her yoke-fellow."

An Athenian, named Pericles, who was now one of the chief citizens, did all he could to make the people refuse to send help to Sparta, but Cimon's entreaties were successful. He was himself sent at the head of the Athenian troops to help the Spartans to subdue the Helots.

The rebels had taken refuge in a fortress, and Cimon tried in vain to expel them from their stronghold.

Always ready to suspect an Athenian, the Spartans began to think that Cimon did not really wish to dislodge the Helots. They accused him of treachery, and roughly bade him return with his troops to Athens, as they no longer wished for his help.

During Cimon's absence, Pericles and a statesman named Ephialtes had made several changes in the ancient courts of Athens. These changes did not meet with the approval of Cimon, and he tried to restore the old customs.

THE ELOQUENCE OF PERICLES

The citizens soon grew angry with the two leaders because each tried to govern Athens in a different way, and, instead of peace, discord ruled in the city. They determined that one of them should be ostracised.

In 461 B.C. it was resolved to put the matter to the vote. The citizens assembled in the market place, and shells were given to them on which to write the name of the leader they wished to be banished. When the names were counted it was found that Cimon was ostracised.

Soon after Cimon left Athens, Ephialtes was slain in his own house, and it was believed that this cruel deed had been done by the order of some of Cimon's friends, in revenge for the ostracism of their chief.

Pericles was now left alone to govern Athens.

He was not rich, so he could not himself do all that Cimon had done for the people, but he used the public money for the good of the citizens. And he pleased them by taking from the court of the Areopagus most of its ancient power, and giving it to the popular assembly.

Tickets, too, were given by his orders to the poorer folk in Athens, so that they might be able to go to the theatres and other places of public amusement. By these and other acts, Pericles soon won the goodwill of the people.

When he was a boy Pericles had been trained by a philosopher named Anaxagoras, who had taught him much wisdom. When storms arose they seemed unable to disturb the calm of the philosopher's pupil.

One day, as he was busy in the market place with affairs of State, a rude fellow never ceased to mock and to speak ill of him.

Pericles heard all that the man said, but he took no notice, and when he had finished his task he set out for home. The rough fellow followed, throwing at him, not stones, but cruel, wicked words.

It was dark when Pericles reached his house. Turning to one of his servants he bade him take a light and see that the man reached home in safety. And this he did although he had been treated so badly.

Because he was a great orator, Pericles was named the Olympian, but by some it was said that he was so called because of the beautiful buildings with which he adorned Athens.

At this time comedies were acted on the stage, and in these comedies great statesmen were often ridiculed; that is, fun was made both of themselves and of their actions.

Those who wrote these plays were allowed to use their wit on any one or anything that they chose. It was soon seen that the Athenians could laugh heartily at themselves, and that is a good thing that some people can never learn to do.

Pericles was too well known to be left alone by the writers of comedy. Sometimes hard words

THE ELOQUENCE OF PERICLES

were spoken of him, as when a writer said that he had a "dreadful thunderbolt in his tongue." But he who said this knew that the eloquence of Pericles was a great power, and that the orator could make people believe almost anything that he wished them to believe.

It is said that one of the kings of Sparta once asked a noble citizen, named Thucydides, if he or Pericles were the stronger wrestler.

"When I," answered Thucydides, "have thrown him and given him a fair fall, by persisting that he had no fall he gets the better of me, and makes the bystanders, in spite of their own eyes, believe him." Thucydides said this in jest, to show what wonders Pericles could work by his eloquence.

But although others might make fun of Pericles' great gift of speech, he himself thought of it with reverence. "He was very careful what and how he was to speak, insomuch that, whenever he went up to the hustings, he prayed the gods that no one word might unawares slip from him, unsuitable to the matter and the occasion."

Pericles encouraged the Athenians to war against many of the Greek States, and when they had subdued them, he bade these States pay tribute to Athens. Year by year, under his guidance, the city grew more powerful.

In 449 B.C., Cimon, who had been recalled from exile, sailed with a fleet of two hundred ships to Cyprus, where several cities still owned Artaxerxes, the Persian king, as their master. He laid siege to the town of Citium, but before it was taken he fell ill. Although he was forced to stay in bed, he still sent orders to his men, which helped them to gain two brilliant victories.

Cimon did not recover from his illness, and after the death of its commander the fleet returned to Athens.

CHAPTER LVII
PERICLES AND ELPINICE

ATHENS was at first the leader of the Delian League; she soon became its ruler.

Many of the allied cities offered to send, as their contribution to the league, money instead of ships. To this Athens agreed gladly, and with the money she added ship after ship to her own fleet. So the navy of Athens continued to grow while that of the other states dwindled until they possessed only a few vessels.

The treasury of the league, which had been kept in the small but sacred island of Delos, was moved to Athens with the consent of the allies.

But after a time the other cities grew discontented. They complained that the money they sent to the league was not spent on ships alone. Some of it, at least, was used to build beautiful temples for the city of Athens.

So dissatisfied were they that they declared that they would leave the league. But they soon found that it would be difficult to carry out their threat, for Athens was too anxious to receive their contributions of money to let them go.

When the people who lived on the island of Samos revolted, Pericles went with an army to besiege their capital town, and after nine months the Samians were forced to surrender. The walls of the city were pulled down, the ships belonging to the island were seized, and the inhabitants were forced to pay a heavy fine.

On his return to Athens, Pericles was welcomed by his own party, but Elpinice, the sister of Cimon, was indignant that the citizens should rejoice at a victory gained over their own countrymen.

One day, soon after his triumphant return, Elpinice waylaid Pericles as he was walking along the streets, and said to him, "These are brave deeds, Pericles, that you have done, and such as deserve our chaplets, who have lost us many a worthy citizen, not in a war with Phoenicians or Medes, like my brother Cimon, but for the overthrow of an allied and kindred city."

Elpinice hoped to make Pericles ashamed that he had fought with people of his own race.

And now for two years, from 447 B.C. to 445 B.C., loss after loss befell Athens. While she was struggling with her other enemies, the king of Sparta marched into Attica with an army. Athens herself was in danger.

But before the army reached the city, it was ordered to halt, and soon after it withdrew from Attica.

No one knew what had made the Spartans spare Athens, but it was said that Pericles had paid their king a large sum of money on condition that he took his army back to his own country.

In 445 B.C. Athens signed a Thirty Years' Truce with Sparta, and at the same time peace was made with Persia.

Pericles was now able to devote himself to the work which was his greatest pleasure. He spent fourteen years in making Athens so beautiful that it became the wonder city of the world.

CHAPTER LVIII

THE CITY OF ATHENS

WHEN the Persians entered Athens they destroyed her temples. Some of these temples had been hastily repaired, others had been hastily built, when the Athenians returned to their own city.

But now that peace had been made with the Persians, Athens determined to show her gratitude to the gods by building in the city, temples, "exceeding magnifical," more beautiful indeed than any that had yet been built.

The most famous of these temples was the Parthenon or Temple of the Virgin, built on the Acropolis, and sacred to the virgin goddess Athene.

This marvellous temple was planned by a great architect named Ictinus, and adorned by a yet greater sculptor called Pheidias.

The architecture of the Parthenon was Doric, which was the oldest, the strongest as well as the most simple, of the four kinds of Grecian buildings.

THE CITY OF ATHENS

There were two rooms in the Parthenon with no entrance from one to the other.

The figure of the goddess, fashioned by the magic hands of the sculptor Pheidias, was a colossal one. Calm, majestic, with a smile upon her face, she stood in her wondrous temple, clad in a robe of gold.

On her head she wore a helmet, in her right hand she held fast a little golden figure of the goddess of victory, while her left lay upon her shield. At her feet a snake lay coiled.

Neither of marble nor of bronze was the statue, but of ivory and pure gold, ivory being used for the flesh, gold for the robe and armour, which was studded with precious stones.

Nowhere was there so marvellous a statue as this of the goddess Athene wrought by Pheidias, save perchance the Zeus at Olympia, which was also moulded by the famous sculptor.

The statue of Zeus had a strange power over those who gazed upon it.

"Let a man sick and weary in his soul, who has passed through many distresses and sorrows, whose pillow is unvisited by kindly sleep, stand in front of this image; he will, I deem, forget all the terrors and troubles of human life."

Close to the Parthenon was an older temple, built not in the Doric but in the Ionic style of architecture. It, too, was sacred to Athene and also to Poseidon.

The figure of the goddess was a colossal one

THE CITY OF ATHENS

This temple, which was called the Erechtheum, was held in awe and reverence by the Athenians, for in it was kept an ancient wooden image of the goddess. So ancient was this "most holy idol" of the people that it looked more like a rough block of wood than a carved figure. The holy olive tree, too, was there, which the Persians had cut down, but which they had been unable to kill, as well as the living snake, the symbol of the presence of the goddess.

The Erechtheum was to the Athenians a shrine, in which lay hidden the story of their past, the Parthenon was to them a sign of the power and the splendour of the age of Pericles.

On the western side of the Acropolis rose a magnificent marble wall called the Propylaea. The marble had been pierced at intervals to make five great gateways, the centre one being for chariots, those on either side leading by steps to the Parthenon. Through these gateways the Athenians marched in solemn procession on their feast days.

A great theatre, sacred to the god Dionysus, was finished in the age of Pericles, and an Odeon or great hall of music was added to it, where contests of song and music were held. The roof of the Odeon was pointed like a tent, and was made of the masts of ships that had been captured from the Persians.

This pointed roof was said by the wits of Athens to be like the helmet of Pericles, whose head was curiously formed, and who often wore a helmet to conceal its strange shape.

"Here comes Pericles," says a comic poet of those days, "with the Odeon set on his crown."

Another great statue of Athene, called Athene Promachos, or Athena Foremost in Battle, stood just within the Propylaea. It was wrought in bronze and showed Athene in armour, holding shield and spear outstretched. This statue, also by Pheidias, was fifty feet high and stood on a pedestal that raised it twenty feet higher, so that it towered above the roofs of the temples. The golden plume on the helmet of the goddess was seen by sailors far out at sea.

With these and many other great works of art, Pericles adorned the city of his love. The Acropolis he said should be no longer a fortress, but a sanctuary.

Some of the Athenians, among them Thucydides, grumbled because Pericles spent the public money on these beautiful buildings.

Pericles heard that the citizens were discontented, and in the open assembly he rose and bade them tell him if they thought he used more money that he ought, to adorn the city.

"Too much a great deal," was the speedy retort.

"Then," said Pericles, "since it is so, let the cost not go to your account but to mine, and let the inscriptions upon the buildings stand in my name."

But the people, surprised at his generosity, and perhaps wishing to share in the glory of his work, were ashamed that they had complained. They bade him spend as much of the public money as he deemed right and "spare no cost until all was finished."

In 479 B.C. the Persians had reduced Athens to ruins. Fifty years later she had been built anew and adorned with temples and statues that made her the wonder of the world.

Marble was found in Attica, gold and ivory were bought with money out of the treasury, but without the magic hand of Pheidias, marble, gold, and ivory had been bought in vain.

CHAPTER LIX

GREAT MEN OF ATHENS

ATHENS, in the age of Pericles, was the home of literary men as well as of sculptors and architects.

Æschylus, one of the greatest men of the age, was a diligent writer of tragedies or serious plays. You will think that he was diligent indeed, when I tell you that he wrote ninety plays, although only seven are known to us now. His tragedies were acted in the great theatre of Dionysus. The *Persae*, his first play, was written eight years after the great sea-fight at Salamis, to tell of the victory the Athenians had won over the Persians.

Just as races were run, and music was written by competitors to win renown and gain prizes at the festival of Dionysus, so plays were written and prizes were awarded to the successful author at this great feast. These plays might be about the things that were taking place in Greece at that very time, or the plot might be taken from the old-world stories of Troy. Proud and dauntless were the men and women whom Æschylus made to live upon the stage of Athens. Of many of these you will some day read yourself.

Sophocles and Euripides also wrote tragedies, and Euripides is known, too, for the beauty of his songs. He was a magician who made all that he touched radiant with beauty. Many people loved Euripides because of the wonderful songs and plays which he wrote, but some hated him.

Aristophanes, the writer of comedies or amusing plays that made the Athenians laugh with uncontrollable glee, was one of those who disliked Euripides and held up some of his works to scorn. But Socrates, a greater man than he, loved Euripides and called him his favourite poet.

Herodotus was the first great Greek historian. He was not born in Attica, but he lived some years in Athens. He wrote the story of the Persian wars, while Thucydides wrote that of the Peloponnesian war.

Some of the greatest teachers in Greece at this time were called Sophists. A Sophist meant, at first, one who was clever in any special art. It did not matter what the art was; it might be cooking, gardening, teaching.

Protagoras was one of the most famous Sophists, but the Athenians did not treat him well. For he wrote a book which displeased them, so that they condemned it and accused him of writing against the gods of Greece. So angry were his enemies that Protagoras knew that he could no longer live safely in

Athens. He fled from the city and set sail for Sicily, but he was drowned before he reached the island.

It was of his dead friend Protagoras that Euripides was thinking when he wrote in one of his plays, "Ye have slain, O Greeks, ye have slain the nightingale of the muses, the wizard bird that did no wrong."

These are a few of the great men who, with Ictinus, Pheidias, and many another of whom I have not told, made the glory of Greece known throughout the wide world.

CHAPTER LX

THE THEBANS ATTACK THE PLATAEANS

THE cause of the Peloponnesian War was jealousy—jealousy between Athens and Sparta. Each wished to be the chief State in Greece, and the only way to settle the dispute in those days was by an appeal to arms.

Athens had a great navy and much wealth. She was at the head of an empire, but the States which she had subdued, and which she had forced to pay tribute, were discontented and unlikely to prove useful allies.

Sparta was the head of the Peloponnesian States. She had a strong army, but she had not money with which to carry on war, nor had she, or any of her allies save Corinth, a fleet that would be of any use against the large, well-equipped fleet of Athens.

As long as Athens could keep the mastery of the sea, she would be able to defy the enemy. Famine would soon subdue her if she lost this mastery, for much of her corn supply came from abroad, and if the corn ships did not reach the Piraeus with their precious freight, the people would starve.

On land Athens could not hope to hold her own against Sparta. Pericles knew this well, and so he urged the Athenians to place their trust in their ships.

"Let us give up lands and houses," he said, "but keep a watch over the city and the sea. We should not, under any irritation at the loss of our property, give battle to the Peloponnesians, who far outnumber us. Mourn not for houses or lands, but for men; men may give these, but these will not give men. If I thought that you would listen to me, I would say to you, "Go yourselves and destroy them, and thereby prove to the Peloponnesians that none of these things move you." Such is the power which the empire of the sea gives."

The Peloponnesian War began in the early spring of 431 B.C. when the citizens of the little town of Thebes made a treacherous attack upon the town of Plataea.

Thebes belonged to the Boeotian League, which was on good terms with Sparta, upon bad terms with Athens.

Plataea was in alliance with Athens, but there were traitors among the citizens, and these determined to betray their city into the hands of the Thebans.

THE THEBANS ATTACK THE PLATAEANS

One dark, stormy night the gates of the city were opened to admit a band of three hundred Thebans. The main body of the Theban force was still some distance off. At midnight the citizens of Plataea were awakened by the sound of trumpets. They dressed in haste, and then rushing to the market place found it in the hands of the Thebans, who were calling upon the citizens to forsake Athens and to join the Boeotian League.

At first the Plataeans thought it would be useless to resist the enemy, but before long they found that there was only a small band of Thebans in the market place. Heavy rains had made the river Asopus rise, and the main body of the enemy was still on the farther side of the river, looking in vain for a ford.

So the Plataeans shut their gates, barricaded their streets with wagons, and then boldly attacked the enemy.

The Thebans were soon separated from one another and lost their way in the unknown and dusky streets. To add to their confusion, from windows and roofs, heavy missiles were hurled down upon them by the angry Plataean women. A few scaled the city wall and escaped, but the greater number, rushing through a large door which they mistook for one of the city gates, found themselves in a granary from which there was no escape save by the door through which they had entered. It was already held by the Plataeans, and the Thebans were taken prisoners and commanded to lay down their arms.

Meanwhile the main body of the Thebans had reached the city gates to find them guarded by the inhabitants. A herald was sent to bid them withdraw, after releasing the prisoners whom they had taken on their march to the city. Unless this was done without delay, the Plataeans threatened to put to death the Thebans whom they had captured.

It was plain that their plot had failed; so, to save their comrades, as they believed, the Thebans released their prisoners, recrossed the Asopus, and went back to their own city. Then the Plataeans did a cruel and treacherous deed, for they slew two hundred of their Theban prisoners.

The Plataeans sent to Athens to ask for help when the Theban army appeared without their walls, but the danger was over before help could reach them.

Yet, lest the Thebans should return, the women and children were taken to Athens for safety, while eighty Athenians were sent to garrison the walls of Plataea.

CHAPTER LXI

ATTICA IS INVADED BY THE SPARTANS

IN the month of May 431 B.C. Attica itself was invaded by a large Spartan army, under King Archidamus.

Before he crossed the border into Attica the king bade his army halt, while he sent an ambassador named Melesippus to the Athenians, to offer them terms if they would submit to him. But Pericles persuaded the council to refuse even to listen to Melesippus, who had been told to return to his own army before the setting of the sun. As he turned away from the council, Melesippus said to the Athenians, "This day will be the beginning of many woes to the Greeks."

Pericles knew that the Spartans would march into Attica, as soon as their ambassador had returned, so he ordered the country folk to hasten within the strong walls of Athens for safety. Their cattle he bade them send to the island of Euboea.

The Spartans found the Attic farms deserted, but they destroyed and burned them, while they trampled down the cornfields and spoiled the olive groves and orchards.

As the invading army drew nearer to Athens, the people within the city walls could mark its progress by the smoke that rose from burning farms and villas. The men rushed to the gates, eager to go to attack the enemy, and it was all but beyond the power of Pericles to restrain them.

As winter drew near, Archidamus was forced to retreat, for he had neither money nor food to keep his troops longer in the country of the enemy.

Then Pericles knowing that the way was clear, sailed from Athens with thirteen thousand men, and surprised many villages on the Peloponnesian coast. He also burned the farms and houses in the district of Megara.

When Pericles returned from Megara, a public burial was given, as was the custom, to those who had been slain in battle.

A cedar box, in which were placed the bones of the fallen, was carried without the walls of the city and buried. For those whose bodies had not been recovered, there was an empty bed covered with a pall. The funeral oration, or Panegyric as it was named, was spoken by Pericles.

Here are a few of the sentences which Thucydides, the historian, heard, as he stood among the people and listened to the Panegyric.

"Our city is equally admirable in peace and in war. For we are lovers of the beautiful, yet simple in our tastes, and we cultivate the mind without loss of manliness. Wealth we employ, not for talk and ostentation, but when there is real use for it. To avow poverty is with us no disgrace; the true disgrace is in doing nothing to avoid it.

"An Athenian citizen does not neglect the State because he takes care of his own household; and even those of us who are engaged in business have a very fair idea of politics. We alone regard a man who takes no interest in public affairs, not as harmless, but as a useless character. . . .

"I would have you day by day fix your eyes upon the greatness of Athens until you become filled with the love of her; and when you are impressed with the spectacle of her glory, reflect that this empire has been acquired by men who knew their duty and had the courage to do it . . . . they freely gave their lives to her as the fairest offering which they could present at her feast. The whole earth is the sepulchre of famous men; not only are they commemorated by columns and inscriptions in their own country, but in foreign lands there dwells also an unwritten memorial of them, graven, not on stone, but in the hearts of men. Make them your example."

CHAPTER LXII

THE LAST WORDS OF PERICLES

WHEN the Spartans marched out of Attica, the country folk left the sheltering walls of Athens to go back to their fields, to dig, to plough, to sow.

They hoped in due time to reap a plenteous harvest, for their last year's crops had been destroyed by the enemy. But before the corn was ripe they knew their hopes were vain. The Spartans had come back, and once again the people were forced to leave their fields and take refuge within the walls of the capital.

But in the city itself an enemy appeared, an enemy that worked more dreadful havoc than even the Spartan army. The plague had come to Athens. It spread rapidly, for the people were crowded together, some in sheds, some in tents, and these rough shelters were not kept clean. Squalor and lack of room added to the misery of the sick folk.

THE LAST WORDS OF PERICLES

Thousands of those who had fled for safety to the city were stricken by the plague, and at first few recovered. For fear seized upon those whom the plague spared and they left the sick untended, to die, tortured by thirst, and alone.

At length even the Spartans grew afraid, lest upon them too the plague should fall, and they again withdrew from Attica.

Then Pericles sailed to Peloponnesus and attacked the enemy in its own country, but with little or no success. But in Thrace, the town of Potidaea, which had been besieged by the Athenians for a year, was forced to surrender.

No breach had been made in the walls, but the famine-stricken people could no longer bear the pangs of hunger, nor had they strength left to defend their city.

The Athenians allowed the miserable inhabitants to leave Potidaea, but the men were forbidden to take anything with them save one garment, while the women were permitted to take two. Before long Athenian families were sent to settle in Potidaea, which then became a colony belonging to Athens.

During the war the popularity of Pericles began to wane. It was he who had advised the Athenians to carry on war with the Spartans, and they now accused him of causing all the misery which they had to endure.

While he was absent with the fleet in 430 B.C., Cleon, the head of those who were opposed to Pericles, tried to make peace with the enemy, but his efforts were in vain.

Cleon was determined, if it were possible, to cause the downfall of Pericles. So when he returned to Athens, he accused him of using public money for his own ends.

When the public accounts were examined a small sum was missing and Pericles was fined by the law courts, but no stain was left on his character.

The Athenians were a fickle people, and before long they forgot their anger and Pericles found himself as popular as ever. They were even eager to carry on the war with Sparta.

Once before Pericles had been attacked by his enemies. He was accused, along with Pheidias the sculptor, of having kept some of the gold which was intended to adorn the statue of Athene in the Parthenon. But it was easy to prove that the charge was false, for the gold had been fixed to the statue in such a way that it could be easily detached.

Pericles demanded that this should be done, so that the gold might be weighed. His enemies could not refuse the test. So the gold was taken off the statue, weighed, and found to be correct.

Against Pheidias there were other charges, one being that in the frieze of the Parthenon there were sculptured portraits of himself and Pericles. In 432 B.C. the great sculptor was thrown into prison, where he died before the day fixed for his trial.

THE LAST WORDS OF PERICLES

The plague, which had disappeared for a year, broke out again in 429 B.C. with new violence.

Pericles had already lost two sons through the terrible scourge. When Paralus, his favourite child, died, he placed a garland upon his body, and shut himself in his house to mourn. Nor could he be persuaded afterward to take much interest in the affairs of the State.

A year later, he was himself stricken by the plague. He recovered, but was soon after attacked by fever which he was too weak to resist.

As he lay dying, his friends gathered around his bed. Thinking that he did not hear what they said, they began to speak to one another of the great things he had done during his life.

But Pericles heard, and interrupting them said, "What you praise in me is partly the result of good fortune, and, at all events, common to me with many other commanders. What I am most proud of, you have not noticed. No Athenian ever put on mourning for an act of mine!" These were his last words.

Plutarch tells us that "Pericles was indeed a character deserving our high admiration, not only for his equitable and mild temper, but also for the high spirit and feeling which made him regard it the noblest of all his honours, that, in the exercise of such immense power, he never had treated any enemy as irreconcilably opposed to him. And it appears to me," says Plutarch, "that this one thing gives that otherwise childish and arrogant title a fitting and becoming significance; so dispassionate a temper, a life so pure and unblemished, might well be called Olympian, in accordance with our conceptions of the divine beings to whom, as the natural authors of all good and of nothing evil, we ascribe the rule and government of the world."

CHAPTER LXIII

THE SIEGE OF PLATAEA

THE Peloponnesian War began with an attack upon the little town of Plataea. Two years later, in the early summer of 429 B.C., Plataea was again attacked, this time by the Spartans, who were led by their king Archidamus. The town, small though it was, was an Athenian fortress, so the Spartans were eager to raze it to the ground.

But Plataea stood on sacred territory; for Pausanias, after his great victory over the Persians, had declared that in time of war it should ever be left undisturbed.

The Plataeans reminded the king of the promise of the Spartan general, and begged him to withdraw his troops.

Archidamus would not lead his army away, but he promised to do the Plataeans no harm if they would become allies of Sparta, or if they would give up their alliance with Athens and fight on neither side. But the Plataeans would not agree to either of these plans.

Then the king offered to let them leave the town. He promised that their homes, their orchards, their fields would be kept in good order as long as the war lasted, and that they would be given back to them when peace was made.

It was a generous offer, and the Plataeans begged to be allowed to send to Athens to ask her advice. Her answer speedily settled the matter.

"Athens," so ran the message, "never deserted her allies, and would not now neglect the Plataeans, but succour them with all her might. Wherefore the alliance must stand and the attack of the Spartans be withstood."

When Archidamus heard what Athens had said to the Plataeans, he determined to besiege the town. The Thebans who were with the Spartan army rejoiced that war was to begin, for they were ever bitter enemies of the Plataeans.

The little town prepared to defend herself against the enemy, sending away the women and children to a place of safety. A hundred women slaves only were kept to cook and wash for the garrison, which was small. Yet few in number as they were, the doughty citizens withstood the attacks of the Spartans for two years.

When Archidamus ordered his men to raise a mound as high as the wall around the town, the Plataeans at once added to the height of their

THE SIEGE OF PLATAEA

defences. They also dug beneath the mound of the enemy, and so undermined it that it was continually sliding down.

Then lest the walls should at length be scaled by the enemy, the citizens built an inner wall to protect the city yet more strongly.

Often the little garrison looked wistfully for the help that Athens had assured them would be sent, but month after month passed and no help came from the plague-stricken city. Yet the Plataeans did not dream of surrender.

Archidamus was in despair, for he knew that his soldiers were seldom able to take a walled town. His pride was hurt at the thought of being beaten by a mere handful of men. He had with him the whole Peloponnesian army, yet a garrison of five hundred had been able to defy all his efforts to capture the city.

The king determined, since he could not take the town by assault, to starve it into submission. So he now ordered two great walls to be built round the city, placing on them here and there towers or battlements. The walls were a certain space apart, and this space was covered over, so that the soldiers could live in it as in a camp, while armed sentinels paced up and down on the roof.

When the second year of the siege began, food grew scarce in Plataea. Either the little garrison must force its way out or die of hunger. To escape, the soldiers would have to scale the wall, without attracting the attention of the sentinels, and reach the ground on the other side.

More than half the garrison resolved to stay where it was, but about two hundred determined to make the perilous attempt.

So one cold, dark night in the month of December, when the sentinels had retreated into the towers for shelter, the brave two hundred stole out of the town, carrying ladders on their backs. They wore little clothing, that they might climb and run the easier. That they might step the more quietly their right feet were bare, while on the left each wore a shoe to keep him from slipping in the mud.

Stealthily they made their way across a ditch and reached the wall unseen, unheard. Twelve of the bravest scaled the wall and killed the sleepy sentinels, who had sought shelter in the towers from a storm of wind and rain.

The others then mounted the wall, fixed their ladders on the farther side and reached the ground in safety, while the twelve, who had waited to the last, began to descend.

All would have been well, had not one man slipped and knocked a tile off the top of the wall. It rattled and fell to the ground with a noise that roused the Spartans, who scrambled up the wall in great haste. But the darkness was so dense that they could see nothing.

Those of the garrison who had stayed in the city did all that they could to perplex the enemy, by making a sally on the side of the town farthest from that by which their friends had fled. And when the Spartans lit torches and flashed danger signals to the Thebans whose city was not far off, the Plataeans lit beacons, so that the signals were confused.

Meanwhile the fugitives, having reached the ground in safety, were met by a band of three hundred Spartans. These were carrying lights, so the Plataeans were able to send a shower of arrows among them with sure and deadly aim. In the confusion that followed, all save one archer succeeded in crossing a ditch, covered with ice, but too thin to bear the weight of the fugitives. They struggled through the icy water, and after many narrow escapes two hundred and twelve weary men reached Athens in safety.

Plataea held out gallantly until the summer of 427 B.C., when famine at length forced her to surrender.

Five judges were sent from Sparta to decide the fate of the prisoners. But the trial was a mere form, for the Thebans had already persuaded the Spartans how to treat the unfortunate men.

Each prisoner as he was brought before the judges was asked if he had helped the Spartans in their war against Athens. As each one answered "No," he was led out and put to death. In this way two hundred Plataeans and twenty-five Athenians lost their lives, while the city they had so bravely defended was razed to the ground.

CHAPTER LXIV

THE SENTENCE OF DEATH

In the fourth year of the Peloponnesian War the city of Mytilene threw off the yoke of Athens. Mytilene was the capital of Lesbos, an island near the coast of Asia. The city had belonged to the Delian league, and when the league became the empire of Athens, the city remained faithful to the empire. But as time passed the Mytileneans became afraid lest Athens should treat them as she had treated the Samians, and should make them subjects instead of allies.

While Athens was at war with Sparta she would have little time, thought the Mytileneans, to trouble about their small island, so they revolted and asked the Spartans to support them, if that should be necessary. The Spartans promised to help the Mytileneans if the Athenians should punish their disloyalty, but, as so often happened, they did not attempt to keep their promise until it was too late.

Athens was angry when she heard of the revolt at Mytilene. Although she could ill spare the men, she sent an army under a general named

Paches to blockade the town by sea and by land and so to starve her into submission. At all costs Mytilene must not fall into the hands of Sparta.

Before long, so strict was the blockade, food began to run short in the hapless island, and the Spartans failed to send the help they had promised.

But when the citizens were desperate with hunger, a messenger from Sparta reached the town. He had passed the Athenian army unnoticed and had entered Mytilene, to the delight of the starving people. When he assured them that ships laden with corn were on the way and would reach them soon, their joy was unbounded.

Day after day, week after week passed, but the Spartan ships did not come, and hope began to die out of the hearts of the Mytileneans. It was plain that they must either surrender or starve to death; so they determined to surrender.

They sent for Paches, and agreed to give up the city, and to leave their fate to be decided by the Athenian assembly. In the meantime about one thousand of the inhabitants were sent as prisoners to Athens.

The Athenians had been bitterly angry with the Mytileneans for revolting when their hands were already full with war at home and with the misery caused by the plague. They were in no mood now to deal mercifully with them.

Cleon, a leather-merchant, who by his own efforts had risen to a high position in the State, roused the temper of the people by his rough and noisy eloquence, and Pericles was no longer alive to restrain it, as he had so often done, by his wiser, calmer speech.

When the assembly met, it was Cleon who proposed that all those able to bear arms should be put to death, and that the women and children should be sold as slaves. In its angry mood the assembly voted as Cleon wished.

No sooner was the sentence of death passed, than a ship was dispatched to the island to bid Paches, the Athenian general, carry out the terrible decision of the assembly.

But a little later, when the assembly broke up and escaped from the influence of Cleon's eloquence, the members began to be ashamed of their cold-blooded sentence.

Ambassadors from Mytilene had come to Athens to plead the cause of their people. When they saw that the Athenians were uneasy, they persuaded them to call another meeting of the assembly the following morning, to reconsider the sentence that they had passed.

Cleon had felt no regret at the fate of the rebels, and he was indignant that the assembly should dream of revoking its decree. When it met on the following day he spoke even more vehemently than before, urging the members to see that the sentence was carried out.

THE SENTENCE OF DEATH

But Diodotus, a noble Athenian, whose name has never been forgotten, spoke as well as Cleon. So wise were his words that those who had already wished to alter the sentence for pity's sake, were now sure that wisdom also demanded that the Mytileneans should be spared. Diodotus won the day, for Cleon was defeated by a small majority.

No sooner was the sentence revoked than in hot haste a ship was manned, and the crew was bidden to do its utmost to overtake the vessel which was carrying the sentence of doom to Mytilene. Already it was twenty-four hours since the ship had left Athens. Was it possible to carry the good news in time?

The ambassadors promised large rewards to the oarsmen if they reached the city before the terrible sentence had been carried out. In their anxiety they provided barley, wine, oil for the crew.

There was no lack of zeal on the part of the sailors. They rowed with all their strength, taking but scant rest, and eating the barley, which had been soaked in wine and oil and made into cakes, as they sat at their oars. They knew that on their speed depended the life or death of thousands.

Swifter and swifter flashed the oars of the second ship. In the first vessel the sailors pulled slowly, for they were in no haste to deliver the dread tidings which they carried. And it was well that they had no heart for their task, for with every muscle strained to the utmost the crew of the second boat reached Mytilene only just in time.

The death sentence had already reached Paches, and he was preparing to carry it out, when with a glad, triumphant shout the second boat swung into the harbour, and the Mytileneans were saved.

But even so they paid heavily for their rebellion, for about thirty of their leading citizens were executed, their fleet was taken by the Athenians, and the walls of their city were destroyed.

CHAPTER LXV

BRASIDAS LOSES HIS SHIELD

IN 425 B.C., the seventh year of the war, an Athenian fleet of about forty ships, under an admiral named Eurymedon, was forced by stormy weather to seek shelter on the promontory of Pylos in Messenia. Pylos stood on the Bay of Pylos, which you now know as the Bay of Navarino.

To give the men something to do until the storm allowed them to sail, Demosthenes, an officer on board one of the ships, bade them begin to build a fort. But it was not only to employ the men that he did this, but because he believed that Pylos would make a good fortress from which to attack the western shore of Peloponnesus.

At first the men took little interest in the work, for they expected each day to leave Pylos. But as the storm continued, they began to work with a will, and soon a fortress that looked fit to defy an enemy was finished.

It had not been easy work, for the men had no iron tools. They could not cut stones, but were forced to pick out those that fitted into each other.

When mortar was needed they had to carry it on their backs, bending forward that it might not fall, and clasping their hands behind to help to keep it in place.

At length the storm was over and the fleet sailed away, leaving Demosthenes with five ships to hold the new fortress. Now the entrance to the Bay of Pylos was almost blocked by a narrow, thickly wooded island called Sphacteria.

The Spartans soon heard that the Athenians had taken possession of Pylos, which was on their territory. They determined to expel them, and an army under Epitadas was at once sent out and took possession of the wooded island of Sphacteria, while a Spartan fleet sailed into the Bay of Pylos. On board one of the ships was a famous Spartan named Brasidas.

Demosthenes had just time to send to Eurymedon to beg him to return with his forty ships, when the Spartans sailed up to the promontory, meaning to attack and capture the fort.

But it proved impossible to land. Again and again the Spartan admiral made the attempt, but each time he was forced to withdraw, lest his ships should be dashed upon the rocks.

Brasidas refused to give in, and he bade his men wreck their vessels rather than be beaten back.

"Be not sparing of timber," he cried, "for the enemy has built a fortress in your country. Perish the ships and force a landing."

Spurred on by his words, the men drove their ship upon the beach, while Brasidas stood fearlessly on the gangway ready to leap upon the shore. But the Athenians saw the bold figure too well, and he became a target for every arrow.

As he fell back wounded, his left arm hung helpless over the side of the vessel and his shield slipped off and fell into the water. The waves washed it toward the shore, whereupon the enemy dashed down to the edge of the water and drew it in triumph up to the beach.

After a desperate struggle the Spartans were forced to withdraw, and the Athenians celebrated their victory by erecting a trophy of their spoils, placing, where every eye could see it, the shield of Brasidas.

For two days the Spartans still fought to gain the fortress but in vain. On the third day, Eurymedon returned with the Athenian fleet, and as the Spartan ships did not come to meet him he sailed in at the two entrances to the bay of Pylos: for the openings had not been secured by the enemy.

A desperate battle took place. Many of the Spartan ships were empty, as their crews were on shore. The Athenians tried to drag away these empty vessels, so that the enemy would have no way of escaping from Sphacteria.

He became a target for every arrow

But the Spartans knew that they must save their vessels at all costs, so they fought with redoubled fury and succeeded in rescuing most of the deserted ships. Yet their efforts proved of little use in the end, for though only five ships were captured, the rest of the fleet was so damaged that the Athenians were left in possession of the bay. They at once began to blockade Epitadas and his army in Sphacteria.

CHAPTER LXVI

THE SPARTANS SURRENDER

WHEN Epitadas found that he was shut up on the island of Sphacteria, he sent a messenger to Sparta to tell what had befallen him. The ephors were so disturbed by his tidings that they at once sent some of their number to the Bay of Pylos to see what could be done to set free Epitadas and his men.

They soon saw that it would be too difficult a task to relieve the island, so they begged Eurymedon to grant a truce until they sent ambassadors to Athens to sue for peace.

Their request was granted, and the Spartan ambassadors at once set sail for Athens.

When they entered the assembly, Athens, had she but known it, might have ended the war with honour. But Pericles was no longer there to tell her that to do so would be well. Cleon still ruled the assembly with his rough eloquence. Nicias, the leader of those who desired peace, although he bitterly disliked Cleon, was not strong enough to overthrow him.

The assembly, urged by its leader, offered the Spartan ambassadors terms which it knew they would not accept. After rejecting them as the Athenians expected, the ambassadors returned indignant to Pylos, and the truce was at an end. But Sphacteria was not taken so easily as the Athenians had dreamed. In spite of the strict blockade, food was taken to the island, so that the Spartans were in no danger of starving.

Sometimes swimmers carrying with them linseed, poppy seeds and honey, reached the island. Sometimes Helots, tempted by promise of freedom, would manage, when the sky was dark and the sea stormy, to sail past the enemy's ships, taking cheese, meal and even wine to the Spartans.

In Athens, the people were growing impatient of the long blockade. When Demosthenes sent messengers to the city to ask for reinforcements, they began to be sorry that they had not offered more reasonable terms to the ambassadors. They looked darkly at Cleon, and began to whisper that but for his counsel peace would certainly have been made.

A meeting of the assembly was called, and Cleon, losing his temper when Nicias urged that peace should be arranged without delay, said, "It would be easy enough to take Sphacteria if our generals were men. If I were general I would do it at once."

Nicias was a quiet man, but these scornful words roused him to anger, and he retorted that if Cleon thought he was able to take the island it would be well that he should go and do so. He was himself a general, while Cleon was only a leather-merchant, but he was willing to resign in his favour.

At first Cleon thought that Nicias was but jesting, and he pretended that he really wished to go to the help of Demosthenes. But when he found that his opponent was in earnest, he declined the honour, saying that while Nicias was a general, he himself had no training in military affairs.

But the people were not willing to let the leather-merchant escape the consequences of his rash words. They shouted that he must go and prove that he could do as he had said.

When Cleon saw that there was no escape he grew reckless, and boasted that he would not only go to Sphacteria, but that he would take the island within twenty days, and either kill all the Spartans on it or bring them prisoners to Athens.

Some there were who mocked at his words, others laughed. But all were glad that the merchant should go, for they were tired of his rough ways and rougher speech. If he went he might return with his promise unfulfilled and his power with the people would then be lost. If he came back in triumph, the Spartans would have been defeated.

Before long, Cleon set out at the head of an army for Pylos. When he arrived he found Demosthenes already prepared to attack the island.

THE SPARTANS SURRENDER

A large part of the forest on Sphacteria had just been burned down by some Athenian soldiers. They had been sent to the island to reconnoitre, and while making a fire to cook their dinner the trees were accidentally set alight.

The wood had sheltered the Spartans from the enemy, and the fire spoiled their chief defence, so that they were the less prepared to face the army of nearly fourteen thousand Athenians, which, led by Cleon and Demosthenes, now landed on the island.

Outnumbered as the Spartans were, for their army consisted of only about four hundred and twenty soldiers and the same number of Helots, they fought bravely as was their custom.

But the arrows of the Athenians soon greatly reduced their number, while to add to the distress of the wounded, as well as of those who had escaped, the ground over which they marched was hot with still smouldering ashes of burnt wood.

At length Epitadas, the Spartan general, was slain, and the few soldiers who were still able to fight retreated to a hill on which was an old ruined fort. Here they took their stand, determined to keep the enemy at bay. And they did so until the Athenians found a path up a steep crag, from the top of which they could command the Spartan fort.

Unseen by the brave defenders, the enemy scaled the almost precipitous path, and when they reached the top they at once began to shoot arrows down upon the startled soldiers.

But soon Cleon bade them stay their arrows while he sent a herald to the Spartans to bid them surrender.

Spartan troops had never yet yielded to a foe. Ever they had conquered or fought to the death. Cleon believed that now, as their brave fellows at Thermopylae had done, they would rather die than yield.

But the Spartans dropped their shields and waved their hands above their heads to show that they would cease to fight. They begged to be allowed to ask the advice of their friends on the mainland. Their request was granted, and their friends bade them "to take counsel for themselves, but to do nothing disgraceful."

Two hundred and ninety-two Spartans, who were all that were still alive on Sphacteria, then surrendered, one hundred and twenty of these belonging to the noblest families in Sparta. Never after this surrender were the Spartans considered invincible.

Cleon was now able to return to Athens, which he reached within twenty days from the time he left the city, bringing with him, as he had boasted that he would do, his Spartan prisoners.

The Athenians rejoiced at the success of their army, but they laughed as they thought of the strange general who had led it to victory.

As for the prisoners, they were glad to hold them as hostages. The Spartans would be less likely to invade Attica while their comrades were in Athens.

CHAPTER LXVII

BRASIDAS THE SPARTAN

THE Athenians were encouraged by the victory they had gained at Sphacteria to hope for still greater success to their arms, and in 424 B.C. they marched boldly into the country of Boeotia. At Delium they seized and fortified a temple, sacred to Apollo.

Now the Boeotians were indignant with the Athenians for invading their land, but they were still more angry that they had dared to enter their temple. They at once marched against the enemy and defeated them with great loss, but the temple was still left in the hands of the Athenians.

As was the custom in those days, the defeated generals asked the victors to allow them to bury their comrades who had fallen on the battlefield. But the Boeotians answered "When you give us back our temple you shall bury your dead."

The Athenians refused to do this, saying that Delium, the site on which the temple stood, belonged to Attica, and they had a right to stay in their own land.

"If you are in your own land," retorted the Boeotians, "do as you wish without asking our consent." It was easy to say this, for they knew that the defeated army was not strong enough to defy them.

When the invaders still refused to leave the temple, the Boeotians determined to drive them away by setting fire to the wooden barricades with which the Athenians had fortified the temple.

So they took a large beam of wood, and scooping out the centre made it into a hollow tube. To one end they fastened, by an iron chain, a huge caldron. In the caldron they placed charcoal and sulphur, while to the other end of the tube they tied bellows, by which a strong current of air could be blown through to the other end. When this was done the charcoal and the sulphur in the caldron were fanned into a great blaze, and the fortifications of the temple were soon on fire.

The Athenians tried to quench the flames in vain, and at length they were forced to flee, leaving the temple to the triumphant Boeotians, who no longer refused to let them bury their comrades.

The defeat of Delium was followed by many other disasters, and was the beginning of the downfall of the empire of Athens.

Meanwhile Brasidas had recovered from the wound that he had received at Pylos.

Never had there been so strange a Spartan as Brasidas. His countrymen spoke as little as possible, and what they did say they said in a brief, concise manner. In later days such short, pithy speech was termed laconic. This name was used because Sparta was also called Laconia. But Brasidas was not laconic, he spoke quickly and with ease, and while his comrades liked to do things in the way their fathers had done, Brasidas loved new ways and bold adventures.

Spartans were seldom liked by strangers, for they were rough, often even discourteous in their manner; but Brasidas had winning ways, and wherever he went he made friends. He was not only pleasant, he was also just, and strangers soon learned that his word could be trusted.

This was the man who was now sent with an army through Thessaly. The country was for the most part loyal to Athens, yet the Spartans reached Macedon unhindered.

Brasidas had been told that the city of Acanthus was ready to fling open her gates to him, but he found them guarded. He asked to be allowed to enter that he might tell the people why he had come to their city, and they, won by his kind and simple manner, admitted him.

His first words pleased them, for he told them that he knew how powerful they were, and that if they refused to throw off their allegiance to Athens many other cities would be encouraged by their example.

BRASIDAS THE SPARTAN

If they would trust themselves to Sparta, he promised that their city should be free. "But should you refuse," and his voice grew stern, "and say that I have no right to force an alliance on a people against its will, I will ravage your land, and force you to consent. And for two reasons will I do this. The tribute you pay to Athens injures Sparta by making her foe stronger, and your example will make other cities resist the claims of Sparta."

The Acanthians were afraid that Brasidas would fulfil his threat and destroy their fields, and trample on their grapes which were now ripe and ready to pluck, so they determined to trust Sparta and throw off their allegiance to Athens.

Brasidas was pleased, for, as he had foreseen, other cities quickly followed the example of Acanthus.

Encouraged by his success the Spartan general now determined to attack Amphipolis, an important town in Thrace, standing on the bank of the river Strymon.

CHAPTER LXVIII

AMPHIPOLIS SURRENDERS TO BRASIDAS

AMPHIPOLIS belonged to the Athenians, who had sent Thucydides and Eucles to guard the city lest it should be attacked by the Spartans. Thucydides had not only the city but a large district also to protect, and he was at this time stationed with his troops at some distance from Amphipolis, while Eucles was in the city itself.

The bridge over the Strymon, which led to the city, was carelessly guarded. So when, on a cold and wintry day, Brasidas reached the river, he took the bridge without difficulty, making prisoners the few soldiers who held it.

Messengers were at once sent to Thucydides to tell him that the Spartans had seized the bridge, and to beg him to come as quickly as possible to protect the city. Before the day was over, Thucydides had reached Eion, at the mouth of the Strymon. But his speed was of no avail, for Amphipolis had

AMPHIPOLIS SURRENDERS TO BRASIDAS

already surrendered, tempted by the easy terms that Brasidas had offered.

When the Athenians heard that the city was lost, they were indignant with Thucydides, and chiefly through the influence of Cleon, who disliked him, he was sent into exile.

The punishment was severe, but Thucydides was not idle during his banishment. He traveled from place to place, and everywhere he went he paid great attention to the ways of the people and to the manner in which their cities were governed. He himself wrote, "Associating with both sides, with the Peloponnesians quite as much as with the Athenians, because of my exile, I was thus enabled to watch quietly the course of events."

After having studied the "course of events," Thucydides began to write about the Peloponnesian war, and he became the greatest of all the historians of Greece.

After the surrender of Amphipolis in 424 B.C., city after city forsook its allegiance to Athens. Scione did not even wait for the Spartans to demand admission, they opened their gates and begged Brasidas to enter. His presence pleased the people well, and when he had spoken to them their enthusiasm knew no bounds. They sent for a crown of gold and placed it on his head, calling him the "liberator of Hellas." Many of the people, too, cast garlands, over him as they were used to do to victors at a race.

Until now Brasidas had fought loyally for the sake of his country, but after the crown of gold had rested on his head he grew more ambitious to win fame for himself than glory for his country. It was his ambition that made him now do all that he could to keep Sparta from making peace with Athens, as she wished to do.

Cleon, too, was eager that the war should continue, not in order to win renown for himself, but rather that Athens might regain the empire that Brasidas was snatching from her grasp.

Two years after the surrender of Amphipolis, Cleon urged the Athenians to make an effort to retake the city. His rough eloquence persuaded them to undertake the task. He was himself appointed general, and was sent to Thrace at the head of a large army.

As he marched through the country he took several towns before he reached Eion, at the mouth of the river Strymon.

Here he halted, meaning to wait for reinforcements. But his soldiers had little respect for their general. Was he not after all only a leather-merchant? What could he know about war? And they clamoured to be led at once against the enemy. Cleon did not dare to refuse to do as his army wished, and he ordered his whole force to march toward Amphipolis to find out the strength of the enemy.

Brasidas was encamped with his army on the top of a hill, near to the city, from which he could watch every movement of the enemy.

AMPHIPOLIS SURRENDERS TO BRASIDAS

When he saw the Athenians approaching, he ordered his men to march into the town where the Spartan Clearidas was now governor.

Cleon at once supposed that Brasidas had taken shelter within the walls of Amphipolis so as to avoid a battle. Feeling no longer anxious, he left his army near the city, but not drawn up ready for battle, and himself rode carelessly forward to look at the surrounding country.

Meanwhile some Athenian soldiers heard the restless movement of men and horses within the walls, others looking under the gates saw many feet gathering together. It was clear that preparations were being made by the Spartans to sally out and attack them.

A messenger was sent in haste to find Cleon. The general no sooner heard the report than he hurried back to his army, and commanded it at once to retreat toward Eion. To do this the Athenians had to march past Amphipolis with their right sides unprotected, for their shields were carried always on their left arm, which was now the farthest from the walls of the city.

The men had no confidence in their general, and they began to retreat in disorder. From within the city, Brasidas was watching with keen eyes the movements of the enemy. Suddenly he cried, "These men will never withstand our onset. Look at their quivering spears and nodding heads. Men who are going to fight never march in such a fashion as this.

Open the gates at once that I may rush on them forthwith."

So the gates of the city were flung open and out dashed Brasidas followed by his men, as he charged right into the centre of the Athenian army. The left wing, seized with panic, fled. Clearidas meanwhile led a body of men against the right wing, and a fierce struggle followed.

Cleon, less at home on a battlefield than in the assembly at Athens, grew frightened at the unusual sights and sounds, and fled, leaving his army without a leader. As he fled an arrow pierced him and he fell to the ground, wounded to death.

Brasidas also, as he turned to go to the help of Clearidas, was wounded. His followers carried him within the walls of the city. He lived long enough to know that the Athenians were utterly defeated.

The people of Amphipolis had learned to love Brasidas, and he was buried with great splendour in the market-place. A temple was built to his honour, and every year sacrifices were offered and games were held in memory of the brave soldier.

So deep was the affection of the people that they determined to forget that their city had been founded by an Athenian, and henceforth to count Brasidas the Spartan the true founder of Amphipolis.

As Cleon and Brasidas were both dead, the peace party, with Nicias at its head, was able to arrange terms with the king of Sparta, and in spring, 421 B.C., the Peace of Nicias was signed. The first part of the Peloponnesian War, which had begun ten years before, was ended.

CHAPTER LXIX

ALCIBIADES THE FAVOURITE OF ATHENS

THE Peace of Nicias, which was made for fifty years, did not last more then six. Thucydides tells us that it did not really last even so long. For although for six years neither Spartans nor Athenians invaded each other's land, yet they did as much harm as they could to one another.

"So that," says the wise historian, "if any one objects to consider it a time of war, he will not be estimating it rightly."

Almost as soon as peace was signed, Sparta and the State of Argos quarreled. Each wished to get help from Athens, so each sent ambassadors to her. The Argives boldly begged Athens to join them against Sparta; the Spartans were content to remind her that she had signed the Peace of Nicias.

In Athens at this time there was a rich young noble named Alcibiades, who wished the Athenians to make an alliance with the Argives.

But the Spartan ambassadors had already been welcomed by the Athenians, because they had come with full power to arrange fair terms. Alcibiades was as determined as he was angry. To gain what he wished he resolved to play a trick on the Spartan ambassadors. So he went to them in secret, and told them how foolish they had been to tell the Athenians what great powers they had, for the assembly would certainly wrest from them more than they wished to give.

"When the assembly meets, tell the people," said Alcibiades, "that you have no power, but that you will send their demands to the Spartan council. I will support you and all will be well, for you will have time to think over their wishes."

The ambassadors thought that the young noble knew better than they how his countrymen should be treated, and they promised to follow his advice.

So when the assembly met the next day, the Spartans declared that they had come only to report what the Athenians should say, that they had no power to arrange terms until they had heard from their own council.

No sooner had they spoken than Alcibiades jumped to his feet, and to the dismay of the ambassadors he pointed to them with scorn, saying, "These men say one thing one day, and another thing the next day; they are not to be trusted. Let us refuse to have anything more to do with them."

The Athenians at once agreed with Alcibiades that it was useless to treat with such unreliable ambassadors, and they then made an alliance with the Argives.

When the Spartans reached their own country they told how they had been deceived by Alcibiades, and how rudely they had been treated by the assembly. And this, as well as the alliance which the Athenians had made with the Argives, was the cause of the second part of the Peloponnesian War.

The Spartans were thirsting to avenge the battle of Sphacteria, and to wipe out the memory of their surrender. When they met the Athenians in 418 B.C. at Mantinea they fought with the courage and the fierceness that had made them invincible until the fatal day of Sphacteria.

Alcibiades, whose trick had been the cause of so much mischief, was the son of an Athenian, named Clinias.

While Alcibiades was still young his father died, and Pericles became one of his guardians. He was a beautiful baby, a handsome boy, and when he grew to be a man he was so brave and so winning in his ways that he made friends very easily.

But he made enemies as well as friends, for he was wild and wayward, while his pride often made him behave with scant courtesy even to those whom he should have treated with reverence and respect.

Staid, sensible folk were shocked at his careless, extravagant ways. Nicias distrusted him. But the

ALCIBIADES THE FAVOURITE OF ATHENS

citizens loved him and forgave him much, for he spent his wealth freely among them, and often entertained them with public shows.

"They love and hate and cannot do without him," wrote Aristophanes, as he watched the Athenians now cherishing, now chiding, their favourite.

One day, he was a mere lad at the time, he was wrestling with a playmate, when, thinking he was going to be thrown, he suddenly bit his companion's hand with all his strength. His friend quickly let go his hold, crying, "You bite, Alcibiades, like a woman."

"No," answered the boy, "like a lion."

Another day he was throwing dice in the street with his playmates, when a wagon pulled by two horses approached. It was the turn of Alcibiades to throw, and he shouted to the driver to stop, but the man paid no heed to the boy and drove on. The other children scampered out of the way, but the wilful little noble flung himself down in front of the horses and cried to the driver to go on now if he pleased.

Afraid lest he should hurt the boy the man at once pulled up his horses, while those who had been looking on in terror rushed forward and dragged the foolish little fellow out of danger. But Alcibiades had made the driver pull up and he was content.

His want of self-control became greater as he grew older. When he was at a grammar school he one day asked the schoolmaster to lend him one of

Homer's books. The master said that he did not possess it, whereupon the rude boy struck him and then turned and walked away. Some years later he struck a citizen whose talent in the theatre had outshone his own.

When he was a young man he walked into the assembly with a pet quail hidden under his cloak. This would have raised a storm of indignation had it been done by anyone else.

In the law court one of Alcibiades' friends was accused, when the favourite at once seized the writ and tore it in pieces before the face of the judge.

The young nobleman was rich, and much of his wealth he spent on horses. He sent seven chariots to the Olympic games, and once, to the great delight of the Athenians, their favourite won the first, second, and third prizes.

Euripides, the poet, sang of the triumph of Alcibiades in these lines:

> "But my song to you,
> Son of Clinias, is due.
> Victory is noble; how much more
> To do as never Greek before;
> To obtain in the great chariot race
> The first, the second, and third place;
> With easy step advanced to fame,
> To bid the herald three times claim
> The olive for one victor's name."

At one time Alcibiades owned a very large, handsome dog, for which he had paid an enormous price. He ordered his tail, which Plutarch tells us was "his principal ornament," to be cut off.

His friends said that it was a stupid deed, and told him that every one in Athens was angry that he had spoiled the noble appearance of his dog. But Alcibiades only laughed, saying, "Just what I wanted has happened then. I wished the Athenians to talk about this, that they might not say something worse of me."

It was natural that so reckless and generous a youth should be surrounded by a crowd of flatterers, ready to applaud his foolish and sometimes insolent acts.

But Alcibiades had no love for these careless admirers, although he would spend hours with them at feasts and revels. His affection he gave to one whom you would scarcely have expected the gay young nobleman to notice—to Socrates, the great philosopher and teacher of Athens.

CHAPTER LXX

SOCRATES THE PHILOSOPHER

SOCRATES was born in 469 B.C. He was not a noble like Alcibiades, but a man of humble birth. Nor was he handsome as was his disciple, but plain, even ugly, the people said. He was small, too, and dressed with little care.

If anyone wished to find the philosopher, he knew that he had only to go to the market-place or into the streets. Here, from early morning until late at night, Socrates was to be seen, and always he was talking, talking to all who were willing to listen. And there were ever many who were not only willing but eager to hear what the teacher had to say, for his words were so wise, his conversations so strange.

Socrates believed that the gods had sent him to teach the Athenians. From his boyhood he had heard a voice within him, bidding him to do this, not to do that. He often spoke of this voice to those who became his disciples. It became known as the dæmon of Socrates.

SOCRATES THE PHILOSOPHER

The philosopher was a soldier as well as a teacher, and his philosophy taught him how to endure hardship as well as or even better than could the ordinary Athenian.

In heat or in cold he wore the same clothing, and in all weathers he walked with bare feet. He ate little and drank less whether he was in the camp or in the city.

Xanthippe, the wife of Socrates, had not a good temper, and she would often scold the philosopher. That may have been because while he was teaching wisdom in the market-place, Xanthippe was at home wondering how to provide food for her husband and their children with the few coins she possessed. Socrates was never paid by his disciples, and so it often happened that Xanthippe found it difficult to get food and clothing for her household.

The philosopher taught for many years, but at length, in 399 B.C., his enemies accused him of speaking against the gods of Athens. He had even dared, so they said, to speak of new gods whom the people should worship, and that was a crime worthy of death.

Socrates took little trouble to defend himself against the accusations of his enemies. His dæmon, he said, would not allow him to plead for his life. So he was condemned to death, but only by a majority of five or six votes out of six hundred.

For thirty days Socrates was in prison, and he spent the time in talking to his friends just as he had been used to do in the market-place.

He drank the contents as though it were
a draught of wine

SOCRATES THE PHILOSOPHER

One of his disciples, named Crito, bribed the jailer to allow his prisoner to escape, but Socrates refused to flee. He did not fear death, but faced it calmly as he had faced life.

On the day before the sentence was carried out, he talked quietly to his disciples of the life to which he was going, for he believed that his soul, which was his real self, would live after he had laid aside his body as a garment.

When the cup of hemlock, a poisoned draught, was brought to him, his friends wept, but he took the cup in his hand, and drank the contents as though it were a draught of wine.

His last words to Crito were to remind him to pay a debt. "Crito, we owe a cock to Asclepius," he said. "Discharge the debt and by no means omit it." Asclepius was the god of medicine, and in this way Socrates showed his reverence for the religious customs of his country.

This was the man who found in Alcibiades, despite his wild ways, a noble mind and a kind heart. These he determined to educate. And his pupil was quick to see that Socrates spoke truth to him. He soon learned to appreciate his kindness and to stand in awe of his virtue. Sometimes, indeed, the words of his master "overcame him so much as to draw tears from his eyes, and to disturb his very soul."

So dear did the philosopher become to Alcibiades that he often lived in the same tent with him and shared his simple meals. Yet sometimes he was tempted by his flatterers when they begged him to come to spend the days in pleasure and the nights in feasting. Then he would yield to their entreaties and for a while desert and even avoid his master.

But the philosopher did not leave his pupil unchecked to do as he wished. He "would pursue him as if he had been a fugitive slave.... He reduced and corrected him by his addresses, and made him humble and modest, by showing him in how many things he was deficient, and how very far from perfection in virtue."

CHAPTER LXXI

ALCIBIADES PRAISES SOCRATES

ONE of the most famous disciples of Socrates was Plato. He loved his master well, and wrote down many of his conversations, so that his words may still be read.

In a book, named the *Symposium*, Plato tells us that Socrates and his friends met at a banquet one day and spoke to each other in praise of love.

When it came to Alcibiades' turn to speak, he was eager to tell of the love he had for Socrates. He began by begging the others not to laugh if he said first of all that Socrates was like the images of the god Silenus, which they had often seen in the shops of Athens.

Now Silenus was a satyr, a strange figure that was half man, half goat. In his mouth were pipes and flutes upon which he played, while his images were made to open, and within each might be seen the figure of a god.

As the gay company thought of the uncouth figure of the satyr, at which they had often stared in shop windows, they could not but laugh at Alcibiades for comparing his master to such an image.

But when the young nobleman went on to speak of the god that was hidden in Socrates, just as the image of one was concealed in the body of the satyr, it may be that the laughter of the gay company was hushed. For in truth the disciple could say no greater thing about the master he loved than this, that within him he bore the likeness of a god.

But Silenus was not the only satyr that reminded Alcibiades of his master. Marsyas, a wonderful flute-player also made him think of Socrates. "For," said Alcibiades, "Are you not a flute-player, Socrates? That you are, and a far more wonderful performer that Marsyas. He indeed with instruments used to charm the souls of men by the power of his breath. But you produce the same effect with your voice only, and do not require the flute; that is the difference between you and him."

Pericles, and other great Athenian orators, Alcibiades had heard, he said, unmoved, while Socrates' words, "even at second hand and however imperfectly repeated, amaze and possess the souls of every man, woman and child who comes within hearing of them."

Alcibiades then told his astonished listeners how his master's eloquence held him as with chains of gold.

"This Marsyas," he says, "has often brought me to such a pass that I have felt as if I could hardly endure the life which I am leading. . . . and I am conscious that if I did not shut my ears against him, and fly from the voice of the siren, he would detain me until I grew old, sitting at his feet. For he makes me confess that I ought not to live as I do, neglecting the wants of my own soul, and busying myself with the concerns of the Athenians; therefore I hold my ears and tear myself away from him."

So greatly did the words of Socrates disturb Alcibiades that sometimes he even wished that his master were dead and could trouble him no more, and "yet I know," he adds quickly, "that I should be much more sorry than glad if he were to die; so that I am at my wit's end."

But it was not only his master's eloquence that Alcibiades praised before the gay company of revellers, it was his deeds as well.

During the Peloponnesian War both Socrates and Alcibiades were present at the siege of Potidæa.

"There we messed together," said Alcibiades, "and I had the opportunity of observing his extraordinary power of sustaining fatigue and going without food. In the faculty of endurance he was superior not only to me, but to everybody; there was no one to be compared to him, yet at a festival he was the only person who had any real power of enjoyment."

"Cold, too," Alcibiades said, "Socrates could bear without flinching. The winter at Potidæa was severe, the frost intense. The Athenian soldiers stayed indoors when they could; when they were forced to be out they put on as many extra clothes as they could find, their feet they swathed in felt and fleeces."

But Socrates, "with his bare feet on the ice and in his ordinary dress, marched better than the other soldiers who had shoes, and they looked daggers at him, because he seemed to despise them."

Yet another tale of his endurance Alcibiades told to the listening company.

"One morning," he said, "Socrates was thinking about something which he could not resolve; he would not give it up, but continued thinking from early dawn until noon—there he stood, fixed in thought; and at noon attention was drawn to him, and the rumour ran through the wondering crowd that Socrates had been standing and thinking about something ever since the break of day. At last, in the evening, after supper, some Ionians out of curiosity (it was now summer) brought out their mats and slept in the open air that they might watch him, and see whether he would stand all night. There he stood all night until the following morning, and with the return of light he offered up a prayer to the sun and went his way."

Not even yet had Alcibiades exhausted the praises of his master, and the gay company listened spell-bound and bewildered to the young noble. They had not guessed how well he loved, how gravely he had studied the words and ways of Socrates. Now it was of the courage of his master that he wished to tell, for Socrates had saved his life in battle.

"This was," said Alcibiades, "the engagement in which I received the prize of valour; for I was wounded and he would not leave me, but he rescued me and my arms; and he ought to have received the prize of valour which the generals wanted to confer on me, partly on account of my rank, and I told them so (this Socrates will not impeach or deny), but he was more eager than the general that I and not he should have the prize."

When the Athenians fled after the defeat of Delium, the young nobleman was on horseback, and being himself safe, he watched Socrates, who was among the foot-soldiers.

"There you might see him," said Alcibiades, "just as he is in the streets of Athens, stalking like a pelican, and rolling his eyes, calmly contemplating enemies as well as friends, and making very intelligible to anybody even from a distance that whoever attacked him would be likely to meet with a stout resistance; and in this way he and his companions escaped."

With one more tribute to his master, Alcibiades ended his discourse on love:

"His absolute unlikeness to any human being that is or ever has been is perfectly astonishing. His are the only words which have a meaning in them, and also the most divine, . . . extending to the whole duty of a good and honourable man. This, friends, is my praise of Socrates."

You will be glad to know that Socrates valued the love of his disciple and returned it.

"I only love you," said the philosopher, "whereas other men love what belongs to you; and your beauty, which is not you, is fading away, just as your true self is beginning to bloom. And I will never desert you, if you are not spoiled and deformed by the Athenian people: for the danger which I most fear is that you will become a lover of the people, and will be spoiled by them. Many a noble Athenian has been ruined in this way."

CHAPTER LXII

THE IMAGES OF HERMES ARE DESTROYED

IN the island of Sicily there were many different states. In some of these dwelt Greeks who owned Corinth as their mother-city. Trade between Sicily and Corinth was good, and because of this Corinth was growing more powerful than Athens liked.

War broke out in 416 B.C. between Segesta and Selinus, two cities in the west of Sicily. When Selinus was joined by another town named Syracuse, the Segestans in dismay sent to the Athenians to ask for their help.

It had long been the ambition of Alcibiades to conquer Sicily. He believed, too, that it would add to the glory of Athens if the island became part of the Athenian empire.

So he now urged the assembly to send a fleet to Sicily, reminding them that if it could conquer Syracuse, it would then be in its power to ruin the trade of Corinth with Sicily.

He did not tell the Athenians how great his ambitions were, but he told them enough to make them wish to help the Segestans, that they might in this way gain new territory for Athens.

The assembly made up its mind to send ambassadors to Segesta, to find out if the town was able, as she said she was, to provide money to carry on the war, if the Athenians provided soldiers.

When the ambassadors returned in the spring of 415 B.C. they brought back with them a sum of money from the grateful Segestans. They reported, too, that the wealth of the city was far greater than they had dreamed. But although the ambassadors did not know until too late, they had been deceived by the townsfolk.

For the rich plate and splendid ornaments with which the Segestans had adorned each feast to which the ambassadors had been invited, were taken secretly from house to house. So that the gold and silver dishes that dazzled the eyes of the Athenians were always the same, although they believed that each of their hosts owned the splendid dishes with which his table was laden.

The sacred treasures of their temples, too, the Segestans pretended were of gold, while in reality they were of silver.

But the ambassadors were convinced that the people they had visited were rich, and their report made the Athenians ready to do as Alcibiades and his party wished. So it was agreed that sixty vessels should be sent to the help of Segesta.

THE IMAGES OF HERMES ARE DESTROYED

Nicias, bent as ever on peace, did all he could to hinder the expedition. But when, in spite of all he could say, the assembly still determined to send a fleet to Sicily, he persuaded it at least to increase the number of ships from sixty to a hundred. Nicias himself, along with Lamachus and Alcibiades, was appointed commander of the expedition.

But the night before the fleet was to sail a strange event took place.

All over the city, at the corner of streets, in some niche of a public building, in front of the houses of the citizens, stood statues or busts of the god Hermes, on short pedestals or pillars.

These figures were reverenced by the Athenians, just as the image of the Madonna by the roadside or in villages and towns abroad is worshipped by Roman Catholics.

On the night before the expedition the statues of Hermes were chipped and broken, so that the god could no longer be recognized.

In the morning as the Athenians went along the streets of the city, bent on their usual business, these poor defaced images stared them in the face. Little groups gathered at street corners, before public buildings, wherever they had been used to see the statues of Hermes. At first they gazed at their mutilated god in fear, but fear soon changed to anger.

Who had dared to do this impious thing, they asked one another. It would surely bring down the wrath of the gods on the Sicilian expedition.

It was perhaps natural that the people should suspect their favourite Alcibiades. Was he not often reckless and ever a mischief maker? They were too excited to remember that he was not likely to do anything to delay the expedition on which his heart was set.

When he heard that the people thought that he had defaced the images, Alcibiades demanded to be brought to trial. But no proof had yet been found of his guilt, and it was decided that the fleet should sail, and that Alcibiades should go with it.

CHAPTER LXXIII

ALCIBIADES ESCAPES TO SPARTA

A GREAT crowd gathered at the Piræus to see the fleet set sail for Sicily. Groups clustered together, talking eagerly of the new empire that was to be won in the West, and the glory that Athens would gain from her conquests. It was a noisy, happy crowd.

Suddenly the heralds called for silence, and a hush fell upon the light-hearted folk as the priests prayed to the gods for the success of the expedition. Sacrifices, too, were offered by officers and sailors alike. Then to the strain of a hymn, in which the crowd of onlookers joined, the anchors were raised and the fleet sailed slowly away.

When the ships reached Sicily each commander had a different plan to propose.

Nicias, having learned how the ambassadors had been deceived, wished to sail homewards, without helping the Segestans. Lamachus, a brave, blunt soldier, wished to sail at once to Syracuse, and take the city by a sudden attack. Alcibiades proposed that they should do nothing until they had made allies of those cities that were not friendly to Syracuse, and to this plan the other commanders at length agreed.

Meanwhile two ships from Athens had followed Alcibiades to Sicily, for the assembly had determined to arrest him, and bring him home to be tried for the destruction of the images of Hermes.

Alcibiades went quietly on board one of the ships, but he knew that if he went back to Athens he would be condemned to death. So daring a deed as the spoiling of their god was more than the Athenians could forgive even to their favourite. And there were many who believed he was guilty.

So when the ship reached a seaport town in Italy, Alcibiades slipped on shore and escaped from his enemies. In his absence the Athenians condemned him to death and confiscated his property, while the curses of the gods were called down upon his head.

Alcibiades was very angry when he heard what his countrymen had done, and in his wrath he cried, "I will make them feel that I am alive." And he fulfilled his threat. For he went at once to the Spartans, the enemies of his own country, and told them the plans of the Athenian generals. He bade them send a clever general, named Gylippus, with an army to Syracuse, to help the city to withstand the attacks of the Athenians. He also advised them to build a fort at Decelea, a town in Attica, and to send troops there to harass the Athenians as much as possible.

To betray his country in this way would have been an unworthy deed for any Athenian; it was the more unworthy in Alcibiades, because he had learned from Socrates the true meaning of honour and righteousness.

The Spartans were eager to profit by the advice of the traitor, and they saw for themselves the wisdom of his words. But in their hearts they did not trust the man who had betrayed his country.

Alcibiades stayed in Sparta for some time, and while he was there he tried to win the confidence of the people by doing as they did.

"People who saw him wearing his hair cut close, bathing in cold water, eating coarse meal and dining on black broth, doubted or rather could not believe that he had ever had a cook in his house, or had even seen a perfumer or had worn a mantle of purple."

It was said that Alcibiades was like a chameleon; because just as it can change its colour as it chooses, so could the Athenian change his dress and his customs as he willed.

CHAPTER LXXIV

THE SIEGE OF SYRACUSE

NICIAS and Lamachus now determined to attack Syracuse without delay.

They succeeded in seizing the high ground which joined the town to the mainland of Sicily. Across this ground they began to build a wall, meaning to cut the Syracusans off from help by land. The Athenian fleet then sailed into the harbour of Syracuse, that so no help might reach the city by sea.

But before the wall was finished, two things had happened to frustrate the plans of the Athenians.

The Syracusans did not mean to let the enemy finish the wall if they could prevent it, so they sailed out of the city to drive them away. In the struggle which followed Lamachus was killed, and Nicias was left alone to carry on the siege.

But what was perhaps even worse for the Athenians than the death of their general, was the arrival of Gylippus the Spartan commander.

THE SIEGE OF SYRACUSE

Almost before the Athenians were aware, Gylippus, at the head of his troops, marched into Syracuse. Nor did he rest until he had driven them from the hill on which they were encamped, and forced them to take up their position close to the harbour.

Nicias was ill, and his illness made him more hopeless than perhaps he would otherwise have been. He wrote to the assembly to tell it that the Spartans had wrested from the Athenians all that they had gained, and that they were now themselves in danger of being besieged.

The fleet, he said, had been drawn up on the beach for months, and would have to be repaired before it was seaworthy. Even then it would be difficult to man the vessels, for many of the crew had died and many more were out of practice.

So faint of heart was the Athenian general that, at the end of his gloomy report, he urged that the whole enterprise should be given up, or if not, that at least a new fleet might be sent out without loss of time. For himself he begged that he might be recalled, as he was ill and unfit for his duties.

The assembly refused this last request, but it sent a new fleet to his help, commanded by Eurymedon and Demosthenes.

Meanwhile Gylippus was not idle. He attacked the Athenians both by land and sea. By land he was victorious, but at sea he was defeated.

Undaunted, he at once ordered that the bows of the Spartan vessels should be made heavier and shorter. When this had been done he again attacked the enemy's fleet, and when the battle ended Gylippus held the entrance to the harbour.

The Athenians were now in great peril, for they were besieged both by land and sea. They could not leave the harbour unless they cut their way through the fleet of the victorious Syracusans, and this they had no courage to attempt.

But on the day after the battle which had seemed to seal their fate, hope awoke once more in the Athenian ranks, for the new fleet, under Eurymedon and Demosthenes, came in sight.

The new commanders at once determined that the hill above Syracuse must be retaken. So on a moonlight night the attempt was made. But although a band of Athenians gained the hill, took a fort and repulsed six hundred of the enemy, they were soon afterwards put to flight. Many of the soldiers flung away their shields, as they were driven down the hill, and fell over the cliffs. Others were pushed back upon their comrades who were still climbing upwards, so that soon the whole army was in confusion.

This disaster crushed the spirit of the Athenians. Many of the soldiers, too, had fever caused by the marshy ground on which their camp was pitched. Many more were ill or wounded.

Eurymedon and Demosthenes advised Nicias to order the whole army to sail away before the

THE SIEGE OF SYRACUSE

entrance to the Great Harbour was entirely blockaded, but to this he would not consent. It seemed that he was afraid to return to Athens to tell that the expedition had failed.

Demosthenes then urged Nicias at least to leave the harbour and sail to a point where their supplies could not be stopped by the enemy. This too, Nicias refused to do.

But soon after his refusal, large reinforcements reached the Spartans, and the general's obstinacy gave way. He ordered the fleet to prepare to leave the harbour.

The men were glad to desert their unhealthy quarters and got ready in haste, but secretly, that the Syracusans might not suspect their plans.

All was ready, when, on 27th August 413 B.C., the night before the fleet was to sail, an eclipse of the moon took place.

Nicias was filled with superstitious fears. What might the eclipse not portend? He sent to the soothsayers, who said that the fleet must on no account leave the harbour for twenty-seven days. To disobey the oracle would be fatal, so Nicias believed, and he at once forbade the fleet to sail until the twenty-seven days had passed.

CHAPTER LXXV

THE ATHENIAN ARMY IS DESTROYED

THE Athenians made their preparations to retreat as secretly as possible, but the Syracusans soon discovered their plans. When they heard that their departure was delayed for twenty-seven days, they determined to attack the Athenian fleet once more, and again they were successful.

On land the Athenians repulsed Gylippus, but they gained little by this success, for the Syracusans had made up their mind that the whole Athenian army should be destroyed.

So, as Demosthenes had foreseen, they barricaded the entrance to the Great Harbour, drawing their ships across it and lashing them together with chains.

Nicias saw that a battle must be fought, and he ordered a great number of the land troops to go on board the fleet. At all costs he must strengthen his navy.

THE ATHENIAN ARMY IS DESTROYED

The first thing the Athenians had to do was to break through the ships that were lashed together at the mouth of the harbour. But before the chains could be broken the enemy was upon them, surrounding them on every side. Despair gave the Athenians courage, and so desperately did they fight that for a time it seemed that they might yet escape.

Above the crash of vessels rose the cheers or groans of those who watched the battle from the shore.

Thucydides gives us a picture of the hopes and fears, the triumph and despair of those who fought as of those who watched. He says:

"The fortune of the battle varied, and it was not possible that the spectators on the shore should all receive the same impression of it. Being quite close and having different points of view, they would some of them see their own ships victorious; their courage would then revive, and they would earnestly call upon the gods not to take from them their hope of deliverance. But others, who saw their ships worsted, cried and shrieked aloud, and were by the sight alone more utterly unnerved than the defeated combatants themselves.

"Others again who had fixed their gaze on some part of the struggle which was undecided were in a state of excitement still more terrible; they kept swaying their bodies to and fro in an agony of hope and fear, as the stubborn conflict went on and on; for at every instant they were all but saved or all but lost. And while the strife hung in the balance, you might hear in the Athenian army at once lamentation, shouting, cries of victory or defeat, and all the various sounds which are wrung from a great host in extremity of danger."

At length the Athenians were pushed back and yet further back, until the fleet was stranded on the shore. The soldiers who had been left on land now rushed forward and succeeded in saving sixty of their ships from the enemy.

Demosthenes urged the men to embark and try once again to cut their way out of the harbour, but they refused, so crushed were they by their defeat. To retreat by land was all that the Athenians could now try to do, yet in their hearts they knew that the retreat must end in slavery or in death.

The sick and the wounded were left behind. But those who were stricken with fever, caused by the marsh land on which they had been encamped, clung to their comrades, and scarce knowing what they did, begged that they might not be left behind. But their strength soon failed, and they sank down by the wayside to die.

Nicias, ill as he was, did all in his power to encourage and cheer his men. He himself led the van, Demosthenes brought up the rear.

After marching for several days, the Athenians were parched with thirst. When at length they reached a stream, it was to find the enemy awaiting them on the farther bank.

THE ATHENIAN ARMY IS DESTROYED

But their thirst was intolerable, and paying no heed to the foe, the soldiers rushed to the water. As they stooped to drink, the Syracusans fell upon them and put them to death.

Demosthenes and his men had fallen behind the rest of the army, and had already been forced to surrender. Nicias now saw that he, too, must submit to Gylippus.

Seven thousand prisoners were sent by the Spartans to work in stone quarries. These quarries were like dungeons, but they were open to the sky, and during the day the scorching sun beat down piteously on the miserable prisoners, while at night the cold was so intense that sleep was impossible.

Here they were kept for seventy days, with only enough food to keep them alive, and with scarcely any water to drink. Many of the men died, those who survived were sold as slaves.

Nicias and Demosthenes were both put to death. It is said that they were tortured, although Gylippus did all he could to save them from the angry Syracusans. Thus in disaster and defeat ended the expedition that sailed forth so bravely from Athens two years before.

Thucydides says that this expedition was "the greatest adventure that the Greeks entered into during this war, and, in my opinion," he adds, "the greatest in which the Greeks were ever concerned; the one most splendid for the conquerors and most disastrous for the conquered, for they suffered no common defeat, but were absolutely annihilated—

land-army, fleet and all—and of many thousands only a handful ever returned home."

CHAPTER LXXVI

ALCIBIADES RETURNS TO ATHENS

ALCIBIADES fled from the Athenians to Sparta, but he did not stay there long, for he soon grew tired of living as simply and frugally as the people of that country. He had, too, made an enemy of one of the kings of Sparta, so in the autumn of 412 B.C. he fled to Miletus in Asia Minor, where Tissaphernes, the Persian governor, ruled for the great king.

Tissaphernes was a cruel man, but he was easily pleased by flattery. Alcibiades soon discovered the governor's weakness, and he determined to win his favour by his agreeable speeches. He succeeded so well that the Persian named some of his parks and pavilions Alcibiades, in honour of the eloquent Athenian.

The luxury and ease with which the Persians were surrounded pleased Alcibiades after his course of Spartan fare and discipline, and he indulged for a time in even greater magnificence than did Tissaphernes. His anger against the Athenians had gradually grown less vehement, and he now began to wish that they would forget their hatred of him and recall him from exile.

But they had little thought to spare for the traitor, for troubles were pouring in upon them on every side. They had but lately heard of the complete overthrow of their fleet and army in Sicily, and they were now building a new fleet with money which Pericles had put aside long before, lest at any time Attica should be invaded by sea.

The Spartans, too, were still at Decelea, where they had built a fort, not fourteen miles from the city. Town after town that had been allied with Athens in the time of her prosperity now became her enemy.

In their despair the Athenians had taken a desperate step—they had asked their old enemies the Persians to come to their aid.

It was then that Alcibiades saw an opportunity, as he thought, to help the people whom he had so cruelly betrayed, and at the same time to please the Persians.

So he sent a message to the Athenians to say that if they would place the government of Athens in the hands of a party named "The Four Hundred," he would be able to persuade Tissaphernes to make an alliance with them. For his master, the great king, would make no terms with Athens as long as she was a democracy.

ALCIBIADES RETURNS TO ATHENS

The Athenians followed Alcibiades' advice, and the government of the city was entrusted to The Four Hundred for a short time. But Alcibiades had not so much influence as he had believed, and the Persian government still refused to help the Athenians.

Partly perhaps in anger with Tissaphernes, partly because the Athenians were not satisfied with the rule of The Four Hundred, Alcibiades helped to overthrow them and to make Athens once again a democracy.

So grateful were the people for his help, that they declared his exile was at an end, and bade his return to Athens.

But although Alcibiades longed to go back to Athens, he was content to wait until he could return covered with glory. By his own request he was given the command of a few ships, and with these he set sail for the Hellespont. Mindarus, the Spartan admiral, with a large army was there, hoping to stop the corn supply of Athens on its way to the city from the Black Sea. If the corn supply was stopped, Athens would starve, and Mindarus knew that the city would then soon be in the hands of the Spartans.

The Athenian fleet was in three divisions, and the one commanded by Alcibiades passed the Hellespont unseen by the enemy and took Mindarus by surprise.

By land and sea desperate battles were fought, and in both the Athenians were victorious. Mindarus was slain, and the Spartan fleet was destroyed. The

Hellespont was not blocked, and Athens was no longer in danger of starving.

The Spartans in their own laconic way sent a brief message to Sparta to tell of their defeat. The dispatch was seized by the Athenians before it reached its destination. This is what the victorious people read: "The ships are gone; Mindarus is slain; the men are starving; we know not what to do."

For two years, from 409 B.C. to 407 B.C., Alcibiades stayed at the Hellespont retaking cities which had thrown off their allegiance to Athens and joined Sparta. Then feeling that now he might return with glory, he set sail for Athens.

Plutarch tells us that as Alcibiades drew near to the Piræus he was afraid to venture on shore, until he saw friends waiting to welcome him:

"As soon as he was landed the multitude who came out to meet him scarcely seemed so much as to see any of the other captains, but came in throngs about Alcibiades and saluted him with loud acclamations, and still followed him; those who could press near him crowned him with garlands, and they who could not come up so close, yet stayed to behold him afar off, and the old men pointed him out and showed him to the young ones."

In the assembly, crowns of gold were placed on his head, and he was created general, with absolute power, over both the land and the sea forces.

ALCIBIADES RETURNS TO ATHENS

The multitude saluted him with loud acclamations

His estates were given back to him, and a "holy herald" was bidden to absolve him from the curses which had been pronounced against him.

The high priest alone refused to obey, for he said, "If he is innocent, I never cursed him."

CHAPTER LXXVII

ANTIOCHUS DISOBEYS ALCIBIADES

THE king of Persia was not pleased with his governor Tissaphernes, because he had made an alliance with neither the Athenians nor the Spartans. So he now sent his younger son Cyrus to take the place of Tissaphernes, bidding him make terms with the Spartans.

Lysander was now in command of the Spartan fleet. He was as brave and as skilful an admiral as Brasidas had been, although he could not win the trust of strangers as his famous countryman had done. But he gained the affection of his men and cared for their welfare.

Cyrus invited Lysander to a feast and tried to bribe him to join the Persians, but in vain.

The Persian prince then offered to give him whatever he chose to ask. Lysander wished nothing for himself, but, to the surprise of all who were present, he begged that the daily wage of his sailors might be increased.

In September 407 B.C., the Spartan sailed with his fleet close to the harbour of Ephesus. About the same time, Alcibiades, with the Athenian fleet, arrived at Notium, from which port he could watch the movements of the enemy.

As he had little money with which to pay his men, he determined to leave the fleet in charge of his pilot, Antiochus, while he, taking with him a few ships, sailed away to plunder a neighbouring city. In this way he hoped to find the money that he needed. Alcibiades strictly forbade Antiochus to risk a battle.

No sooner, however, had the admiral gone than the pilot disobeyed his orders, and with a number of ships he sailed past the Spartan fleet, challenging Lysander to fight.

The Spartan in reply merely sent a few vessels to drive away the reckless pilot, but the ships that had been left at Notium soon noticed that Antiochus was being chased, and they at once hastened to join him.

In a short time the two fleets were engaged in battle. Antiochus was slain, and fifteen of the Athenian ships were taken or sunk. Those that escaped sailed to Samos, where Alcibiades soon joined them. He determined, if it were possible, to avenge the punishment the Spartans had inflicted on the Athenian vessels, so he sailed to Ephesus and offered battle to Lysander. But the Spartan had won a great victory and he did not mean to risk a defeat. He refused to fight again.

Alcibiades still had enemies in Athens, and they were so angry with him for having left the charge of the fleet to Antiochus that they clamoured for his command to be taken from him. The assembly was forced to yield to them, and Alcibiades was deposed, while the command was given to an Athenian named Conon.

The admiral then fled to a city on the Hellespont, where he had long ago bought a castle, lest at any time he should need a place of refuge from his enemies.

Conon, the new commander, gained a great victory, at the island of Arginusæ, on the coast of Asia. After the victory a storm arose, and a dozen Athenian vessels which had been disabled in the battle went down with all their crews on board.

No attempt was made to rescue the unfortunate sailors, and eight Athenian generals were ordered to come home to be tried for neglect of duty. Six only obeyed.

The assembly met and condemned the generals, but their sentence was left undetermined. On the day after the trial a festival was held in the city, at which solemn family gatherings took place.

When the relations of those who had perished at Arginusæ appeared, clad in black, their number roused the people to fresh fury against the condemned generals.

The assembly met shortly afterwards, and one of the members demanded that the people should vote without delay, and if the generals were found guilty that they should be put to death.

Now the generals had not yet finished their defence; moreover, there was a law in Athens that prisoners should be judged and sentenced one at a time.

At first the assembly wished to obey this law, but the mob was so fierce that it yielded, and pronounced sentence of death on all the generals at once. To each was brought a cup of hemlock.

Socrates was present in the assembly, and he was not afraid to denounce the sentence as unlawful. Nor would he withdraw his protest in face of the angry crowd. This was a brave deed, such as you would expect from the great philosopher.

CHAPTER LXXVIII

THE WALLS OF ATHENS ARE DESTROYED

THE last battle of the Peloponnesian War was fought in the Hellespont in 405 B.C. The Athenians had drawn up their ships near a desolate spot named Ægospotami, and they soon found that it was an awkward place from which to get provisions for the army. There were no houses near, from which they could demand help, so the sailors were forced to leave their ships and scour the country round about for food. So dreary was the spot that the Athenians longed to fight at once.

But Lysander was in a strong position on the other side of the strait; he had, too, a plentiful supply of food, so that he did not mean to let himself be forced into a battle.

Again and again the Athenians sailed across the strait, hoping to tempt the Spartans to fight, but Lysander refused to move.

As the weeks passed, the Athenians grew careless of an enemy that seemed too lazy or too cowardly to fight. They left their ships well-nigh unguarded, and wandered over the country in large numbers in search of food.

Alcibiades, from his castle not far off, saw that the Athenians were in a dangerous position, and that they were leaving their ships unprotected. He rode over to Ægospotami to warn the generals to seek a safer position. At Sestos, a town but two miles off, they would be better able to defend themselves from the Spartans, should they be attacked. They would also be able to command provisions.

But the generals did not wish to listen to Alcibiades, and their pride forbade them to follow his advice. They spoke rudely to him, telling him to be gone, that now not he but others had the command of the forces.

The very day after Alcibiades had warned them, the Athenians, leaving their ships for the most part unmanned, set out to search the countryside for food.

Lysander knew how the enemy usually spent the afternoons. Now that they had grown heedless of danger he determined to attack the forsaken ships without further delay.

So he ordered his vessels to row quickly across the strait and he found, as he expected, the Athenian fleet utterly unprepared for battle.

THE WALLS OF ATHENS ARE DESTROYED

There was indeed no battle fought, for the Spartans easily captured one hundred and seventy ships, and took more than four thousand prisoners, among whom were three or four admirals.

Conon alone, with eight ships, succeeded in escaping. But he dared not return to Athens with tidings of the disaster, for he knew that if he did so he would be condemned to death. So he sent a ship to carry the terrible news to the city.

It was evening when the vessel reached Piræus.

"The noise of wailing spread all up the Long Walls into the city, as one passed the tidings on to another; that night no one slept." For now there was no fleet to hinder the Spartans from stopping the supply of corn, and the Athenians knew that they must starve or surrender.

For a little while the city refused to yield. But she had no allies, no ships, no money, and no corn could enter the town. The wretched people were dying of hunger before Athens surrendered to the Spartans in March 404 B.C.

She expected no mercy from her conqueror. Even as she had destroyed many a Spartan town, so she thought that now she herself would be utterly ruined.

But Sparta proved less harsh than Athens had deemed was possible. The city was indeed to be "rendered harmless for ever, but not destroyed."

All that was left of her fleet was taken away, and the walls of Piræus and the walls leading to Athens were pulled down.

Lysander stood near, looking on, as the Athenians and the Spartans together began to break down the walls.

It was not so gloomy a scene as you might have expected. Perhaps the Athenians were glad that at length the long and desperate struggle had come to an end. Flute players and dancers were present, and added a strange touch of gaiety to the crowd.

Soon after the surrender of Athens, Lysander was ordered to put Alcibiades to death, lest he should encourage the Athenians at any time to throw off their allegiance to Sparta.

Plutarch tells us that "those who were sent to assassinate him had not courage enough to enter the house, but surrounded it first and set it on fire.

"Alcibiades, as soon as he perceived it, getting together great quantities of clothes and furniture, threw them upon the fire to choke it, and having wrapped his cloak about his left arm, and holding his naked sword in his right, he cast himself into the middle of the fire, and escaped securely through it, before his clothes were burnt.

"The barbarians, as soon as they saw him, retreated, and none of them durst stay to wait for him, or to engage with him, but, standing at a distance, they slew him with darts and arrows."

CHAPTER LXXIX

THE MARCH OF THE TEN THOUSAND

In 404 B.C., soon after the disaster of Ægospotami, Darius, king of Persia, died. His eldest son Artaxerxes succeeded to his father's throne.

Cyrus, the younger son, who was present at his father's death, was accused by Tissaphernes of trying to secure the throne for himself.

Artaxerxes believed Tissaphernes, and Cyrus was arrested, and would have been put to death had not his mother pleaded that his life might be spared.

The king listened to his mother's request and set his brother free. He even allowed him to govern the provinces that had been his in his father's lifetime.

But Cyrus felt no gratitude to his brother, he hated him, and was determined if it were possible to seize his throne.

So he hired a large number of Greek soldiers, for now that there was peace between Athens and Sparta, many of them were idle and glad to take service under Cyrus.

The prince pretended that he was going to fight against Tissaphernes, and no one save himself and the Spartan, Clearchus, who was the leader of the Greeks, knew that the army was going to Babylon to fight against Artaxerxes, king of Persia.

Among the Greek soldiers was Xenophon, a scholar and a pupil of Socrates, who wrote the story of this expedition.

Early in 401 B.C., Cyrus assembled his troops at Sardis. When they arrived at Tarsus, a city on the coast of Cilicia, the soldiers began to suspect that Cyrus was going to lead them against Artaxerxes. They were not afraid of the great king, but they were afraid to leave the sea behind them, for that was ever a terrible thing to the Greeks. So they refused to march farther.

Clearchus, who was a stern commander and no favourite with his men, tried in vain to quell their rebellion, but all his efforts were vain. Not a step forward would they march.

He had used his authority and failed, now he resolved not to command but to persuade. So he called his men together again, and as he looked at them he wept.

Their grim, stern commander shedding tears! The soldiers stared at him in open-eyed wonder.

Then Clearchus bade them see in how difficult a position they had placed him, for he must either fail Cyrus or forsake them. Forsake them he could not, so he declared, for were they not "his country, his friends, and his allies"?

These words pleased the soldiers well, but what pleased them even more was that when Cyrus sent to ask their commander to go to his tent, he refused to go.

But they were less content when Clearchus reminded them that as they refused to follow Cyrus, they could no longer expect him to give them food or wages. What, he asked them, did they mean to do?

All that they could do was to send a few of their number to the prince to ask him where he intended to lead them.

Cyrus answered that he was taking them to the river Euphrates, to fight against a Persian rebel, and at the same time he offered to increase their wages if they would obey Clearchus.

The Greeks were far from home, and not knowing what else to do, they agreed to follow their commander. But they did not trust Cyrus, and they still suspected that he wished to march beyond the river Euphrates. And when they reached the river their suspicions proved true, for Cyrus told them plainly that he was going to Babylon to dethrone his brother Artaxerxes.

As the Euphrates was unusually shallow, the army was able to cross over on foot, and soon afterwards it was in the desert of Arabia.

Xenophon tells us that the desert was "smooth as a sea." There were no large trees in all the great expanse, but there were many shrubs that had a pleasant scent.

The soldiers did not find the march across the desert dull, for they saw many strange beasts, unlike any they had ever seen—wild asses, ostriches, antelopes,—and these they hunted with zest.

When the desert lay behind them they found themselves in a land where fields had been dug and gardens tended. Here, too, a little before them, was Artaxerxes, with a great army, ready to fight to the death for his crown.

The king was encamped at a place called Cunascæ, where in the summer of 401 B.C. a battle was fought. Strange as it may seem, before a blow was struck, the Persians were seized with panic and turned to flee. Only Tissaphernes at the head of the cavalry stood firm.

Cyrus with a small body of men, about six hundred in number, dashed upon the centre of the army, for there, surrounded by six thousand horsemen, was Artaxerxes. The guards scattered before his fierce attack, and the king turned to fly with them.

THE MARCH OF THE TEN THOUSAND

Then Cyrus, careless of aught save his desire to slay his brother, and gain his crown, galloped after him, attended by only a few of his own bodyguard.

As he drew near to the king, he hurled a javelin at him and wounded him slightly. Almost at the same moment Cyrus himself was wounded in the eye, and shortly after he fell from his horse and was slain.

Cyrus was dead, and ten thousand Greek soldiers were left alone with their generals in a strange land, surrounded by enemies. Tissaphernes pretended to be a friend to the Greeks, and offered to guide them safely home. So the two armies set out together, but before long the Greek soldiers grew suspicious of the Persians. To reassure the men, Tissaphernes invited Clearchus and his captains to his tent.

The Greek general accepted the invitation, and, never dreaming of treachery, he went to the Persian's tent with four other generals, twenty captains and a few soldiers.

No sooner had they entered than the captains and soldiers were seized and put to death by the order of Tissaphernes. Clearchus and the other generals were loaded with chains and sent to the king. Artaxerxes commanded that they, too, should be put to death.

The Persians believed that the Greek army would now be forced to surrender. For, alone in an unknown land, without a leader, how could they hope to reach their own country?

But the greatness of their danger roused the courage of the Greeks. Xenophon, who was at the time only a young man, made an eloquent speech to the army, bidding them choose new generals and obey them, for in this way only could they hope to escape from their enemies.

The men did as he advised, choosing Xenophon himself as one of the new generals.

And now began the retreat of the ten thousand through untold difficulties. To go back the same way as they had come was impossible, for the roads would be guarded by the Persians. So they turned to the north and marched through a wild and barren country, where fierce hillmen held the narrow passes through which they must pass.

Sometimes the savage tribes hurled down upon them from the heights great pieces of rock, and the soldiers lived in dread of being crushed to death by their unseen foes.

When they reached Armenia it was December and bitterly cold. They were overtaken by a snowstorm so severe that many of the men lost their way. In vain they tried to rejoin their comrades, and at length, utterly worn out, they stumbled into great snowdrifts or lay down on the road to die.

Still the army struggled bravely on, in the face of the biting north wind, until at length it reached a tributary of the river Euphrates. This they crossed in safety, to find that most of their difficulties were over, for soon after they reached a city called Gymnias.

Gymnias was a prosperous mining town, and the inhabitants welcomed the ten thousand gladly and gave them food and shelter, after they had heard of the terrible difficulties through which the men had come.

But the soldiers did not linger long at Gymnias. They were eager to set out again, for a guide promised that in five days he would bring them to the sea.

"On the fifth day the Greeks came to a hill, and when the van reached the summit a great cry arose. When Xenophon and those at the rear heard it they thought that an enemy was attacking in front; but when the cry increased as fresh men continually came up to the summit, Xenophon thought it must be something more serious, and galloped forward to the front with his cavalry.

"As he drew near he heard what the cry was—'The Sea, the Sea.'"

A few days more and the ten thousand were on Greek soil. Here they rested for a month, offering glad sacrifices of thanksgiving to Zeus, who had brought them back in safety to their own land.

CHAPTER LXXX

PELOPIDAS AND EPAMINONDAS

WHEN Sparta heard that Artaxerxes had been able neither to force the ten thousand to surrender nor to slay them, she thought that his army could not be very powerful. So, confident in her own strength she went to war against the great king, dreaming that she would conquer Persia and add it to her dominions.

But instead of conquering the country, the Spartans were so often defeated that, in 387 B.C., they were willing to make peace on any terms which Artaxerxes chose to make.

And the king saw to it that the terms were severe, for he demanded that the Greek cities in Asia, which had now been free for ninety years, should once again acknowledge him as their lord.

To those Greeks who loved their country truly, it seemed better to fight to death than to accept such terms. Nor will you wonder at this as you read the proud words in which the king couched his demands.

"King Artaxerxes thinks it just," he wrote, "that the Greek cities in Asia should belong to him. He also thinks it just to leave all the other Grecian cities both small and great independent, except three cities which are to belong to Athens as of old. Should any parties refuse to accept this peace I will make war upon them, along with those who are of the same mind, both by land and sea, with ships and with money."

The states of Greece accepted these terms, which were carved on stones and placed in their temples, so that it could be seen by all that Greece was no longer free.

Although Sparta had been defeated by the Persians, she was the most powerful state in Greece. Wishing to add to her possessions, she determined to seize the little town of Thebes, which at this time was friendly with Athens.

The two governors of Thebes, Leontiades and Ismenias, did not get on well together. Leontiades disliked his colleague so bitterly that he was ready even to betray his city, if by doing so he could injure Ismenias.

In September 382 B.C. a Spartan army, led by a general named Phœbidas, chanced to be marching through Bœotia. Not far from the walls of Thebes the soldiers halted to rest.

Leontiades thought this was the opportunity for which he had been waiting. He would be able to get rid of Ismenias with the help of the Spartans. They had already determined to seize the town, but this the traitor did not know. He went secretly to the camp, asked for Phœbidas, and was admitted to the general's tent. He at once offered to open the gates of Thebes to the Spartans on the following day.

It would be an easy matter to seize the citadel if the gates were opened, for on the morrow a festival kept by women alone was to be held there, while at noon the men would be in their houses dozing during the hottest part of the day.

The Spartan general was as eager to take the city as Leontiades could desire, and the traitor slipped back to the city thinking of nothing save that Ismenias would soon be out of his way.

At noon on the following day, the Spartans marched to the gates of Thebes, and there, according to his compact, was Leontiades waiting to admit them. Silently he drew the keys from under his cloak, unlocked the gates, and Phœbidas at the head of two thousand men entered the city. They made their way at once to the citadel, took possession of it, and made the women, who were keeping the festival, prisoners.

Before long the men of Thebes roused themselves from their noontide nap, to find, to their dismay, that their wives and daughters were in the hands of the Spartans.

Leontiades ordered his rival Ismenias to be arrested, and soon after the miserable governor was sent to Sparta and cruelly put to death.

Three hundred Thebans, who were determined not to submit to Sparta, succeeded in escaping from the city and reaching Athens. Many who wished to flee did not dare to do so, lest in their absence harm should befall their wives and daughters.

Leontiades was rewarded for his treachery by being still allowed to rule in Thebes, along with a Spartan general. So harshly did Leontiades use his power that the people hated him, but years passed before the tyrant's power was wrested from him.

During these years those who had fled to Athens often heard from the miserable Thebans of the hardships they suffered under the stern rule of Leontiades.

Among the exiles was a young nobleman named Pelopidas. Often he would tell his fellow exiles that it was dishonourable to dwell in comfort in Athens while their city was not free, and he would urge them to march against the Spartans, and banish them from Thebes.

Pelopidas had a great friend in Thebes named Epaminondas. And although the two friends did brave deeds not only for their city, but for Greece, they are remembered most of all for the great love they bore each to the other.

Both were of noble birth, but Pelopidas was rich, while Epaminondas was poor. Pelopidas had a generous nature, and used his money to help those who were not so well off as he was. Even among his friends many were quick to accept his kindnesses, but Epaminondas would never take from him either gold or gifts.

Pelopidas resolved that if Epaminondas would not share his wealth, he would share his friend's poverty. So he bade his slaves lay aside his soft, silk robes, that he might clad himself in garments as simple as those of Epaminondas. He would allow no rich dishes to be set before him at table, but he ordered that his food should be both plain and scanty. In the camp he endured hardships as a common soldier, in war he showed himself bold as a lion.

The friends were clever and well-trained, both in mind and body, but Pelopidas was often to be found in the fields, while Epaminondas was listening to lectures.

Each longed to serve his country well, but no touch of jealousy disturbed the beauty of their friendship. It was founded deep on reverence and love.

Some years before the treachery of Leontiades, when the Spartans were at war with Athens, the Thebans had sent a troop of soldiers to the aid of Sparta. Among the soldiers were the two friends Pelopidas and Epaminondas.

PELOPIDAS AND EPAMINONDAS

The company with which the Theban soldiers fought was beaten, and many fled from the field. But Pelopidas and Epaminondas joined their shields together and fought on bravely. Pelopidas was wounded seven times, and at length, faint with the loss of blood, he fell to the ground.

Epaminondas thought that his comrade was dead, but he resolved that the enemy should have neither the arms nor the body of his friend. So he stood over him with his shield, willing rather "to die than forsake his helpless Pelopidas."

Soon Epaminondas himself was so severely wounded that he was no longer able to defend the body of his friend. Had not the king of Sparta chanced to see his danger, and with a few followers dashed to his rescue, he would have been slain by the foe. But the king carried off both Epaminondas and Pelopidas, who was then found to be still alive.

Pelopidas recovered, although his wounds had been severe, and never did he forget that it was his friend who had saved his life.

CHAPTER LXXXI

THE SEVEN CONSPIRATORS

THREE years passed before the Theban exiles, encouraged by Pelopidas, formed a plot to deliver their city from the Spartans.

They were helped in their plans by Phyllidas, a Theban who had stayed in the city and become secretary to the Spartan governors Archias and Philippus. He had taken this position under the enemy that he might be able the better to help his own countrymen. He agreed with Pelopidas that the time to act had now come.

Epaminondas was also in Thebes, but he would have nothing to do with the plot. He would fight when the time for fighting came, but to slay even tyrants unawares was not to his liking.

Pelopidas and six other exiles did not share the scruples of Epaminondas. They disguised themselves as farmers or country folk, and one evening reaching Thebes as it began to grow dark, they slipped one by one at different times into the city.

THE SEVEN CONSPIRATORS

They then found their way to the house of a citizen named Charon, who had promised to shelter them.

Snow was falling and the streets were nearly deserted, so that the return of the exiles was unnoticed.

On the following day, Archias and Philippus were to be present at a great banquet. Phyllidas, the secretary, had promised to bring to the feast seven beautiful Theban women. He told no one that the promised guests were the seven exiles, who had resolved to don a second disguise to enable them to be present at the banquet.

The day of the feast passed slowly for the conspirators, but at length evening came, and the exiles were putting on the garments that were to make them appear like beautiful women, when a loud knock came to the door.

Already the long day had tried them sorely, and the knock filled them with foreboding.

When the door was opened their hearts beat quicker, for there stood a soldier who bade Charon come to the banqueting hall without delay.

Had Charon betrayed them? The exiles looked uncertainly one at the other. Then they grew ashamed of their distrust and bade their host hasten to Archias to allay his suspicions, if indeed they had been aroused.

Charon was brave and true and he knew that the lives of the seven men were in his hand. He hoped that they trusted him, yet he wished to dispel any doubt that they might have. So he hastened to the nursery of his little son, and carrying the child to Pelopidas, he placed him in his arms, saying, "If you find me a traitor, treat the boy as an enemy without any mercy."

But the exiles protested, and truly, that they trusted him well and needed no such hostage, while Pelopidas bade him take the child back to his nurse.

Then Charon, staying only to ask the help of the gods, hastened to the banqueting hall.

Archias and his secretary were awaiting him, and Archias said, "I have heard, Charon, that there are some men just come lurking into the town. We fear lest they have come to stir up the citizens."

"Who are they? Where are they hidden?" asked Charon. For he wished to find out how much Archias knew.

But Archias knew nothing. It was but a rumour that had reached him.

"Do not disturb yourself because of a rumour," said Charon, who had now no fear of discovery. "There are many tales told in the market-place. But I will find out if there is truth in what you have heard."

Archias was glad to leave the matter to Charon, for he was impatient to go back to the feast. So Charon hastened back to his house to tell Pelopidas and his comrades that their fears were needless, for Archias suspected nothing.

THE SEVEN CONSPIRATORS

But although Charon did not know it, a letter was at that moment being placed in the hands of Archias that might easily have ruined both him and the conspirators. For it told Archias the whole plot, as well as the names of those who were to take part in it.

The letter had been sent from Athens, and as the messenger handed it to the Spartan governor, he said, "The writer of this desired that it might be read at once; it is on urgent business."

But Archias could think of nothing that night save the banquet and the beautiful Theban women, who should now soon arrive.

Thrusting the letter unopened under the cushion on which his head rested, Archias cried, a smile upon his face, "Urgent business to-morrow." And these words were ever after used as a proverb by the Greeks.

The conspirators had now reached the hall. Their beautiful dresses were wide and loose, for beneath their splendour they wore armour. On their heads were garlands of pine and fir, so that their faces might not be seen.

Archias and his guests clapped their hands gleefully. Here at last were the beautiful Theban women whose presence Phyllidas had promised should grace the banquet.

But in a moment the conspirators had torn off their disguise. Archias and Philippus were slain almost before they had time to realise their danger, while the guests who had rushed to their aid were also put to death.

Pelopidas and his comrades then hastened to the house of Leontiades. But he heard them knocking at the door, and when they rushed into his room a few seconds later, he met them with his sword drawn, and slew the first man who entered.

A terrible struggle then took place between Leontiades and Pelopidas, but at length the traitor was wounded to death.

The conspirators then ran to the prison, ordered the gates to be opened, and the prisoners to be set free and armed, for their only crime had been loyalty to their city.

As day began to dawn, troops from Athens poured into the city to help the Thebans. The Spartans fought fiercely, but after a few days the garrison was forced to surrender, and once again Thebes was free.

The grateful citizens then assembled in the market-place, where the priests crowned Pelopidas and Charon, while the people appointed them governors of the city.

CHAPTER LXXXII

THE BATTLE OF LEUCTRA

THEBES had always been a dull, unambitious, little town, but now her ambition awoke. She was not content only to be free, she wished to become the most important town in Bœotia.

And there was one of her citizens who was so great a soldier and so wise a statesman, that he was able to do for Thebes more than she dreamed. Epaminondas not only made Thebes the chief city in Bœotia, but several years later, he conquered the Spartans, and so made her the most important town in Greece.

Pelopidas, too, fought for the glory of his country. He became the captain of a band of three hundred young Thebans, who had sworn to defend their city with their lives.

These three hundred soldiers, more strictly trained than other youths, were named the Sacred Band, because each member was a friend to the other. As they had sworn to defend their city so they had promised to stand by one another unto death.

After many victories, of which you will read, the Sacred Band fell on the battle-field. Even their conqueror, as he looked upon them shed tears, saying, "Perish any man who suspects that these men either did or suffered anything that was base!"

For two years after Thebes won back her freedom, Sparta never ceased to try to wrench it from her. But at the end of two years she was forced to leave the Thebans alone, for all her soldiers were needed to fight against the Athenians, who had once more declared war against their ancient foe.

While the Spartans and the Athenians waged war one against the other Epaminondas was not idle, for he subdued the Bœotian cities which had dared to help Sparta while Thebes was in her power.

Pelopidas, too, won a great victory in 375 B.C. against the Spartans at Orchomenus. He had with him only the Sacred Band and a small company of cavalry when he found himself unawares facing a large Spartan army.

"We are fallen into the midst of the enemy," cried one of the Band. "Why so, more than they into the midst of us?" said Pelopidas.

The rare confidence of their captain inspired the Band to fight even more valiantly than usual, and to win a great victory over the large army of the Spartans.

This victory encouraged the Thebans so much that in the following year they succeeded in banishing the Spartans from Bœotia.

Thebes was now at the head of the Bœotian Confederacy, just as Sparta was ruler of the Laconian Confederacy. Four years later, in 371 B.C., the Greek States met to arrange terms of peace among themselves.

It was agreed that each city should be treated as independent. But when Agesilaus, king of Sparta, rose to take the oath, he took it not alone for his own city, but for the cities that belonged to her allies as well.

Epaminondas sprang to his feet to remonstrate, saying that if Agesilaus was allowed to take the oath for the allied cities, he too must be permitted to take it for all the cities of Bœotia.

The Spartan king, angry with the bold demand of the Theban, taunted him with taking away the liberty of the Bœotian cities.

"And what do you do with the liberty of the cities of Laconia?" retorted Epaminondas.

Agesilaus was astonished at what he considered the insolence of the Theban. In a rage he snatched up the treaty of peace, struck out the name of Thebes, crying that if the Thebans wished war they should have it. The other cities signed the treaty, so Sparta and Thebes were left to settle their quarrel alone.

Epaminondas hastened back to Thebes, where he was at once chosen general of the Theban army.

Without delay he set out to secure a pass by which he thought the Spartans would attempt to enter Bœotia.

But the Spartans, led by Cleombrotus, one of their kings, did not try to enter by the pass. Finding a narrow mountain track, they succeeded in eluding Epaminondas, and marching within eight miles of Thebes.

Here, on the plain of Leuctra, the Spartans encamped in 371 B.C.

Near to Leuctra were the tombs of two Bœotian maidens. Many years ago they had slain themselves, because of the cruelty with which the Spartans had treated them.

An old prophecy said that some day the Spartans would be defeated at the tombs of the maidens. Epaminondas, although he did not greatly believe in soothsayers, encouraged his captains to fight by reminding them of this old saying.

Before the battle Pelopidas had a strange dream. In his dream he saw the two maidens of Leuctra alive and wandering about the plain. Their father, too, was there, and Pelopidas heard him say that if the Thebans wished for victory, they must sacrifice to the gods a maiden with chestnut hair.

When he awoke, Pelopidas told his dream to the other captains, and as they were wondering what to do, a colt of a bright chestnut colour ran through the camp.

"So," cried a soothsayer, "the sacrifice is come. Expect no other, but use that which the gods have sent."

Then the colt was solemnly offered in sacrifice at the tombs of the maidens. And the army was content, for the gods, they were sure, would give them the victory.

Until now a Greek army had always been drawn out in a long, narrow line. But Epaminondas arranged his men in a new way. His left wing was only a few men wide, but it was fifty men deep, which made it unusually strong.

Pelopidas with his Sacred Band was placed in front of the heavy left wing, while the rest of the army was arranged as usual.

The Spartan cavalry attacked the Theban horse, but it was soon driven from the field. Cleombrotus was with his right wing and he now led it against the strong left wing of the enemy.

Bravely as the Spartans fought, they could not withstand the onslaught of the left wing, led by the Sacred Band.

Cleombrotus fell and was carried from the field, wounded to death. The Spartans still struggled bravely, although their king was slain. But when Epaminondas called to his men, "Give me a step more and the day is ours," the Thebans spurred on to one more effort, broke the Spartan line and put it to flight. The Thebans had won the day, with but little loss of life, while four hundred Spartans had been slain.

Cleombrotus was the first Spartan king who had fallen on a battlefield since the fatal day of Thermopylæ.

The terrible news of the defeat of Leuctra was sent to Sparta, but the citizens were too well disciplined to show the dismay which they must have felt.

They had been beaten by the inhabitants of the dull little town of Thebes, yet no sound of grief was heard in their streets, nor was any sign of mourning to be seen.

It was on a festive day that the fateful tidings reached the city, and sacrifices were offered and games held as though nothing had happened to interrupt the usual rites.

Those whose friends had fled looked sullen and ashamed, for it was counted a disgrace to leave a lost battlefield alive. Those whose friends had fought to the death were to be seen in the streets the following day, with faces that were calm and content. Of such stern stuff were the Spartans made.

CHAPTER LXXXIII

THE DEATH OF EPAMINONDAS

THEBES was now the most powerful city in Greece. But Epaminondas was not yet content. He wished to invade Sparta.

In November 370 B.C. he marched with his army into Arcadia, which lay to the north of Laconia. Here he was joined by all those who wished to throw off the Spartan yoke. His army soon numbered forty thousand, some even say it was seventy thousand strong.

Sparta could hardly believe that any one had dared to invade her territory. She was used to fighting in other states of Greece or in other countries, but it would be a new experience if she was forced to fight for her own homes. Yet there was Epaminondas and his army encamped within sight of the city.

The Spartan women had never before seen the smoke of an enemy's fire camp, and they gave way to despair, in spite of their stern training in self-control.

But the Theban general was too wise to attack the city. He knew that the Spartans had gathered together a large army, and that they would fight to the death for their homes. So, satisfied that he had encamped in sight of Sparta, he turned away, destroying the land through which he passed. The Spartans were eager to follow and fight with the enemy who had defied them, but their king refused to lead them to battle.

Epaminondas was not yet ready to leave Spartan territory. He led his army to the country of Messenia, which the Spartans had conquered many centuries before, banishing or making slaves of the people.

The Theban general roused the descendants of these slaves, and encouraged them to build a new city on Mount Ithomé, where Aristomenes had made his gallant stand against the Spartans.

While the first stones of the new city were being laid, the sound of flutes was heard. When it was finished it was named Messenia. A large piece of ground which belonged to Sparta was given by Epaminondas to the citizens of the new town. Those who had been slaves or Helots were now free men.

The army then marched back to Thebes, which it reached four months after the time for which Epaminondas had been appointed commander.

THE DEATH OF EPAMINONDAS

In spite of all that he had done for his country, his enemies wished him to be punished, because he had not laid down his command on the proper day. But he appealed to the people, and they gladly made him, along with Pelopidas, general for another year.

When the year had passed, Epaminondas was treated coldly, not only by his enemies but by the people also, because he had failed to surprise and take the city of Corinth.

In Thessaly at this time there was a cruel king named Alexander. So badly did he treat his subjects, that they begged the Thebans to come to their help.

Pelopidas was sent to Thessaly to punish Alexander, unless he promised to treat his people less harshly. The king was forced to listen to the Theban general, but he was angry because Pelopidas had dared to interfere with him and he resolved to punish him.

For some time the king found no opportunity to reach his enemy, but at length Pelopidas was foolish enough to go through Thessaly with only a few followers.

Alexander was overjoyed to have the general in his power, and he at once sent a band of men to capture him and throw him into prison.

But the Thebans were very angry when they heard that their favourite general was a prisoner, and they determined to set him free. So they sent a large army into Thessaly to rescue Pelopidas.

Epaminondas went with the army as an ordinary soldier, and you can imagine how he must have longed to be at its head, so that he might himself deliver his friend.

The Theban generals were not clever, and though they did all they could to conquer the army that Alexander sent against them, they soon saw that the battle was going against them.

Then they showed that if they were not clever they were wise, for they went to Epaminondas, and begged him to take command of the army.

But it was too late for even a clever general to rescue Pelopidas, and all Epaminondas could do was to save the Theban army from being destroyed.

The Thebans were so grateful to Epaminondas for his help that they made him general once more, and sent him back to Thessaly with a larger army that he might save his friend.

Alexander knew that he need not hope to conquer the great Theban general, and a few days after Epaminondas entered Thessaly, the king set Pelopidas free. He then asked the Thebans to make peace with him.

Three years later, in 364 B.C., Pelopidas was ordered to go at the head of an army against his old enemy.

As he was ready to leave Thebes, the sun was eclipsed and the soothsayers did not hesitate to say that this was a bad omen. Many of the soldiers were afraid to march, and Pelopidas was too angry to wait

THE DEATH OF EPAMINONDAS

to force them to go with him, so he set out with only a few men. When he reached Thessaly he bade all those who hated the tyrant to join him.

Thousands who had groaned under the cruelty of the king flocked to his side, but even then the army of Alexander was twice as large as his.

The two forces met at a place called Cynoscephalæ, where a great battle was fought.

Pelopidas led his men well, and himself fought so bravely that the battle was all but won in spite of the greater strength of the enemy. Suddenly Pelopidas caught sight of Alexander, and forgetting everything save his desire to avenge his imprisonment, he sprang forward to slay the tyrant. Ere his followers could reach him, he himself was struck down and killed.

Alexander was defeated and his kingdom was taken from him. But the Thessalians could not rejoice, because Pelopidas, to whom they owed their deliverance, had been slain. They buried him with great pomp on the field where he had fallen.

Epaminondas was filled with grief at the loss of his dear friend. He tried to forget his sorrow in serving his country.

In 362 B.C. he fought at Mantinea against the Spartans, on the field where long before he had saved the life of Pelopidas.

Never had Epaminondas fought more bravely than on this day, leading the Bœotians against the foe "as a war-galley ploughs through the waves with its beak."

The victory was well-nigh gained, when a Spartan thrust his pike through the breast of Epaminondas. He fell, and his men carried him off the field to a little hill, from which the battle could be seen.

For a short time the great general lay unconscious, but at length he opened his eyes and asked if his shield was safe. He was told that it was safe and that the battle was won.

Then he begged to see his two chief officers. They had fallen on the field, and when the news was broken to him, the dying man said,

"Then you had better make peace."

The head of the spear that had struck the general was still in the wound. As it was withdrawn he breathed his last.

It was Epaminondas who had made Thebes great. After his death she slowly slipped back into her old insignificant position.

CHAPTER LXXXIV
THE TWO BROTHERS

THE city of Corinth stood upon the narrow isthmus that joined the mainland of Greece to the Peloponnesian peninsula. She had two harbours, a large fleet, and she carried on a prosperous trade with other countries.

As the city grew strong and populous, she began to plant colonies in other lands. One of the wealthiest of these colonies was the town of Syracuse in Sicily.

In 346 B.C. Syracuse was in the power of a tyrant named Dionysius. The other cities in Sicily would have been in the same plight had their inhabitants not fled to a neighbouring town, and sought the aid of a powerful prince named Icetes. Icetes had a large army, and with its help they hoped to be able to overthrow Dionysius.

But trouble after trouble overtook the people, for the Carthaginians had sailed from Africa and had reached their shores. Sicily was in despair lest they should conquer the island and make it their own.

In their distress, the Sicilians sent messengers to Corinth, their mother-city, to beg her to help them to get rid of both the Carthaginians and Dionysius.

Icetes pretended to approve of this, but no sooner had the ambassadors set out for Corinth than he made friends with the Carthaginians. He hoped that if they drove Dionysius away, he himself would become tyrant of Sicily.

In Corinth, about twenty years earlier, there dwelt two brothers of noble birth—one was named Timophanes, the other Timoleon. Never were two brothers more unlike save that both were brave. Timophanes was cruel and ambitious, while Timoleon was gentle and content. Yet under his quiet ways Timoleon had one strong passion and that was the love he bore his country.

Timophanes was a captain in the Corinthian army; his brother served in the ranks.

Once when the captain was sent against a neighbouring state, he was thrown from his horse, which had been wounded. He fell close to the enemy and his men fled, leaving him in danger of being taken prisoner.

Timoleon saw what had happened, and rushing from the ranks, he stood over Timophanes with his shield, and defended him from the spears which were being hurled at him by the enemy. Although he

THE TWO BROTHERS

himself was sorely wounded, he never flinched. But at length his comrades rushed to his aid and drove off the foe. Timoleon had saved his brother's life.

Not long after this, Timophanes was given the command of four hundred foreign soldiers. This pleased the captain, but to the dismay of the citizens he used the troops to make himself tyrant of the city.

All who dared to oppose him he put to death, while he ruled so harshly that he was hated and feared by everyone.

Timoleon was ashamed of his brother's behaviour. He begged him to treat the people more kindly, and if he must rule at least to rule with justice. But Timophanes first mocked at his brother's words, and then he grew angry and refused to listen to them.

Gentle as Timoleon was, he could be strong when there was need to be so. In a short time he went again to his brother, taking with him two friends who used to admire Timophanes.

Together the three men besought the tyrant to give up the power he had so wrongfully seized, and to serve his country in an upright way.

Again Timophanes laughed at his friends, but when they persisted in their entreaties he grew angry, and rudely bade them begone. Then Timoleon hid his face in his cloak and wept, while the others put his brother to death.

The Corinthians, for the most part, praised Timoleon because he loved his country so well that he sacrificed his brother for her sake. But there were some citizens who blamed Timoleon for allowing his brother to be put to death before his eyes. His mother refused to see him and called down upon him the curses of the gods. This pained Timoleon more than anything else, and he begged her to see him, if it were but once. But she would not allow him to enter her house.

Timoleon loved his mother, and her treatment made him so sad that he refused either to eat or to drink. He resolved to starve himself to death rather than endure his mother's reproaches.

His friends did all they could to comfort him, and at length they succeeded in persuading him to eat. But his sorrow was too great to let him stay in Corinth, so he left the city, and for several years he lived by himself. Even when he returned to Corinth, he still refused to take part in any public business.

Timoleon was fifty years old when in 346 B.C. the Syracusans sent to the Corinthians to beg for help against the Carthaginians.

The Corinthians determined to send an army to Sicily to help their fellow-countrymen, but they could find no one willing to go at its head.

Some one proposed that Timoleon should be made commander of the force that had been raised, and he was at once appointed.

Perhaps Timoleon thought that it was now time that he should do something for his country; in any case he undertook the task that was given him with goodwill.

One worthy citizen bade Timoleon act "like a man of worth and gallantry. For," said he, "if you do bravely in this service we shall believe that you delivered us from a tyrant; but if otherwise, that you killed your brother."

CHAPTER LXXXV

TIMOLEON SENDS DIONYSIUS TO CORINTH

TIMOLEON was ready to sail to Sicily with a fleet of seven vessels and a force of about one thousand men, when a message from Icetes reached the Corinthians.

The traitor told them it was useless to try to help the people of Sicily, for he had joined the Carthaginians, and their combined army would easily crush any force that was sent against them.

This made the Corinthians so angry that they at once added two hundred soldiers to Timoleon's small army, as well as three vessels to his fleet.

Even so, Timoleon's task seemed hopeless. Athens, with hundreds of ships and with tens of thousands of men, had failed to take Syracuse. How then could the Corinthian hope to do so with his handful of men and his small fleet?

Before he sailed, Timoleon journeyed to Delphi to offer sacrifices to Apollo. As he prayed in the

TIMOLEON SENDS DIONYSIUS TO CORINTH

temple, a wreath slipped from its place and fell upon his head. It seemed to Timoleon that Apollo was already crowning him with victory.

At length all was ready, and the army embarked and set sail with a favourable wind. Suddenly a bright flame leaped out from the sky and hovered over the ship in which Timoleon sailed. The flame soon changed into a torch which guided the ships until they reached Rhegium, a town in Sicily.

Here Timoleon learned that Icetes had already defeated Dionysius, who was now shut up in the citadel of Syracuse, and that he had sent the Carthaginians with twenty warships to Rhegium to keep the Corinthians from reaching Sicily.

Timoleon had only ten vessels, and he knew it would be impossible to leave Rhegium unless he could in some way cheat the enemy.

So he pretended to agree to Icetes' demands, and then begged the Carthaginian generals to go with him to the assembly to tell the people what they had agreed. Meanwhile he had given orders to his fleet to be ready to sail the moment he returned.

In the assembly the generals and the people of Rhegium began to talk, and they grew so interested in what they were saying that they paid very little attention to Timoleon. The generals indeed forgot all about him, which was just what the Corinthians had hoped would happen.

By and by when the conversation seemed most engrossing, Timoleon slipped quietly out of the hall and hastened to the harbour. The moment he was on board his ship, the fleet set sail and before long reached Sicily in safety.

Without their generals, the Carthaginians had not known what to do, and while they had hesitated Timoleon had escaped. But when the Carthaginian generals found out how they had been tricked, their indignation knew no bounds.

Not far from the small town at which the Corinthians landed was a city named Adranum, where there was a temple consecrated to the god Adranus. This deity was reverenced throughout the whole island.

The city was divided into two parties, one of which sent for Icetes, the other for Timoleon, to help them each against the other.

Both generals at once set out for Adranum, Icetes with five thousand, Timoleon with only twelve hundred men. On the second day the Corinthians found that in spite of all their haste they had been outstripped by the army of Icetes. It was already encamped close to the city.

The Corinthian officers begged Timoleon to order a halt, as there seemed no need for further haste, and their men needed food and rest after their hurried march.

But Timoleon wished to take the enemy by surprise. He thought that if they did not delay they would reach Icetes and his men while they were putting up their tents and preparing supper. So instead

TIMOLEON SENDS DIONYSIUS TO CORINTH

of listening to his officers, he seized his shield, and going to the head of his army he bade them follow him and he would lead them to victory. The enemy's camp was still three and a half miles away, but the Corinthians marched on bravely.

As Timoleon had hoped, he reached the camp of the enemy while the men were getting ready a meal and were unprepared to fight.

Before they were aware of his approach, Timoleon had fallen upon them and put them to flight, taking the camp as well as many prisoners.

The people of Adranum at once opened their gates to the victorious general, and told him that when the battle began, the doors of their temple suddenly opened of their own accord. On the threshold stood their god, holding his javelin in his hand. It was trembling as though the god was weary with its weight.

Other cities, when they heard of the victory of the Corinthians, gladly entered into alliance with them.

Meanwhile Dionysius, shut up in Syracuse by Icetes, was growing tired of his position, and food was becoming scarce in the citadel. He, too, thought it would be well to make terms with Timoleon.

So he sent to the Corinthian general to offer to surrender the citadel if he would promise to send him in safety to Corinth.

When Timoleon heard this he felt more than ever sure that the gods were on his side. He gladly accepted the tyrant's offer, and at once sent two of his officers and a company of men to receive the keys of the citadel.

Dionysius treated the Corinthians well, leaving to them a number of horses, a store of weapons and two thousand soldiers. He himself escaped from the city and fled to the camp of Timoleon. Soon afterwards he set sail for Corinth.

Tidings of his arrival was sent before him, and as the ship drew near to the harbour, the people gathered there in excited groups. They had often shuddered at the tale of the cruel deeds of the man who was now coming to their city, shorn of his power. They were eager to see him.

A few weeks later they wondered if this man had really been as cruel as they had been told. They saw him contentedly loitering in the market-place or spending long hours in the shops of the perfumers, and it seemed to them as though he must always have been as harmless as he was now. In later years the tyrant is said to have taught the boys and girls of Corinth to read, and he also trained those who wished to sing in public.

Timoleon had not been fifty days in Sicily before Dionysius was on his way to Corinth. The Corinthians were so pleased with their general that they determined to send him reinforcements, both of cavalry and infantry. But it was some time before the fresh troops reached Timoleon, for the Carthaginian fleet was waiting near the coast of Italy to bar the way.

CHAPTER LXXXVI
ICETES TRIES TO SLAY TIMOLEON

THE small band of Corinthians who now held the citadel of Syracuse was closely besieged by Icetes. But soon he grew tired of waiting for it to surrender and hit, as he thought, on a quicker way of driving the enemy out of the island.

Without Timoleon he would not fear the Corinthians, so he resolved to get rid of him without delay. He hired two foreign soldiers and sent them to Adranum with orders to kill the general.

Timoleon went about without a bodyguard, as Icetes knew. When the assassins reached the city, he was in the temple, sacrificing to the gods, for it was a festival.

With their daggers hidden beneath their cloaks, the men slipped in among the crowd of worshippers and were soon standing together, close to the altar.

As they hesitated to strike the fatal blow, a sword flashed out behind, and one of them fell slain to the ground.

His companion, in his terror, forgot to kill Timoleon, and laid hold of the altar lest he too should be slain by an unseen foe.

When his terror grew a little less he did not try to obey Icetes' orders, but begged Timoleon to spare his life and he would tell him everything.

Timoleon promised that his life should be safe, and then the miserable man confessed that he and his friend had been hired by Icetes to kill the Corinthian general.

Meanwhile the stranger who had killed one of the assassins had fled to the top of a great precipice that overlooked the city. Here he was captured, and as he was hurried before Timoleon he told the guards that the man he had slain was one who years before had killed his father. He pleaded that he had done right to punish the evil-doer.

It may be that the Corinthians and the citizens of Adranum agreed with their prisoner; in any case they were so grateful that he had saved the life of Timoleon that they gave him a gift of money and set him free.

As the attack on Timoleon had failed, the Carthaginians thought they would try to frighten the citadel of Syracuse into surrendering. So they decked the masts of their ships with wreaths, and hung Grecian shields over the sides of their vessels. Then with shouts of victory they sailed toward the harbour.

From the citadel, the garrison saw the ships and heard the shouts, but it was not so easily deceived as Mago, the general of the Carthaginians, had expected. The Corinthians were sure that Timoleon would have managed to let them know had he been defeated, so they laughed at the enemy's trick and stayed safe within their walls.

Soon after this the reinforcements sent from Corinth joined Timoleon, and he then marched to Syracuse.

Mago had already begun to doubt the loyalty of Icetes. He feared that he was trying to make terms with Timoleon. When, a little later, he saw the soldiers of both generals talking together in a friendly way as they fished for eels in the marshes near the city, he grew more suspicious. Day by day his fears grew, until at length in a panic, he ordered his troops to embark and set sail for Africa.

The very day after Mago had deserted his post, Timoleon himself reached Syracuse. He looked at the empty harbour. Where was the enemy? Not a single Carthaginian vessel was to be seen.

When Timoleon learned how Mago had fled, he laughed at his cowardice, and still laughing he offered a reward to anyone who would tell him where the Carthaginians had hidden.

But although Mago had fled, Icetes and his men still held the city. But the wisdom of Timoleon and the valour of his troops soon put them to flight, and without the loss of one Corinthian soldier the city was taken.

This wonderful success was said by everyone to be due to the good fortune that followed all that Timoleon undertook.

The citizens of Syracuse thought that Timoleon would now make himself tyrant. To their surprise as well as to their joy, he proclaimed that they themselves were to govern the city. He ordered the public crier to go through the streets, bidding all those who were willing, to come with pickaxe and hammer to pull down the citadel which Dionysius had built.

The people did not need to be asked twice. With right goodwill they destroyed not only the citadel, but the palaces in which the tyrants of Syracuse had dwelt. And while they pulled down the walls, flutes sounded and women danced and sang. On the places where the palaces had stood, Timoleon ordered courts of justice to be built.

So neglected and forsaken had the city been during the rule of the tyrants, as well as during the siege, that grass was growing in the market-place, grass enough to feed the soldiers' horses.

All over Sicily, cities had been deserted, and in some of them deer and wild boars wandered up and down the streets.

Timoleon saw that if the island was to grow prosperous again, those who had fled must be brought back, and new citizens must come and settle in the different cities.

So he sent to Corinth to ask her to send out colonists to the island. This she did, and she also sent vessels to Asia to bring back to their island home those who had taken refuge there. Soon sixty thousand citizens were added to the inhabitants of Sicily.

CHAPTER LXXXVII

THE BATTLE OF CRIMISUS

THE exiles who had returned to Sicily, and the colonists who had come to settle there, were needed, not only to till the ground but to defend the island. For the Carthaginians, angry with Mago's failure, now sent to Sicily an enormous army, seventy thousand strong.

The Syracusans were frightened to see so large a force, and not more than three thousand men were willing to go with Timoleon against the enemy. He hired four thousand soldiers, but of these one thousand deserted before a battle was fought.

Near the river Crimisus the Carthaginians encamped, and thither Timoleon hastened with his faint-hearted army.

On their way they met a number of mules laden with baskets of parsley. Now the Sicilians were used to place wreaths of parsley upon the tombs of their dead, so they were sure that it was a bad omen to meet the mules, and they grew still more uneasy.

THE BATTLE OF CRIMISUS

But Timoleon laughed at their fears, telling them that in Corinth the victors at the games were crowned with chaplets of parsley. He then lifted some from the baskets, and twisting it into a wreath he placed it on his head, his officers first and then the soldiers following his example.

At that moment two eagles flew toward the army. One carried in its talons a snake, which it had killed, the other uttered loud cries as of victory. Here was a good omen! It was ever a sign of success to see an eagle, and the soldiers thanked the gods and plucked up courage.

Before long Timoleon led his men to the top of a hill that looked down on the river Crimisus. But at first he could see nothing, for a thick mist veiled the river.

The hill was still hidden from sight when the mist lifted from the river, and Timoleon saw that the Carthaginians had begun to cross to the other side, but they had no idea that the enemy was near.

Now was the time, thought Timoleon, to charge the enemy, while it was crossing the river. So bidding the trumpets sound, he seized his shield and ordered his troops to advance.

The courage of the men had returned, and with cheers they rushed down the hill and charged the Carthaginians, who, taken by surprise, yet fought bravely. They wore heavy armour and their breastplates were able to resist the thrust of the Corinthian spears. Soon the men were at close quarters with swords drawn, and a terrible struggle began.

It seemed that now one side, now the other would conquer. While the victory still hung in the balance, a violent storm broke over the battlefield.

The thunder crashed so that the orders of the officers could no longer be heard. Lightning flashed in the eyes of the startled horses and blinded them, while torrents of rain and hail dashed in the faces of the Carthaginians.

As the ground grew muddy, the soldiers slipped and fell to the ground. The Sicilians, who wore light armour, easily struggled to their feet, but their foes found it almost impossible to rise.

Soon the river overflowed its banks and swept across the battlefield. This was more than the Carthaginians could bear, and they turned and fled, but many were overtaken by the swift-footed Sicilians and slain.

The victorious army found more spoil than they had thought possible—a thousand breastplates and ten thousand shields of marvellous workmanship, as well as ornaments of gold and silver were taken.

When tidings were sent to Corinth of the great victory of Crimisus, the richest of the spoil was also sent to the city.

On the booty were written these words, "The people of Corinth and Timoleon, their general, having redeemed the Greeks of Sicily from Carthaginian bondage, make oblation of these to the gods, in grateful acknowledgement of their favour."

Sicily was now free, and the people in their gratitude begged Timoleon to become their king. But this he would not do, nor would he even keep the command of the army. His wife and children whom he had left in Corinth joined him, and for a time he lived with them in Syracuse as quietly as any other citizen. When he left the city it was to live in a beautiful country house which was given to him by the grateful people of Syracuse.

As he grew older, Timoleon's eyesight failed, and at length he became quite blind. But old and blind as he was the people did not forget all that he had done for them, and they loved and trusted him as in happier days.

If trouble arose in the assembly, they would beg him to come to give them his advice. And the old man would order his car, which was drawn by mules, and be driven to the hall. Here he would sit and listen to the troubles of the people, and when he spoke it was seldom that his words were not obeyed.

Three or four years after the battle of Crimisus, Timoleon died. The grief of the Syracusans was deep, for they had loved their deliverer well.

Thousands of men and women, clad in white and crowned with garlands, followed his body as it was carried slowly through the city, past the places where once the palaces of the tyrants had stood.

As the bier was laid on the funeral pile, a herald cried aloud, "The people of Syracuse inter Timoleon the Corinthian at the public expense and decree that his memory be honoured for ever, by games held each year, the prizes to be competed for in music, in horse-races and all sorts of bodily exercises, and this because he suppressed tyrants, overthrew the barbarian, replenished the principalities that were desolate with new inhabitants, and then restored the Sicilian Greeks to the privilege of living by their own laws."

CHAPTER LXXXVIII

DEMOSTHENES WISHES TO BECOME AN ORATOR

Demosthenes, the great Athenian orator, was born in 384 B.C. He was a shy and delicate boy, and often stammered when he spoke. Some of his companions were cruel enough to laugh at him and even to imitate his stammer. So he would often slip away from his playmates, but when they saw that he did not join in their games, they but laughed at him the more.

The father of Demosthenes was a rich man. He died when his little son was seven years old, leaving his fortune to his child. But the guardians who took charge of Demosthenes and his wealth were careless and dishonest men. Some of the boy's money they lost, some they spent on themselves.

As the child grew older, his guardians found that there was little money left to use for his education. They could not afford to get the best teachers, nor did they pay well those whom they employed. So that Demosthenes was often taught carelessly or not at all.

Of the boy's mother we are told little, save that she was kind to her delicate little son and tended him with care. But she, too, died while he was still young.

Demosthenes did not learn his lessons well or quickly, but he was interested in all that went on around him, and he soon began to distrust his guardians. Long before he was sixteen years old, he knew that they had lost his money, and even then he hoped that some day he would be able to punish them.

The boy loved the beautiful city of Athens in which he grew up. Never did he tire of gazing at the wonderful temples, the noble statues which made her renowned throughout Greece.

There were in these as in other days famous orators in Athens, to whom the citizens were ever eager to listen. For they were well pleased to be reminded of the glorious days of Thermopylæ, and of Marathon, though now they were not anxious to win glory on the battlefield. They had grown rich and indolent, and were content to stay at home, content to go to games and to theatres.

Demosthenes often heard his teachers talk of the great orators of Athens, and he wished that he might listen to their eloquent speeches.

One day Callistratus, a famous orator, was to speak at a great trial that was taking place in the city.

The boy begged to be allowed to go, and his tutor at length agreed to find a corner in the hall where the boy might sit to see and to hear all that went on.

Demosthenes could imagine no greater treat than to be there, hidden away in the midst of the crowd, to listen to Callistratus.

The speech was a great one, and when it was over the Athenians crowded round the orator, eager to applaud, while many followed him to his home. Demosthenes came away with his ambition roused. He said to himself, "I too will be an orator and make the people do as I wish. They shall applaud me, even as they have applauded Callistratus to-day."

But another reason that made him wish to speak in public was that he might expose the dishonesty of his guardians in the law courts. For he could not be content until they were punished.

When the boy had made up his mind to be an orator he lost no time in beginning to study. He knew that he must work hard if he would succeed.

For two years he read history, wrote speeches, and when it was possible, went to hear famous orators. When he was eighteen he thought that he was ready to speak in public. So he went to the law courts and accused his guardians of theft.

At first little notice was taken of what the lad said, but he pleaded his cause again and again, until at length he won his suit, and his guardians were punished. But it was too late to recover the money, which was now nearly all lost.

CHAPTER LXXXIX

DEMOSTHENES THE GREATEST ORATOR OF ATHENS

DEMOSTHENES had spoken in the law courts, but he was not content. His great ambition now was to speak in the assembly of Athens. He wished to remind the Athenians of their glorious past, he wished to encourage them to fight against the enemies of their country.

His first attempt was a failure. His voice was weak, his sentences long, and before he had finished what he wished to say, the people were laughing and jeering, so that he was forced to sit down.

As he left the assembly he was so unhappy that he thought he would never speak to the people again. He walked along the streets, scarcely knowing, in his distress, where he went.

Suddenly he felt some one touch his arm, and looking up he saw a very old man who had been in the assembly, and had heard him speak. He had seen how disappointed Demosthenes was as he left the hall, and he had determined to encourage him. So first he praised the crestfallen orator, saying that his speech had reminded him of the great orator Pericles, and then he upbraided the young man for being so easily discouraged by the laughter of the people.

Demosthenes allowed himself to be comforted and made up his mind to try again, thinking that perhaps after all he would be able to make the people listen to him. But in spite of all his efforts he could not hold their attention, and he left the assembly, hiding his face in his cloak that none might see his sorrow.

An actor, named Satyrus, who knew him well, followed him home, for he guessed that Demosthenes would be in despair. The orator did not hide his trouble from his friend. "The citizens will listen to any one, even to those who have not studied, rather than to me," he said in bitter anger. "A sailor with a foolish story will make them applaud, while if I tell them tales of the glorious deeds of their own countrymen they pay no heed."

"You say true, Demosthenes," answered Satyrus, "but I will soon tell you how this is if you will recite to me some lines from one of our great poets."

Demosthenes did as his friend asked. But although he said the words correctly, his voice was dull and his attitude was stiff and awkward.

He left the assembly, hiding his face in his cloak

Satyrus said nothing when his friend ended, but himself began to repeat the same lines. Yet you would scarcely have known that they were the same, for the eyes of the actor flashed, his voice rang clear, then sank to a whisper, his body swayed now this way, now that, as he sought to make the meaning of the poem plain.

Then Demosthenes understood as he had never done before how it was that his carefully studied speeches did not interest the Athenians. He must not only read or recite them, he must act them, so that the things of which he spoke might become real to those who listened.

From that day Demosthenes began to work in a different way. He made one of the cellars of his house into a study, that there, undisturbed, he might practise his voice and gestures. He stayed in this strange study for two or three months at a time, and lest he should be tempted to go to theatres or games, he shaved one side of his head, "that so for shame he might not go abroad, though he desired it ever so much."

At other times to strengthen his voice he would go to the seashore while a storm was raging, and putting pebbles in his mouth he would try to make his words heard above the roar of the waves. He also recited speeches while he was out of breath from running up some steep hill, and at home he would stand before a large mirror to watch his gestures and the expression of his face.

And his hard work and perseverance were rewarded, for Demosthenes became what he most desired to be, the greatest orator of Athens. His enemies learned to fear his speeches, his friends to count upon them to aid their cause.

Demosthenes was thirty-three years of age when he made his first speech against Philip of Macedon, who now, in 356 B.C., invaded Greece.

The king would gladly have made an alliance with the Athenians and gained their goodwill. But they, wishing to recover Amphipolis, which he had taken from them, refused to make peace.

Demosthenes lost no opportunity to speak against Philip. He reminded his countrymen that the king was "not the man to rest content with that he has subdued, but is always adding to his conquests, and casts his snare around us while we sit at home postponing." In another speech he told the Athenians that they chose their captains, "not to fight, but to be displayed like dolls in the market-place."

These and other speeches against the king of Macedon were called "The Philippics" of Demosthenes, and still to-day, if some one makes a speech against a special person, although his name is not Philip, we call the speech a "Philippic."

CHAPTER XC

THE SACRED WAR

PHILIP of Macedon began to reign in 359 B.C. When he was sixteen years of age he was taken by Pelopidas as a hostage to Thebes. Here he stayed for three years, reading Greek literature and learning to love it, studying Greek art and learning to admire it. The craft of war he gained from the great Theban general Epaminondas.

When Philip went back to Macedon as king, he trained his army in the movements he had first seen used by the Theban troops under their famous general.

At this time a war called the Sacred War was going on in Greece.

Delphi, where the temple of Apollo stood, had been seized by the Phocians, who were led by a bold commander named Philomelus. The home of the Phocians was near Mount Parnassus.

In the temple vast treasures had been stored; these, said Philomelus, should be safe as of old. But when he fortified the city and brought a large army of soldiers to guard it, the other Greek states said it was time to interfere—that Delphi must be taken from the Phocians.

Philomelus at once resolved to increase his army, but he had no money to pay more soldiers. The Phocians had already spent all that they possessed on the war, and the citizens of Delphi had been so heavily taxed that they could give no more.

Money Philomelus must have! So he began to borrow from the treasures of the temple, which he had promised should be untouched. As the war went on he took more gold, more of the sacred treasures, none of which he was able to replace.

When the Thebans and their allies met Philomelus, he and his hired troops were soon put to flight. Philomelus fled alone to the top of a precipice, pursued by the enemy. He must either leap into the awful abyss or be captured by the angry soldiers. In a moment he had made his choice, and when the Thebans reached the spot where he had been seen but a second before, he was no longer there.

But other leaders replaced Philomelus, and they too rifled the temple of Apollo.

At length the Phocians grew so bold that they determined to attack Philip of Macedon who had invaded Thessaly, and drive him from Greek territory. They forced the king to return to Macedon, but he soon came back with a large army and the Phocians retreated to the famous pass of Thermopylæ. They hoped that Athens would help them to hold the pass against Philip, but in spite of the Philippics of Demosthenes, she did nothing.

Alone, the Phocians were not strong enough to resist Philip's attack, and they were forced to surrender. The pass, which the king had long resolved to gain, was in his hand.

When the Athenians heard of the disaster they were dismayed, and when Demosthenes again urged them to take up arms against the invaders, his appeal was not made in vain.

In August 338 B.C. the united army of Athenians and Thebans marched against the Macedonians, and met them in the plain of Chæronea, where a great battle was fought.

Philip's famous son Alexander, who was then only eighteen years old, was in command of one of the wings of the Macedonian army. Young as he was, it was his attack upon the Sacred Band of Thebans that determined the battle.

The Sacred Band fought to the last, and was cut down where it stood. Soon the rest of the Greek army fled from the fatal field, Demosthenes, who was among the foot soldiers, taking flight with his comrades.

On the roadside, not far from the town of Chæronea and near to Thebes, is a tomb, where the fallen heroes of the Sacred Band were laid.

Standing over the tomb is the statue of a lion, now partly in ruins, which was placed there as though to protect the bodies of the slain.

The victory of Philip at Chæronea left Athens, and indeed all Greece, at the mercy of the king, and he treated her well. His chief ambition was to conquer the kingdom of Persia, and the army he meant to lead against the great king was to be made up of Greeks as well as of Macedonians.

But in 336 B.C., before his plans could be carried out, Philip was murdered.

When Greece heard the tidings she rejoiced, for now again she hoped to be free. None was more glad than Demosthenes, for he, as you know, had always been a bitter enemy of the king.

The orator was wearing black clothes at the time, because he had but lately lost his daughter. When he heard that Philip had been murdered, he put them away and clad himself in gay garments, while he placed a wreath upon his head.

Only one Athenian was found to reprove the Athenians for their hasty and foolish joy.

Phocion, who was both a general and an orator, said gravely, "Nothing shows greater meanness of spirit than expressions of joy at the death of an enemy. Remember that the army you fought at Chæronea is lessened by only one man."

CHAPTER XCI

ALEXANDER AND BUCEPHALUS

ALEXANDER, the son of Philip of Macedon, became king in 336 B.C. The queen-mother adored her brave son and dreamed of the great things he would do when he became a man. She did all she could to awake his ambition, telling him that he was descended from Achilles, the hero of Troy, and bidding him, when he was older, strive to do nobler deeds than his great ancestor had done. One of his tutors called the young prince Achilles, while he named himself Phoenix, after the tutor of the old Greek hero.

The Iliad of Homer, which tells of the deeds of Achilles, Alexander knew by heart. When he was a man he always carried a copy with him on his campaigns. It is said that he slept with it as well as his sword beneath his pillow.

Alexander might almost have been a Spartan boy, so simple was his training. He learned to ride, to race, to swim, but he never cared to wrestle as did most lads of his time. Nor would he offer prizes for such contests at the games which were held each year.

When the prince was asked if he would run in the Olympic games, for he was fleet of foot, he answered, "Yes, if I could have kings to race with me."

Even as a lad he was eager to win glory, and when he heard of a great victory gained by his royal father, or of a town that had been subdued by him, he was more sorry than glad, and said to his companions, "My father will make so many conquests that there will be nothing left for me to win."

One day, while Alexander was still a boy, a Greek from Thessaly arrived at the court of Macedon, bringing with him a noble horse, named Bucephalus, which he offered to sell for £2600.

Philip went with his son and his courtiers to look at the horse and to test its powers. But when any one approached or tried to mount, Bucephalus reared and kicked, and became so unmanageable that the king, growing angry, bade the Thessalian take the animal away.

The prince had been watching the horse keenly, and as he was being led away, the lad exclaimed, "What an excellent horse do they lose for want of skill and courage to manage him!"

Philip heard what his son said, but at first he took no notice of his words. But when the prince said the same thing again and again, he looked at

Alexander, and saw that he was really sorry that the horse was being sent away.

Then, half mocking, the king said, "Do you reproach those who are older than yourself, as if you knew more and were better able to manage him than they?"

"I could manage the horse better than others have done," answered the prince.

"And if you fail what will you forfeit?" asked the king.

"I will pay the whole price of the horse," said Alexander quickly.

The courtiers laughed at the confidence of the prince, but paying no attention to them, he ran toward the horse and seizing the bridle turned Bucephalus, so that he faced the sun. For the prince had noticed that the steed was afraid of his own shadow as it flitted backward and forward with his every movement.

After speaking quietly to the horse and patting him, the prince flung aside the mantle he was wearing, and nimbly mounted on his back. Using neither whip nor spur, he let the animal choose his own pace. And Bucephalus was content to go at a quiet trot.

Gradually Alexander urged him on to a gallop, with voice and spur. As the pace grew quicker and quicker, the king looked on in fear lest the lad should be thrown. But when he saw that the horse was well

He ran toward the horse and seized the bridle

ALEXANDER AND BUCEPHALUS

under control, and that Alexander had turned and was coming back, he burst into tears of joy, while the courtiers loudly applauded the prince.

As he leaped from the horse, Philip kissed him and said, "O my son, look thee out a kingdom equal to and worthy of thyself, for Macedon is too little for thee."

Soon after this the king sent for a famous philosopher, named Aristotle, to teach his son.

Alexander was quick to learn, and his eager interest in his studies pleased Aristotle. In after days, when the prince had become king and was adding kingdom after kingdom to his possessions, he wrote to his old tutor, "I assure you I had rather excel others in the knowledge of what is excellent than in the extent of my power and dominions."

When Philip was murdered, Alexander was twenty years of age, "a stripling," Demosthenes said, making light of his youth. But had Demosthenes known the character of the prince, he would not have spoken thus slightingly of his years.

The orator not only rejoiced when Philip was murdered, but he urged the people to rouse themselves and throw off the yoke of Macedon. The old days when the Athenians would not listen to Demosthenes were long past. Now his matchless eloquence could hold them spellbound, even when they refused to be guided by his advice. But in Athens, as in many other cities, discontent had long been smouldering, and fanned by his words it broke out into a blaze.

The young king found that he must put down rebellion in Greece before he set out, as he wished to do, to conquer Persia.

CHAPTER XCII

ALEXANDER AND DIOGENES

WHEN Alexander marched at the head of his army into Thessaly, not a blow was struck. His presence seemed enough to gain the allegiance of the Thessalians.

The king then went to Corinth, where ambassadors from many of the Greek states met him. Young as he was, they chose Alexander to be general over the Greek troops which were to go with the Macedonians to invade Asia.

Every one in Corinth was eager to see the king. From the surrounding towns, too, the people crowded into the city, that they might look at the young monarch who was going to lead their soldiers on so great an expedition.

They did not dream of all that he would do, how he would spread their customs, their language, their culture over Asia first, and then over all the world. But looking at him they knew that he would be a conqueror.

Among those who wished to see Alexander were many philosophers and great men. But one strange philosopher, called Diogenes, showed no interest in the king.

Alexander heard of this man, who was said to sit all day in a tub or barrel. As Diogenes did not come to see him, he resolved to go to see Diogenes. He found the philosopher outside the gates of Corinth, sitting in a tub which was placed so that the rays of the sun fell upon him.

When the philosopher saw the king and the courtiers who accompanied him, he roused himself from his meditations and looked at the young sovereign.

Alexander spoke kindly to him, and asked if there was anything he wished.

"Yes," answered Diogenes, "I would have you not stand between me and the sun."

The couriers were indignant at such an answer, but Alexander laughed, and being pleased with the philosopher's indifference to his rank, he said to them, "If I were not Alexander, I should like to be Diogenes."

Soon after this the king, believing that he had secured the fealty of Greece, went back to Macedon. In the spring of 335 B.C. he hoped to set out to invade Asia.

But the wild tribes on the borders of Macedon began to be restless, and the king was forced to subdue these foes nearer home before he went to

Asia. While he was driving them beyond his borders, a rumour that he was dead reached Greece.

If Alexander was dead it was a good chance, thought the Thebans, to drive the Macedonians from their citadel, and without waiting to find out if the rumour was true they revolted. Demosthenes tried to persuade the Athenians to go to the help of the Thebans, but although his eloquence moved them it had not power to make them act.

The Thebans soon found to their cost that Alexander was not dead. He was, indeed, on his way to Greece to punish them for revolting.

Outside the walls of their city he halted, so that the citizens might submit, if so they willed. But they, still dreaming of liberty, refused to surrender.

Then Alexander attacked the city and captured it with little difficulty. He determined to give the other cities in Greece a lesson by punishing the rebels severely. So he pulled down their houses and utterly destroyed their town, leaving untouched only the temples, and a house in which a great poet named Pindar had dwelt.

Demosthenes was bitterly disappointed that the Athenians had not sent to help the Thebans. He feared, too, that Alexander would now march against Athens, and destroy her as he had destroyed Thebes. But the king only sent to demand that eight of the orators who had done their best to incite the people to rebel against him, should be sent to him as hostages.

Demosthenes would have been among the eight, and he urged the Athenians not to "hand over their sheep-dogs to the wolf." But Phocion said that it would be wise to do as Alexander asked.

At length the assembly sent Damocles to the king to plead the cause of his comrades, for he was, after Demosthenes, the greatest orator in Athens.

Alexander listened to Damocles and was persuaded to leave the orators in their own city, for he believed that the fate of Thebes would make Athens afraid to rebel.

Of the loyalty of the Greek troops the king was sure, for were they not going to avenge the invasion of Greece by Xerxes?

The king did not mean to return to Macedon to reign, rather did he dream of a throne in one of the great cities which he was going to conquer. So before he marched away, he divided his royal domain and his wealth among his friends.

Perdiccas, one of his friends, was dismayed at the generosity of the king, and asked him what he was keeping for himself.

"Hope," answered Alexander. Then Perdiccas refused to accept his share of the king's gifts, saying, "We who go forth to fight with you need share only in your hope."

Antipater, one of his father's generals, Alexander left in Macedon to look after his kingdom.

At length in the spring of 334 B.C., after saying good-bye to his mother, whom he dearly loved, the king marched with an enormous force to the Hellespont and crossed it. The great expedition had really begun.

CHAPTER XCIII

THE BATTLE OF GRANICUS

BEFORE Alexander crossed the Hellespont he had seen that the opposite shore was held by his Macedonians. While the army landed he himself sailed to the "Harbour of the Achæans." Midway in the strait he took a golden dish in his hand, and flung from it an offering to Poseidon and to the Nereids. It is said that the king himself steered the ship in which he sailed to the Mysian shore.

Crossing the plain of Troy, the king climbed the hill of Ilion, and here in a forsaken little town he found a temple to Athene, to whom he offered sacrifice. He left his own armour in the temple, taking in its place an ancient suit that had once been hung upon the walls, a trophy of war.

On the tomb of his ancestor, Achilles, he laid a garland, while Hephæstion, his beloved friend, placed one on the grave of Patroclus. The old Greek stories had entered into the very fibre of the young king, and in this way he did honour, as he deemed,

THE BATTLE OF GRANICUS

to his glorious ancestor. He felt ready now to do deeds as great as his hero had done.

When Alexander rejoined his army, it had advanced to the river Granicus, and there, on the opposite bank, was a great force under Darius, king of Persia. Alexander would have to conquer this great host before he could advance into Asia.

One of his officers, named Parmenio, begged the king to wait to cross the river until early the next morning, when the enemy would not be drawn up in battle array.

"I should be ashamed," answered the king, "having crossed the Hellespont to be detained by a miserable stream like the Granicus." He then ordered the army to advance, and himself dashed into the river, followed by his horseguards.

The Granicus was not a river to be despised, for the current was strong, and the horses kept their feet with difficulty.

A storm of arrows was poured upon the struggling horses and their riders, and it seemed as though the attempt to cross in the face of the foe would be useless. But the king refused to be daunted, and the soldiers followed their intrepid leader, until at length they reached the opposite bank.

But to clamber up the bank was no easy matter. The sides of the river were slippery, and the horses having no firm foothold, stumbled and fell. Only after great and repeated efforts did Alexander and those who followed him reach the top of the bank. Wet and exhausted, they had no time to form their ranks before the Persians dashed upon them. A desperate hand-to-hand fight was at once begun.

The enemy was quick to notice Alexander, for he wore a large plume of white feathers in his helmet, while his buckler was more splendid than that of any of his soldiers.

Two Persian officers, wishing to win the glory of having killed the king, attacked him together. One of them, riding close to Alexander, rose in his stirrups, and brought his battle-axe down with all his strength upon the helmet of the king. So fierce was the blow that the crest was torn away along with one of the plumes, while the axe cut its way through the helmet, until the edge touched Alexander's hair.

Again the officer raised his axe, but ere he could strike, Clitus, the foster-brother of Alexander, slew the officer with his sword and the king was saved.

The famous phalanx of the Macedonians now threw itself upon the enemy, and the Persians tried in vain to repel the fierceness of the attack. Soon the whole army was put to flight, all save a band of Greek soldiers who were fighting for Darius.

These withdrew to a height above the battlefield, and sent to Alexander to ask for quarter. But the king refused their request, and ordered his men to attack the little company.

THE BATTLE OF GRANICUS

The Greeks fought desperately, and Alexander lost more men in this struggle than he had lost in all the rest of the battle. His horse, which was not the famous Bucephalus, was killed on the field.

While in this great battle, fought in 334 B.C. on the banks of the Granicus, the Persians lost a great number of men, only thirty-four Macedonians, it is said, were slain.

The spoil was enormous, and Alexander determined that the Greeks should have a generous share. To Athens he sent three hundred Persian bucklers to be offered to Athene, with these words inscribed, "Alexander, son of Philip, and the Grecians, except the Lacedæmonians, won these from the barbarians who inhabit Asia."

Athens accepted the king's offering to their goddess, but they churlishly refused to send ships to help him to conquer the coast towns which he must now attack.

While dividing the spoil of the Granicus, Alexander did not forget his mother. To her he sent all the plate he had taken, as well as beautiful cloth of wonderful purple dye. For himself he kept but little.

CHAPTER XCIV

THE GORDIAN KNOT

AFTER the battle of Granicus, many Persian towns submitted to the conqueror. Those along the coast of Asia Minor that refused to open their gates, the king quickly subdued.

During the winter he reached a city called Gordion, about which a strange story is told.

In the citadel of Gordion was an old, roughly built wagon, which had once belonged to a peasant named Gordius. Long, long ago Gordius had ridden into the town in his wagon, and the oracle had declared that this peasant had been chosen by the gods to be king of Phrygia, in which country Gordion stood.

When Gordius was made king, almost the first thing he did was to dedicate his wagon to the gods, tying the yoke to the pole with fibre taken from the bark of a tree. The Gordian knot, as it was named, was twisted and tangled in a bewildering way, and looked as though it would defy the most

THE GORDIAN KNOT

skilful fingers to untie. Yet an oracle had said that whoever should succeed in undoing this wonderful knot would become king over all Asia.

Many men who wished to wear a crown came to Gordion to try to undo the knot, but not one of them had been able to unravel the twisted fibre.

When Alexander, with his victorious army, rode into Gordion, every one wondered if the king would be able to untie the famous knot.

Alexander was not long in going to see the ancient wagon. He looked at the puzzling knot and soon saw that he would not be able to untie it.

But he did not mean to be beaten. He would solve the problem in his own way. So taking his sword in his impatient hands, with one swift stroke he cut the formidable knot in two.

The onlookers, both Phrygians and Macedonians, shouted with delight for lo! the oracle was fulfilled, and Alexander would become monarch of Asia.

As the knot was cut in twain, a great thunderstorm raged over the town, and the people said, "It is Zeus who sends the storm to show that he is pleased that the prophecy is fulfilled."

While Alexander had been conquering the towns along the coast of Asia, Darius had been gathering together another great army, which numbered, so it was said, six hundred thousand men. The king himself commanded the vast army, and in the spring of 333 B.C. he set out to find Alexander.

Darius was not a skilful general, nor was he a brave king, but he had no doubt that he would conquer Alexander.

When Alexander still lingered in one of the coast towns, Darius deemed that it was cowardice that kept him there, so little did he know of the character of his foe. It was illness alone that kept Alexander from advancing against the great king.

Some said that it was the hardships of the battlefield that had made the king ill, others that while he was still heated after a long march he had bathed in a river, the waters of which were very cold.

To the dismay of his soldiers, who adored their brave leader, the king grew worse and worse. He was so ill that it seemed that he must die.

His physicians were afraid to give the king medicine, for should he die they would be accused of giving him poison.

At length one of the physicians, named Philip, to whom Alexander had shown great kindness, determined that whatever happened to him, he would do his utmost to save the king's life.

Alexander himself was content to take what Philip ordered, so impatient was he to be well and at the head of his army once again.

So Philip left the king for a few moments to prepare the medicine that he believed would cure him.

While he was absent, a letter was brought to Alexander from his officer Parmenio. It besought the king not to trust Philip, as he had been bribed by Darius to poison him. Vast sums of money and the hand of the great king's daughter, said Parmenio, were to be the reward of the physician.

When Alexander had read the letter, he put it under his pillow, showing it to no one, not even to his beloved friend Hephæstion. He had no sooner done so than Philip returned with the medicine. The king took it without hesitation. Then, drawing the letter from beneath his pillow, he bade his physician read it.

Philip was horrified as he read the false accusation, and flinging himself down by the bed, he entreated the king to trust him and to fear nothing.

The drug was a powerful one, and after taking it the king was unconscious for hours. His nurses whispered to one another that he was dead.

But after a time he opened his eyes, weak indeed, but no longer in danger. Philip tended him until his strength returned, and he was at length able to go out to show himself to his Macedonians. For they had been in constant fear lest aught should befall their king, and nothing would satisfy them until they had seen his face.

CHAPTER XCV

DARIUS GALLOPS FROM THE BATTLEFIELD

As soon as he had recovered from his illness, Alexander led his army to meet Darius. He found the great king in the pass of Issus, in October 333 B.C.

Darius had first encamped on the plain of Issus, in a strong position, where his vast army would have had room to fight.

But he dreamed that Alexander would try to escape him, so he ordered his men to march through the narrow mountain passes to meet the enemy.

A Macedonian, who had deserted, begged Darius not to leave the plain. "But," said the king, "if I stay here, Alexander will escape me."

"That fear is needless," answered the Macedonian, "for assure yourself that far from avoiding you, he will make all speed to meet you, and is now most likely on his march toward you."

DARIUS GALLOPS FROM THE BATTLEFIELD

When Alexander knew that Darius had left the plain for the pass of Issus, he was pleased, for he knew that the enemy would now be hemmed in between the mountains and the sea.

Before long the two armies were close together. Alexander led his right wing against the left wing of the Persians. Here he was soon victorious, and free to attack the centre of the enemy, where Darius sat in his chariot, surrounded by a band of Persian nobles.

As the great king saw Alexander and his followers drawing nearer and nearer, he began to grow afraid. Soon he could bear his fears no longer, and leaping from his chariot, he mounted a horse and fled from the field.

When the Persians saw that their king had fled, they stayed to fight no longer. Even the cavalry, which had withstood every attack, now wavered, then broke and fled with the rest.

The great hosts sought to hide themselves from their pursuers among the mountain passes, but thousands were captured and slain.

Darius in his haste had left his shield and his royal cloak behind, but he would not stay to recover them. On and on he fled until he reached a town on the river Euphrates.

Alexander was well pleased with his great victory, but he would fain have captured the Persian king. To a wound in his thigh he paid little attention, nor did it prove dangerous. But it made it impossible for him to overtake Darius.

When the king returned from the pursuit of his enemy, he found his men pillaging the Persian camp. The tent of Darius, which was beautifully furnished, and which also had a great store of gold and silver, was set apart for Alexander himself.

"Let us now cleanse ourselves from the toils of war in the baths of Darius," said the king as he entered the tent of the defeated monarch.

"Not so," answered one of his followers, "but in Alexander's rather; for the property of the conquered is and should be called the conqueror's."

Alexander's early training had been simple as that of a Spartan, and the luxury of the great king's tents amazed him.

In one there were numerous baths and many boxes of ointment, in another a table was spread for a magnificent feast. As Alexander looked at it all, he turned to his followers and said, "This, it seems, is royalty."

But his early training still influenced him, and he kept his simple tastes and cared little for dainty fare or other luxuries.

Once a queen to whom Alexander had been kind sent to his tent, day by day, some of the dishes which had been prepared for her own table. And at length, that he might always fare well, she sent cooks and bakers.

But the king would not accept them, for he said that his old tutor had given him the best possible cooks. They were, "a night march to prepare for breakfast, and a moderate breakfast to create an appetite for supper."

He told the queen, too, how when he was a boy his tutor Leonidas used to look often in his wardrobe, lest his clothes were too fine, and in his room, to see that his mother had not given him cushions for his couch or soft pillows for his bed.

As Alexander sat down to supper on the evening of the victory of Issus, the sound of wailing and weeping fell upon his ear. It seemed to him as the weeping of women, and he demanded to be told at once who was in trouble.

His officers said that it was the mother, and wife and children of Darius who were weeping. For they had heard that Alexander had returned with their lord's shield and cloak, and they thought that he must have been slain.

Then the king bade one of his followers go tell the royal mourners that Darius lived, and that they need fear no harm from Alexander. For he made war upon Darius not because he bore him ill will, but because he wished to gain his dominions. He promised that he would provide them with all the comforts which they had been used to receive from the great king.

When Darius was safe beyond the Euphrates, he remembered that his wife and mother had been left to the mercy of his conqueror. So he wrote to

Alexander, begging that they might be sent to him and offering to make a treaty with the king.

Here is part of the proud answer that Alexander sent to Darius.

"I am lord of all, Darius," he wrote, "and therefore do thou come to me with thy requests. Thou hast only to come to me to ask and receive thy mother and wife and children, and whatever else thou mayest desire. And for the future, whenever thou sendest, send to me as to the great king of Asia, and do not write as to an equal, but tell me whatever thy need be, as to one who is lord of all that is thine. Otherwise I will deal with thee as with an offender. But if thou disputest the kingdom, then wait and fight for it again, and do not flee; for I will march against thee, wheresoever thou mayest be."

CHAPTER XCVI

TYRE IS STORMED BY ALEXANDER

ALEXANDER did not cross the Euphrates in search of Darius. He knew that the great king could do him no harm, even should he again assemble a large army. So for a time he left Darius to do as he pleased, while he himself went on with his own plan.

Nearly all the towns in Syria were ready to open their gates to Alexander. Some that had found Darius a hard master, hailed him as a deliverer.

Tyre alone, while saying that she was ready to do as the king willed, refused to receive either a Persian or a Macedonian into the city.

Alexander wished to offer sacrifice to the deity of Tyre, whose temple was within the city, and when the people refused to open their gates, he was so angry that he at once laid siege to the town.

Tyre stood on an island, about half a mile from the mainland. Near the coast the water was shallow, while close to the walls of the city it was deep.

The Tyrians believed that they could hold their city against Alexander, for the walls were built high, on the top of a steep and dangerous cliff.

As the king had no fleet, he could not attack the city until he had built a causeway from the mainland to the island, so he ordered his men to begin the work without delay.

But when the causeway stretched almost to the island, the Tyrians did all that they could to hinder the workmen. They sent among them showers of arrows, and hurled down upon them great pieces of rock, so that they found it impossible to complete the causeway.

But the king was not easily beaten. He ordered the men to build towers along the causeway, and to tie leather screens from one tower to another, so that they might be protected from the arrows and missiles of the enemy.

Then the Tyrians dragged a ship, loaded with dry wood, as near to the causeway as they dared to venture, and set it on fire. The towers were soon in flames, and while the Macedonians tried in vain to extinguish them, the enemy never ceased to send showers of arrows among the unfortunate men, so that many of them lost their lives.

Although the Tyrians had destroyed the work of months, Alexander still refused to give in. He now sent to the cities round about, and bade them send ships to guard his soldiers until the causeway was finished. In seven months from the time it was begun, the causeway reached to the foot of the rock on which the city stood.

In July 332 B.C. a breach was made in the wall, and, led by Alexander himself, the Macedonians rushed in triumph into the city that had so long defied them.

The Tyrians fought fiercely, for they knew they need not look for mercy if the city was taken. But they were soon overpowered, and the town was given up to plunder. The soldiers were eager for spoil, but spoil alone could not satisfy them. As they thought of the weary months which they had spent in trying to reach the island, they wreaked their rage on the miserable citizens, massacring all on whom they could lay their hands.

After Tyre had fallen, Alexander was master of Syria, and could control the eastern Mediterranean.

From Tyre, the king marched southward until he reached Egypt. Here, after making himself lord of the country, he founded the city, which is still called after him, Alexandria.

During the siege of Tyre, Darius had again sent to Alexander, offering to him a large ransom for his family, as well as the hand of the daughter and all the provinces west of Euphrates.

While Alexander and his generals were talking over the offer of Darius, Parmenio exclaimed, "If I were you I should accept these terms."

"And I," answered the king, "would accept them if I were Parmenio."

To Darius, Alexander's reply was haughtier than ever. "If thou comest," so ran his words, "and yield thyself up into my power, I will treat thee with all possible kindness; if not, I will come myself to seek thee."

Soon after this the wife of Darius died. Alexander had always treated her well, and now he buried her with great honour.

One of her servants fled to Darius to tell him the sad tidings. He told him, too, of the kindness Alexander had ever shown to his royal captive.

"O king," said the servant, "neither your queen when alive, nor your mother, nor children wanted anything of their former happy condition, unless it were the light of your countenance. And after her decease, Statira, the queen, had not only all due funeral ornaments, but was honoured also with the tears of your very enemies; for Alexander is as gentle after victory as he is terrible in the field."

CHAPTER XCVII

THE BATTLE OF GAUGAMELA

It was now almost two years since the battle of Issus, and Alexander determined once more to meet Darius, who had again assembled a large army.

In the spring of 331 B.C. the king went back to Tyre, and by August he had reached Thapsacus, a town on the banks of the river Euphrates. He wished to go on to Babylon, the capital of the Persian empire, but the direct way to the city, which was down the Euphrates, was guarded by Cyrus with a large army. So Alexander struck off across the north of Mesopotamia, and reaching the Tigris marched along the river on the eastern side. Above Nineveh he crossed to the other bank, and after marching southward for several days, he heard that Darius was encamped on a plain near Gaugamela, on the river Bumodus.

Even to the brave Macedonian generals, the vast hosts of the Persians looked formidable.

Parmenio looking at them begged the king to surprise the enemy by a night attack rather than risk a battle in daylight.

"I will not steal a victory," answered Alexander.

The night before the battle the king slept soundly, as though nothing preyed upon his mind. In the morning his generals found him still fast asleep, so without disturbing him they themselves bade the soldiers have breakfast.

At length Parmenio went to wake the king, and having with difficulty roused him, he asked how it was possible he could sleep so soundly when the most important battle of his life had to be fought that day.

"You slept, sire, as though you were already victorious," said the anxious general.

"Are we not so indeed," answered the king, "since we are at last relieved from the trouble of wandering in pursuit of Darius, through a wide and wasted country, hoping in vain that he would fight us?"

Alexander, who was already dressed, now put on his helmet, which was of iron, yet so polished was it that it shone as silver. Great skill had been lavished on the decoration of his belt, which was indeed the most splendid part of his dress. He then ordered his army to be drawn up in battle array, while he mounted Bucephalus, who was old now, yet eager for battle.

Before the king gave the signal to attack, he stretched out his right hand to heaven, and called upon the gods to defend and strengthen the Greeks, if he indeed were the son of Zeus.

By the side of Alexander rode a soothsayer, clad in a white robe and wearing on his head a crown of gold. He pointed to the sky, and the soldiers looking up saw an eagle flying over the king's head and on toward the Persian army. "It is a good omen," they cried, and shouted to be led at once against the foe.

A moment later the order was given, and the Macedonians rushed upon the great hosts of the enemy.

Darius thought that his war-chariots would cause deadly havoc among his enemies, for scythes were fastened to the wheels to mow down all who came within reach.

But the Macedonian archers drew their bows and sped their arrows among the charioteers, while the strongest seized the reins of the horses, and pulled the drivers from their seats. Then the soldiers opened wide their ranks so that those chariots that still had drivers rattled harmlessly past them.

Alexander was already attacking the centre of the Persian army, where, as at the battle of Issus, Darius sat in his chariot, looking on at the struggle.

All at once he saw Alexander with his chosen companions drawing nearer and nearer, and once again his courage failed. Fiercer and fiercer raged the battle, closer and closer drew Alexander to the Persian king.

The horsemen grouped in front of Darius were driven backward and fled, all save the bravest who never flinched, but fell in a supreme effort to keep the enemy from approaching any nearer to the king's chariot.

Even as they fell they still tried to keep back the foe, clinging desperately to the legs of the horses as they galloped over their wounded bodies.

Darius was in immediate danger of being captured. In vain the driver tried to turn the royal chariot, the bodies of the fallen soldiers would not allow the wheels to move. The horses plunged and kicked in an agony of fear, and the charioteer was helpless.

Then, as the king had done on the field of Issus, he did now. He leaped from the chariot, mounted a horse and fled from the battlefield.

Alexander followed the king in swift pursuit; it seemed impossible that he could escape. But Parmenio, who was commanding the left wing, was almost overpowered by the enemy. He sent a messenger to overtake Alexander, and beg him for help.

The king reluctantly gave up his pursuit of Darius, and rode back with his companions to give his general the help he had entreated. But by the time he reached the left wing his aid was no longer needed. Parmenio had wrestled victory from the foe.

So the king again set out in pursuit of Darius, but all that he captured was the chariot, the shield and the bow of the coward king.

CHAPTER XCVIII

ALEXANDER BURNS PERSEPOLIS

THE battle of Gaugamela in 331 B.C. decided the fate of the Persian empire. Darius was no longer the great king, for Alexander took the title as well as the dominions of his foe.

At Babylon, to which city Alexander now marched, the gates were thrown open to welcome him, the people coming out to meet the conqueror, led by their priests.

Alexander received them kindly, and bade the Babylonians not be afraid still to worship their own national god.

Here, in this great city, the king dreamed that he would set up his throne. Babylon should be the capital of his new empire.

Not far from Babylon was the city of Susa, where the Persian kings usually spent the winter months. Susa also surrendered to the great king without a blow being struck.

ALEXANDER BURNS PERSEPOLIS

There were many treasures and much gold in both Babylon and Susa; perhaps the most wonderful treasure was a piece of purple cloth, which was worth an enormous sum of money. Although it had been laid aside for one hundred and ninety years, yet its marvellous colour was as perfect as it had ever been.

The spoils for which the Greeks cared most were some that had been carried away by Xerxes. Among those that they found at Susa were statues of Harmodius and Aristogeiton. By the order of Alexander, they were now sent back to Athens.

But even greater treasures than any the king had yet found were stored in palaces hidden among the highlands of Persia. To these palaces Alexander resolved to march, although the way led through narrow mountain passes which were guarded by a Persian army.

By attacking the enemy both in the front and in the rear, Alexander caught the Persians in a trap. They were speedily cut to pieces or fell down the dangerous mountain tracks in a vain effort to escape.

Then unhindered by any foe, the king marched on to one of the great cities of the Persian kings, which the Greeks called Persepolis, or "the richest of all the cities under the sun."

So great were the treasures stored in the palace of Persepolis, that ten thousand pairs of mules and five thousand camels were needed to carry them away.

For four months Alexander lingered in the city. His soldiers were proud indeed of their king when for the first time they saw him sitting under a canopy of gold on the throne of the Persian monarchs.

A Corinthian, who was a great friend of Alexander's, exclaimed at the sight, "How unfortunate are those Greeks who have died without beholding Alexander seated on the throne of Darius!"

Before he left Persepolis to go in search of Darius, Alexander gave a great feast.

It was then that the king, urged by the excited revellers, allowed the palace to be burned.

With a wreath of flowers on his head and a lighted torch in his hand, the king, followed by his guests, surrounded the palace, and set light to it. The soldiers also seized torches and amid shouts and merriment they, too, helped to destroy the palace of the Persian kings.

The Macedonians thought that the burning of the palace was a sign that Alexander did not mean to dwell among the barbarians, and they rejoiced. For they were growing weary of marching into unknown countries, and they were beginning to think wistfully of their homeland.

Alexander was soon sorry for the wild impulse which had seized him, and he gave orders to put out the fire as speedily as might be.

The officers in Alexander's army had become rich with the spoils of conquered cities, and the king found that they were growing as fond of ease and luxury as the Persians. Their tables were loaded with delicacies, servants attended to their slightest wish. One officer even had his shoes made with silver nails.

Such indulgence annoyed the king and he reproved his officers, telling them that toil was more honourable than pleasure.

"How is it possible," he said, "if you cannot attend to your own body, that you look well after your horse, or keep your armour bright and in good order? You should surely avoid the weaknesses of those you have conquered."

To set his army an example, the king now began to hunt more than was his custom and with less care for his own safety. When the soldiers were sent against an enemy, Alexander himself went with them, and endured the same hardships and dangers as his men.

CHAPTER XCIX

ALEXANDER SLAYS HIS FOSTER-BROTHER

EARLY in 330 B.C. Alexander left Persepolis to go in search of Darius.

After a long and difficult march of three hundred miles, to which his soldiers took only eleven days, the king heard that Darius had passed the defile called the "Caspian Gates." For five days he allowed his men, who were utterly exhausted, to rest, before he again started in pursuit of the fugitive.

After passing through the Caspian Gates, Alexander heard that Bessus, a kinsman of Darius, who was also his officer or satrap, had made him a prisoner. Loaded with chains, Darius was being carried away to the district over which Bessus ruled.

This made the king the more determined to reach the unfortunate captive. For four days he hurried on until at length he reached a village where Bessus and his men had stayed the evening before.

He was told that the satrap was going to make a forced march that night.

The king learned of a shorter road, by which he might overtake the fugitives, but there was no water to be found on the way. Alexander did not hesitate. With only a small company he set out the same evening, and when morning dawned he had ridden forty-five miles. The fugitives were now within sight.

When the barbarians who were with Bessus saw the king in the distance they fled. The satrap quickly took the chains off his captive, bidding him mount a horse and follow them. When Darius refused he stabbed him and rode away, leaving the wretched king to die or to fall into the hands of his enemy.

A few Macedonians who were riding in front of the king reached the wounded man first, and gave him water, for which he begged. Darius then lay back and before Alexander arrived, he had breathed his last.

The king looked at his fallen foe with pity, and then flung over him his own cloak. His body he sent to the queen-mother, that it might be buried beside the other Persian kings at Persepolis.

Bessus was betrayed into the hands of Alexander not long afterwards. Naked and chained he was placed on the road by which Alexander's army must pass.

The king stopped when he reached the satrap, and asked him why he had murdered Darius, who had always treated him well.

Bessus answered that he did it to win Alexander's favour.

His reply won no pity from the king, who ordered him to be scourged and sent to prison. Some time after he was brought to trial and sentenced to a cruel death.

Until now Alexander had lived almost as simply as when he was a lad, and but lately he had reproved his officers for their indolent and luxurious habits. Now he gradually began to adopt the customs of the East. He dressed in purple and surrounded himself with Persian courtiers, and acted as though he was indeed a descendant of the gods. The Macedonians were quick to take offence at the favour their king showed to the Persians.

Philotas, a son of Parmenio, resented the king's deeds, more perhaps than any other of his generals. He was proud and his haughty ways had made his men dislike him.

Parmenio would sometimes say to him, "My son, to be not quite so great would be better." But Philotas would take no notice of the rebuke.

One day he declared that but for him and his father, the king would never have conquered Asia. "Yet it is he, the boy Alexander who enjoys the glory of the victories and the title of king," said the foolish officer.

ALEXANDER SLAYS HIS FOSTER-BROTHER

Alexander was told of the boastful way in which Philotas had spoken, but he neither reproved nor punished him.

A little later a plot was made against his life, and Philotas would not allow those who wished to warn the king to enter his presence. Then Alexander, who knew of this also, ordered Philotas to be seized and imprisoned.

He was tried before an assembly of Macedonians and confessed that he had known of the plot to kill the king, and yet had neither warned him nor allowed others to do so.

The Macedonians condemned him to death, and themselves carried out the sentence, throwing at him their javelins.

Alexander had been patient with Philotas and his punishment was just, but now the king did a cruel deed. For thinking that his old and faithful general Parmenio might have shared in the treachery of his son, he sent a messenger to slay him.

The king's despatch was taken to Parmenio and put into his hand. As he began to read it he was stabbed in the back.

From this time the king's temper grew less and less controlled. At one of the royal feasts he lost it altogether. A guest sang a song which made a jest of some Macedonians who had been beaten by the Persians. The old soldiers were indignant, the more so that Alexander paid no heed to their anger and bade the singer sing on.

Clitus, the king's foster-brother, had a quick temper, and he cried out, "It is not well done to expose the Macedonians before their enemies; since though it was their unhappiness to be overcome, yet are they much better men than those who laugh at them."

"Clitus pleads his own cause," said the king, "when he names cowardice misfortune."

The king spoke half in jest, half in anger, for he knew well that Clitus and all his Macedonians were brave men and no cowards.

But Clitus sprang to his feet at Alexander's words and cried, "Yet, O king, it was my cowardice that once saved your life from the Persians, and it is by the wounds of Macedonians that you are now the great king."

"Speak not so boldly," answered the king, and in his voice there was a threat, "or think not you will long enjoy the power to do so."

Clitus was now too angry to care what he said, and he spoke to the king yet more bitterly, until Alexander could brook no more. He took an apple from the table before him, and flinging it at his foster-brother, felt for his sword. But one of his guards, foreseeing what might happen, had removed it. His guests now gathered around the king, trying to soothe his anger. Alexander pushed them aside, and ordered one of his guard to sound the alarm. This would have assembled the whole army and the man hesitated, whereupon Alexander struck him on the face.

ALEXANDER SLAYS HIS FOSTER-BROTHER

Meanwhile a friend had hurried Clitus out of the room, but he slipped back again by another door, and boldly taunted the king with the way in which he treated his old soldiers.

Then in a passion Alexander snatched a spear from one of his guards, rushed upon Clitus and stabbed him to death.

A moment later the king's anger faded away, and he looked in horror upon the dead body of his foster-brother. He seized the spear again and tried to kill himself, but his guards wrenched it away, and led him to his own room. There he lay all through the long night and all through the following day, weeping for his foster-brother whom he had slain.

CHAPTER C

PORUS AND HIS ELEPHANT

THE Macedonians had now for some time been longing to march homeward rather than into new and unknown lands. But Alexander's ambition was not yet satisfied, and in 327 B.C. he determined to march into India, to add that land also to his conquests.

The army was laden with booty, and the king saw that unless it were left behind the men would not be able to march. It would be no easy matter to make the soldiers give up their plunder, but Alexander knew well how to manage men.

He ordered all his own share of plunder, all his unnecessary clothing, almost all his ornaments, to be burned. His courtiers did as they saw their king do, and when the soldiers were ordered to follow Alexander's example, they did so without a murmur, while some even cheered.

Without the plunder the soldiers marched easily, and soon reached the Punjab, where the king of the district brought to Alexander's aid five thousand men.

The army marched on unopposed, until it came to the river Hydaspes, or as we call it now the Jhelum. Here it was forced to halt, for on the opposite bank was a powerful Indian king, named Porus, and a large army.

Porus had with him a number of elephants, and when they trumpeted, the horses of the Macedonians took flight. The banks of the river were slippery, and the enemy was ready with arrows, should the king order his army to cross the river.

Alexander had made up his mind to cross the Hydaspes, but first he wished to put Porus off his guard.

So night after night, by the king's orders, a trumpet called the cavalry to march. It advanced always to the edge of the river, while Porus, thinking the whole army was going to cross, commanded his elephants to be moved to the bank, and his great hosts to be drawn up ready for battle.

Hour after hour the Indians waited, but the Macedonians never attempted to cross, and so they grew listless and each night less vigilant. Even Porus began to think the Macedonians must be cowards, and he paid less and less attention to their movements. This was what Alexander had expected would happen.

But one stormy night, when the Indians were off their guard, the king with part of his army crossed to a wooded island that lay in the middle of the river. It was a terrible night. Lightning flashed, thunder crashed, and several of Alexander's men were killed as they struggled breast high in the water. With great difficulty the others reached the farther side, to find that Porus had realised his danger. A thousand horsemen and sixty armed chariots awaited the daring king. But Alexander captured the chariots and slew four hundred of the cavalry.

The whole Macedonian army had now joined the king and a desperate battle was fought. Hour after hour the conflict raged, neither side gaining the victory.

At length, when the elephants were dead or their riders slain, when the Indians were flying in every direction, Porus knew that the day was lost.

Yet he disdained to flee and fought on, seated upon an elephant of enormous size, for he himself was more than six feet in height. Only when he was wounded in his shoulder, did he turn to ride away from the field.

It is told that while the battle was raging the elephant took the greatest care of his master. And when the animal saw that the king was faint from his wounds, he knelt down carefully that Porus might not fall. Then with his trunk he drew out the darts that were left in the body of the king.

Alexander had seen how bravely his enemy had fought. As he watched him riding from the field, he thought he would like to speak with so great a warrior, and he sent to ask him to return. He himself went out to meet the king, and was amazed at his great height and at his beauty.

When Alexander asked Porus how he wished to be treated, he answered, "As a king."

"For my own sake I will do that," replied the great king; "ask a boon for thy sake."

"That," said Porus, "containeth all."

As was his way, Alexander treated the fallen king right royally, giving back to him his kingdom and adding to it new territories.

Two cities were built close to the battlefield. One was named Bucephala, after Alexander's famous horse which, some say, was wounded and died after the battle. But others tell that Bucephalus had died shortly before the battle of old age, for he had lived for thirty years. The king grieved for the loss of his noble steed as for the loss of a friend.

This terrible battle made the Macedonians still more unwilling to advance farther into India.

Before them lay a desert which would take eleven days to cross. The soldiers could not face a long march in a strange land, without water and without guides.

When Alexander ordered the army to advance, the Macedonians who had followed him loyally through every difficulty, refused to obey.

Nothing he could say would make them advance a step farther.

"There they stood, looking hard at the ground with tears trickling down their cheeks, yet resolute still not to go forward."

Then Alexander dismissed them in anger. But the next day he sent for them again and told them that he was going to advance. They, if they chose to forsake him in a hostile land, could go back to Macedon.

Still in anger the king left them and went to his tent, and shut himself up for two days, refusing to see any of his companions.

Perhaps he thought his obstinate Macedonians would yield. But although it grieved them to thwart their king, the soldiers remained firm.

On the third day Alexander left his tent and offered sacrifices to the gods, as he always did before beginning a new adventure. But the signs were unfavourable, and against this the king was not proof. So he sent to tell the army that he had determined to lead them in the direction of home.

In a transport of joy the faithful Macedonians hastened to the king's tent. Some of them wept as they thanked "the unconquered king that he had permitted himself to be conquered for once by his Macedonians."

CHAPTER CI

ALEXANDER IS WOUNDED

ALEXANDER determined to begin the homeward journey by sailing down the Hydaspes to the Indus in order to reach the ocean.

The king himself with part of the army embarked in the ships which awaited them on the Hydaspes. The rest of the army was divided into two companies, and marched on either bank of the river, one being under Hephæstion, the king's friend.

On the way the fleet and the army joined their forces in order to subdue some of the warlike tribes that refused to submit to them.

One of these tribes, the Malli, Alexander pursued to their chief city, which stood where the town of Multan has since been built.

The city was easily taken, but not so the citadel in which the Malli had taken refuge.

Before the walls surrounding it could be scaled, ladders were needed, and two were hurriedly brought to the spot. But it was difficult to place them in position, for the Malli hurled upon the soldiers every missile on which they could lay their hands.

Alexander growing impatient, seized one of the ladders, and covering himself with his shield he placed it in position and began to mount.

Peucestas, carrying the sacred shield of Troy, and Leonnatus, two of the companions, followed closely after their king, while Abreas began to climb the second ladder which was now also ready for use.

The king was soon standing alone on the top of the wall, having flung down those of the Malli who were keeping guard at that point.

In despair the Macedonians saw the danger to which their king had exposed himself. He was a mark for every weapon hurled from the citadel.

They rushed in a body to the ladders, and began to mount in such numbers that the ladders both gave way, Peucestas, Leonnatus and Abreas alone having first reached the top of the wall.

His friends called aloud to Alexander, entreating him to come back. But he leaped down on the other side among his foes. Fortunately he landed on his feet, and at once placing his back against the wall, he strove to keep back the enemy as they rushed upon him.

The foremost fell before the swift stroke of the king's sword, as did also those who followed him. At two more the king hurled stones which felled them to the ground. After that the Malli were afraid to approach close to the great king, but they began to throw at him stones and great pieces of rock.

A moment later his three companions had leaped down and were by the side of their king, ready to defend him with their lives.

Abreas fell at his feet almost at once, pierced by a dart. Alexander himself was wounded, but fought on until at length, faint through loss of blood, he fell fainting on his shield.

Peucestas covered him with the sacred shield, while Leonnatus fought on desperately until help came.

A few of the Macedonians, maddened by the thought of their king's danger, scrambled up on each other's shoulders, and leaped down on the other side to rescue him and his three companions if they still lived.

Some ran to the gates, and opened them, and the anxious soldiers poured in and took the citadel. They believed that their king was dead, and they wreaked their fury on the miserable inhabitants, leaving neither men, women nor children alive.

Alexander was not dead, and although his wound was severe, he recovered. But the rumour of his death had reached the camp near the river where the main body of the army had been left. No letters, no messages could make the grief-stricken soldiers believe that their king still lived.

Alexander was brought down the river in a ship. He was lying on a couch in the stern of the vessel as he drew near to the camp, and he ordered the canopy which screened him to be raised that his soldiers might see him.

At first they thought it was but his lifeless body which they beheld, but as he drew nearer still, the king waved his hand. Then a great shout of joy rent the air.

CHAPTER CII

THE DEATH OF ALEXANDER

In the autumn of 325 B.C. Alexander began to march through the desert of Gedrosia on his way to Babylon.

The heat was terrible, and the soldiers were soon parched with thirst, while sinking sand added to the hardship of the march.

Alexander tramped by the side of his men across the dreary waste, sharing all their privations and cheering them by his presence. But before he left the desert of Gedrosia, the king had lost more than a fourth part of the army that had set out with him from India two short months before.

At length the exhausted soldiers reached Susa, and here the king allowed them to rest. He himself found much to do, for many of the satraps whom he had left in charge of different provinces had betrayed their trust. They had treated cruelly those who were in their power, and had formed plots to make themselves kings over their own provinces. It may be that they thought Alexander would never come back from his perilous journey in the East.

When he had punished those who had proved faithless, were they Macedonians or Persians, he turned to a matter on which his heart was set—the union of the peoples of the East and the West.

The king tried to accomplish this in different ways. He had already built cities in the East, and left in them Greeks and Macedonians along with the native Asiatics.

Now he himself wedded Statira, the daughter of Darius, Hephæstion married her sister, while several Macedonian generals, following the example of the king, took the daughters of Persian nobles to be their wives. Many of the soldiers, too, married women of the East.

Alexander hoped that little by little the two races would learn to know each other better and to have the same interests.

In the spring of 324 B.C. Alexander went to Ecbatana, where the Persian kings had been used to spend the summer months. Shortly afterwards he met his whole army at Opis, not far from Babylon, and discharged many of the Macedonian veterans who were no longer fit to fight because of old age or because of the wounds from which they had suffered. The king promised to provide for these old warriors for the rest of their lives. He expected them to welcome their dismissal and their reward.

THE DEATH OF ALEXANDER

But the Macedonians had been growing more and more jealous of the favours Alexander had been showing to the Persians, and now the feelings that they had been forced to hide found words.

They bade the king discharge not only the veterans but his loyal Macedonians. Some even dared to shout, "Go and conquer with Zeus, your father."

The king, in sudden anger, sprang from his seat, down among the angry throng, and ordered thirteen of the ringleaders to be put to death. He then bade the others go away if they wished. They had been only poor shepherds on the hills of Macedon, he reminded them, until his father Philip had made them rulers of Greece. He had shared with them the wealth of the East, and had kept nothing for himself, save his purple robe and his royal diadem.

Alexander then went to his palace, and in three days he sent for the Persian nobles, to whom he gave the posts of honour which until now had been held by the Macedonians.

Plutarch tells us that when the Macedonians, who had stayed in their quarters in spite of their dismissal, heard what Alexander had done, "they went without their arms, with only their undergarments on, crying and weeping, to offer themselves at his tent, and desired him to deal with them as their baseness and ingratitude deserved . . . yet he would not admit them to his presence, nor would they stir from thence, but continued two days and nights before his tent, bewailing themselves, and imploring him as their lord to have compassion on them. But on the third day he came out to them, and seeing them very humble and penitent, he wept himself a great while, after a gentle reproof spoke kindly to them and dismissed those who were too old for service with magnificent rewards, and with recommendation to Antipater that when they came home, at all public shows and in the theatres, they should sit in the best and foremost seats, crowned with chaplets of flowers."

During the summer which he spent at Ecbatana, a great sorrow befell the king. Hephæstion, his dearest friend, took ill, and in seven days he was dead. For three days the king would touch no food. No one could comfort him, for well the king knew that no one would ever fill the place that Hephæstion had held in his heart. The body of his friend the king ordered to be taken to Babylon, where it was burnt on a pyre adorned with great magnificence. Chapels were built in his honour in Alexandria and other cities.

In June 323 B.C., a month after the funeral rites, Alexander, who was preparing for a great expedition by sea, went to the river Euphrates to inspect some new harbours which he had ordered to be built.

The place was unhealthy, because of the many marshes that lay round about the river, and the king was attacked by fever. He refused to take any care

THE DEATH OF ALEXANDER

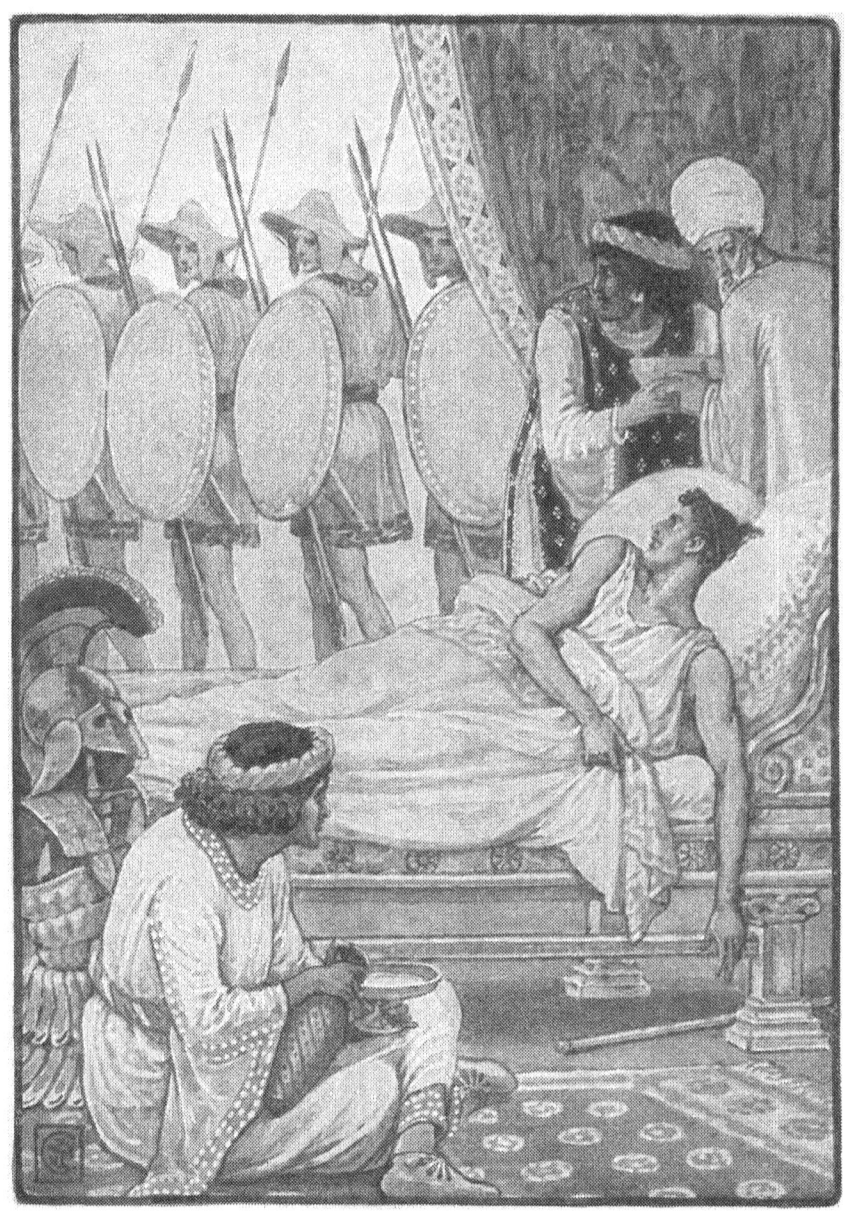

With an effort he looked at them as they passed

and daily he grew worse, until at length he was forced by weakness to stay in bed.

A rumour that he was dead reached the Macedonians, and they hastened to the palace, begging to be allowed to see their king once more.

Alexander was not dead, but he was too weak to speak, as one by one the soldiers were permitted to walk quietly past his bed. With an effort he looked at them as they passed, and feebly raised his hand in farewell.

"After I am gone will you ever find a king worthy of such heroes as these?" he murmured as they slowly filed out of the room.

Then he drew his signet ring from his finger and gave it to an officer, saying that he left his kingdom "to the best man." So the great king passed away at the age of thirty-three.

CHAPTER CIII

DEMOSTHENES IN THE TEMPLE OF POSEIDON

WHEN Alexander set out on his great expedition to Asia, Demosthenes was living in Athens, and for five years nothing happened to disturb the quiet habits of his life.

He loved his city well, and with his own money he had rebuilt the walls of Athens. Many other services he had done for his countrymen, and because of these, one of the Athenians proposed to the people that a hero's crown of gold should be bestowed upon Demosthenes.

This they were very willing to do. So at one of the great Athenian festivals, when the people were assembled in the theatre, a herald proclaimed that a golden crown had been awarded to the orator because of all that he had done for his city.

But Æschines, another great orator, was angry that this honour should have been given to Demosthenes, whom he happened to dislike. So he brought a lawsuit against him, and attacked his enemy in a speech that became famous.

But Demosthenes defended himself in a still more brilliant speech, and won his case, which so annoyed Æschines that he left Athens and never again returned to the city.

Six years later, Demosthenes was accused of having taken bribes. It was not proved that he had done so, yet he was found guilty and sentenced to pay a heavy fine.

As he had not money enough to pay the fine, he was thrown into prison. Before long he escaped and fled to the sea-coast town of Ægina, not far from Athens. Often he would sit on the shore or pace up and down the sands, looking wistfully toward the city he loved.

When tidings of the death of Alexander reached Athens, the Greeks resolved once more to try to fling off the yoke of Macedon. Demosthenes was recalled to the city, and his voice encouraged the Athenians in their determination to fight for liberty.

But Antipater hastened to Attica with an army, and soon put down the revolt of the Athenians. He then condemned Demosthenes to death, for it was well-known that his Philippics had often roused the Athenians to show their hatred of Philip, and he had, too, continually spoken against his son Alexander.

When Demosthenes heard that he had been condemned, he fled to the temple of Poseidon, in

DEMOSTHENES IN THE TEMPLE OF POSEIDON

the island of Calauria. Antipater at once sent soldiers, led by a man named Archias, to capture the fugitive. Archias had once been an actor, and was well known to Demosthenes.

Archias reached Calauria, and going to the temple he begged Demosthenes to come out of the sanctuary, saying that if he did so he would be pardoned.

But Demosthenes knew that this was a false promise and he said, "O Archias, I am as little affected by your promises now as I used formerly to be by your acting."

Now Archias had been proud of his acting, so this made him very angry with Demosthenes, and he began to threaten him with all kinds of evil.

"Now," said the orator, "you speak like an oracle of Macedon; before, you were acting a part. Therefore wait only a little, while I write a word or two to my family."

Then he rose and went into the inner temple, and taking a tablet and his own pen in his hand, he sat down as though to write. He had a habit of putting his pen into his mouth and biting it, and he did so now. It seemed as though he was thinking what he would write. But all the while he was sucking poison which he had concealed in his pen.

Then, knowing that the poison would soon do its work, Demosthenes leaned on the altar, his face hidden in his cloak.

Archias had now grown tired of waiting, and he went into the temple again and bade Demosthenes come, without more delay.

The orator rose, uncovering his head, and looking at Archias, he said, "I will depart while I am alive out of this sacred place." But as he tried to walk toward the door he staggered and fell by the altar. The poison had done its work.

Antipater had no interest in the art or in the culture of Greece, and her glory soon faded under his rule. Athens, Sparta, Corinth, as well as the smaller states, all ceased to be independent.

As the power of Greece grew less, that of Rome was growing greater and greater. In 196 B.C. she conquered Macedon and restored to Greece her liberty.

Fifty years later, Corinth defied the Roman power, and treated her ambassadors with insult. The Roman consuls then sent an army into Greece to conquer the country, and add it to their great dominions.

But although the Romans conquered Greece, and so made her subject to them, they could not escape her influence. The Greek language was spoken by every educated Roman, Greek plays were acted at Rome, Greek literature was read and studied.

Wherever the Romans went they carried with them the habits and the culture of the people whom they had conquered. And the greatest and most precious thing the Greeks had to teach the world was, "the just consideration of the truth of things everywhere."

www.ingramcontent.com/pod-product-compliance
Lightning Source LLC
Chambersburg PA
CBHW030131170426
43199CB00008B/35